The Death of Satan

The Death of Satan

HOW AMERICANS HAVE LOST THE SENSE OF EVIL

Andrew Delbanco

FARRAR, STRAUS AND GIROUX

New York

LIBRARY OF CONGRESS CATALOGING-IN-PUBLICATION DATA
Delbanco, Andrew.
The death of Satan : how Americans have lost the sense of evil /
by Andrew Delbanco. — 1st ed.
p.   cm.
Includes bibliographical references and index.
1. American literature—History and criticism. 2. Evil in
literature.   3. United States—Civilization—Moral and ethical
aspects.   4. Literature and society—United States.   5. National
characteristics, American.   6. Ethics in literature.   7. Devil in
literature.   8. Ethics, American. I. Title.
PS169.G66D45   1995   810.9'353—dc20   95-10007   CIP

The author and the publisher would like to thank the following
for permission to reproduce art included in this book: *Photofest*;
Brancacci Chapel, Santa Maria del Carmine, Florence; Columbia
University Library; Mary Evans Picture Gallery; NBC; Yale University Library; *The New Yorker*; Artists' Rights Society. The ex-
cerpt from "Esthétique du Mal," by Wallace Stevens, is reprinted
by permission of Random House and Faber & Faber.

For Dawn

Contents

Introduction　　　　　　　　　　　　　　　　　　　　3

PART ONE:　*The Age of Belief*

1. The Old Enemy Comes to the New World　　　23
2. The Devil in the Age of Reason　　　　　　　57
3. The Birth of the Self　　　　　　　　　　　91

PART TWO:　*Modern Times*

4. The Loss of Providence　　　　　　　　　125
5. The Age of Blame　　　　　　　　　　　155
6. The Culture of Irony　　　　　　　　　185
7. Prospects　　　　　　　　　　　　　219

Notes　　　　　　　　　　　　　　　　237
Acknowledgments　　　　　　　　　　　263
Index　　　　　　　　　　　　　　　265

The death of Satan was a tragedy
For the imagination. A capital
Negation destroyed him in his tenement

.   .   .   .

It had nothing of the Julian thunder-cloud:
The assassin flash and rumble . . . He was denied.
Phantoms, what have you left? What underground?
What place in which to be is not enough
To be? You go, poor phantoms, without place
Like silver in the sheathing of the sight,
As the eye closes . . . How cold the vacancy
When the phantoms are gone and the shaken realist
First sees reality. . . .

—WALLACE STEVENS

The Death of Satan

Anthony Hopkins as the serial killer Dr. Hannibal Lecter in Jonathan Demme's film
The Silence of the Lambs
(PHOTOFEST)

Introduction

A gulf has opened up in our culture between the visibility of evil and the intellectual resources available for coping with it. Never before have images of horror been so widely disseminated and so appalling—from organized death camps to children starving in famines that might have been averted. Rarely does a week go by without newspaper and television accounts of teenagers performing contract killings for a few dollars, women murdered on the street for their purses or their furs, young men shot in the head for the keys to their jeep—and these are only the domestic bulletins. As I was finishing this book, one could read in *The New York Times* about a prison camp in what is now known as "the former Yugoslavia," where Bosnian male prisoners were marched out naked into a courtyard while Serb women stripped before their eyes; the punishment for any man who got an erection was to have his penis cut off. Not far away, prison guards forced a father and son to have sex with each other as they watched.

The repertoire of evil has never been richer. Yet never have our responses been so weak. We have no language for connecting our inner lives with the horrors that pass before our eyes in the outer world. Philanthropy and protest seem empty gestures, arbitrary in their choice of beneficiary or occasion. It is now commonly remarked (especially since the Cruise missile entertainments of the Gulf war) that technology has carried us to the point where death by fire is indistinguishable from the puffs and crackle of a video game; and when some shocking new cruelty does seize our attention, it is likely to be met with consternation or annoyance. We shudder or wince; then we switch the channel.[1]

How this crisis of incompetence before evil came about and how it has made itself felt in the United States, whose culture is the dominant one

3

of the West, is the subject of this book. It is not a history of crime or criminology, or of philosophical ethics or religious doctrine. Nor is it a call for intervention in this or that human conflict. It takes the form of a kind of national spiritual biography, beginning with America's childhood because, as Tocqueville put it in the most incisive book yet written about this country, if we are to "see the first images which the external world casts upon the dark mirror of [the nation's] mind," we must "watch the infant in his mother's arms."[2] For the "infant" Americans three hundred and fifty years ago, evil had a name, a face, and an explanation. It was called the Fall, it was personified in the devil, and it was attributed to an original sin committed in Eden and imputed by God to all mankind. Sin was understood to have filled the world—sown and nurtured by a devil of "baleful eyes," as Milton described him in *Paradise Lost*, a creature motivated by "obdurate pride and stedfast hate." And no one was immune to his charms.

When American culture began, this devil was an incandescent presence in most people's lives, a symbol and explanation for both the cruelties one received and those perpetrated upon others. But by 1700 he was already losing his grip on the imagination—a process that has continued ever since and that has left us, in the words of the psychologist Henry Murray, with a Satan who is "no more than a vestigial image, a broken-spirited relic of a perished past, a ludicrous ham actor with no greater part to play in man's imagination than the vermiform appendix in his gut."[3] In our disenchanted world, one respected historian has recently remarked (and here he is perfectly representative) that mass murderers like Hitler and Stalin require us "judiciously [to] distinguish mental disorders that incapacitate from streaks of disorder that should not diminish responsibility."[4] This distinction would be meaningless to the scores of millions who died at their hands. What does it mean to say that the inventor of the concentration camps, or of the Gulag, was subject to a "disorder"? What does it mean to call these monsters mentally disordered, and to engage in scholastic debate over whether their brand of madness vitiates their responsibility? Why can we no longer call them evil?

When I think back to my years of growing up in the 1950s, I realize that this process of unnaming evil, though it began centuries ago, has accelerated enormously during my own lifetime. My parents, German-born

Jews who had fled Hitler, spoke only rarely in their native language in our house, in part because it seemed to their children a language full of shouting and bluster in which even endearments could sound harsh. But a few German words did stray into our vocabulary. Among them was the word *übel*. We heard it and used it all the time; we felt *übel*, not nauseated, at the onset of the stomach flu (or grippe, as my parents, having spent a decade in England, called it); if I tried to read in a moving car, I felt *übel*, or if I followed a cream-sauced dinner too quickly with a piece of *Sachertorte*. Only later did I learn that *übel* was the German word for evil—a concept it shared with the rather differently pitched word *Böse*. For the first twenty years or so of my life, *übel* had the trivial meaning of evil as in "evil-smelling," which is how we described my father's favorite cheese, Limburger, known to us as *Stinkekäse*—at least until it was placed safely under the bell jar.

My parents had come of age in a world where evil was not casually confused with a bad smell. My mother told me with tears in her eyes that Joseph Goebbels had been the devil incarnate—Mephistopheles, she called him. Yet even for her, *übel* was becoming a word that diminished evil into a small treatable distress; it denoted a queasiness to be fixed with bicarbonate of soda or a walk in the fresh air. It was a German word, an unassimilated fragment of my parents' native tongue, but it was also, as it turned out, an introduction to the language of the culture that had rescued us, a culture where evil is supposed to be a thing of the jettisoned past.

Every American family has its own terms and stories by which it tries to preserve, undiminished, the moment when it broke away from its particular Old World hell. For my wife, it is the story of her mother, as a young girl in Hong Kong, cutting her hair short and hiding indoors in boy's clothing so that the Japanese soldiers would pass her over in their search for a Chinese girl to rape. Until about 1930, black American children—for whom the hell has always been local—might have known a grandfather who bore whip scars on his back. Some of my friends in 1960 still had a frail aunt or nervous cousin with a hint of terror in her eyes and blue numbers tattooed into her arm. But time is a relentless solvent of memory. For a Jew, thinking about modern Germany today is like walking past a row of sequential exhibits that show burnt woodlands coming back from charred stumps to sprig, then to leaf, and bole, and forest again—until the image of the catastrophe is left behind and it is time to leave the museum. This is as it should be; it is the wisdom of mourning as a regimen preparatory for the resumption of life. But the enormity of the crime and the speed with which it recedes from memory raise the question of whether any evil is large enough to testify against itself.

These old, remembered confrontations with evil are still among the basic sources of identity for Americans, who are a mongrel people; but like any communicated energy, they weaken and eventually dissipate in transmission. Just as the Holocaust becomes an abstraction, the regime of slavery fades, and comparable distances open up between Armenian-Americans and the Turkish massacre, between Chinese-Americans and the Japanese slaughter at Nanking, between Irish-Americans and the war for independence against Britain (though in some respects this last is still going on). We are all left without the moral markers we once depended on for knowing who, and where, we are. As they recede, they leave us in an identity panic that manifests itself as a splintering into ethnic blocs held together chiefly by some history of oppression unsharable with outsiders. More and more groups in American society are engaged in arguments over whose history is the richest in pain and injustice.

This "multicultural" competition tends to be morally fraudulent. It tries to compensate for the receding of the images of evil into the mythic past—Nazi storm troopers, police dogs in Selma—images that once galvanized Americans into common moral purpose. This was acutely evident as President Clinton—a member of the Vietnam generation who did not serve in the armed forces—walked the Normandy beaches where the first waves of D-Day troops landed fifty years ago, and tried to find words for what an earlier generation of Americans had experienced there. One watched the commemorative ceremonies with some measure of doubt about whether Americans were still equipped to recognize evil if it should be visited upon us again.

One evidence of this estrangement is that serious books on the problem of evil now typically begin with careful demonstrations that the problem is real, as if this were a matter of dispute. They read like primers. They offer proof lists ("We see [evil]," according to one contemporary moral philosopher, "in the . . . massacres of Armenians, Cambodians, Gypsies, Indonesians, Jews, and kulaks"[5]) or quote wire-service accounts of more local horrors (suburban parents burning their children with cigarettes, or locking them up, soiled in their own feces, in unlit closets).

Yet as we know from history—most conspicuously from the national failure of sight and hearing that seems to have afflicted most German citizens during the 1930s and 1940s—even the actual removal or torture of one's neighbor can seem as remote as the newspaper statistics of a Peruvian earthquake. Litanies and lists will never convey the experience of what they try to represent.

Everyone knows this—that evil tends to recede into the background hum of modern life, that "the industrial system," as the anthropologist Lionel Tiger puts it, "provide[s] a uniquely efficient lubricant for moral evasiveness." One more homeless person freezes to death under the night sky—and joins a procession of images for which it seems impossible to assign cause. Where does one lay the blame? In a corporate culture that permits, as Tiger says, "individual people with fully fledged private moralities to conduct business without personal liability," where does the savvy investor stop and the criminal insider trader begin?[6] Even where the evidence of "crime" is more palpable than the suspected presence in Switzerland of some unduly large bank balance—say, the body of a child caught in the drug dealers' cross fire—we cannot readily see the perpetrator. We think of him as the agent of some large entity called culture, and we step away, feeling more implicated than incensed. Who, or what, bears the responsibility?

The intransigence of such questions is among the reasons that Hannah Arendt struck a nerve when she announced thirty years ago in *The New Yorker* what she called the *banality* of evil. She found the ultimate symbol of this ordinariness in the person of Adolf Eichmann, one of the chief managers of the Nazis' killing machine—an orderly, loyal, efficient man who sat at his Jerusalem trial impassive in a glass booth, his face set in an expression somewhere between a smirk and a grimace. He seemed the quintessential image of evil in its modern form.

It was a riveting image. It fixed in the mind the truth that the bureaucratic discipline which modern organizations value and reward fosters a sense of exculpatory determinism ("following orders," "doing my job"). The self, Eichmann seemed to say, has become a collection of functions and duties rather than an accountable moral being. He seemed appallingly ordinary, not so much a deformation as a norm. Arendt's most frightening implication was that the concept of evil might actually be incompatible with the very nature of modern life. She confirmed how hard it had become to find the place (as Henry David Thoreau had described it a hundred years earlier) where one can "no longer accuse institutions and society, but must front the true source of evil"[7]—the self.

Yet Eichmann on trial in Jerusalem is finally less chilling, perhaps, than Eichmann before he was captured, when he was living freely in Buenos Aires. It is *before* his capture and trial, when he lived as an inconspicuous citizen, that he is really haunting, and seems a harbinger of our world. Here is the account, written by the chief of the Israeli Secret Service, of the first close look obtained by an Israeli agent (named Kenet) of Eichmann at home in his Argentinian refuge, where he had been under surveillance:

> At about eleven forty-five the man Kenet had seen the day before came walking toward the house from the direction of the main road—the peephole in the tarpaulin was too small for Kenet to see exactly where the man had come from. He was fairly well-groomed, wearing light-brown trousers, gray overcoat, a plain green tie, and brown shoes. Kenet estimated his height at about five feet eight inches. Other details he noted were: "about three-quarters bald, fair hair on either side of his head, large nose, wide forehead, spectacles, maybe a mustache, walks slowly."
>
> The man entered the property from the other side, not through the front, bent down to pass under the wire marking off the boundary of the plot, and walked into the yard. He stopped for a moment next to the child, said something to him, and stroked his head and straightened his clothes—this time the child was fully dressed, perhaps because it was Sunday. With a slow tread the man climbed the steps to the porch, brushed away the flies with a newspaper he was carrying, and was about to open the door when the stout woman opened it from the inside. As he walked in, they both waved the flies away from the open doorway.[8]

One horror of this passage is the unspoken but obscene disproportion between the pedestrian householder "Ricardo Klement" and the murderer Eichmann. The still greater horror is that to see him brush the flies away on his porch is to know that the distinction between the two—in this case soon forcibly reasserted by the Israelis—will become ever more elusive until it disappears altogether. Eichmann-Klement becomes a "postmodern" figure, a man without a center, without a self, merely a subject for observation whose identity fluctuates with the perspective of the observer. When the last Nazi hunter is gone, only Klement will remain, and no one will be able to bring Eichmann back into the field of vision. Evil will have become an epistemological problem. This is the vanishing point to which we seem headed.

So the work of the devil is everywhere, but no one knows where to find him. We live in the most brutal century in human history, but instead of stepping forward to take the credit, he has rendered himself invisible. Although the names by which he was once designated (in the Christian lexicon he was assigned the name Satan; Marxism substituted phrases like "exploitative classes"; psychoanalysis preferred terms like "repression" and "neurosis") have been discredited to one degree or another, nothing has come to take their place. The work of this book is therefore to think historically about the shrinking range of phenomena to which accusatory words like "evil" and "sin" may still be applied in contemporary life, and to think about what it means to do without them.

I have written it out of the belief that despite the shriveling of the old words and concepts, we cannot do without some conceptual means for thinking about the sorts of experiences that used to go under the name of evil. Few people still believe in what the British writer Ian McEwan has recently called a "malign principle, a force in human affairs that periodically advances to dominate and destroy the lives of individuals or nations, then retreats to await the next occasion."[9] We certainly no longer have a conception of evil as a distributed entity with an ontological essence of its own, as what some philosophers call "presence." Yet something that feels like this force still invades our experience, and we still discover in ourselves the capacity to inflict it on others. Since this is true, we have an inescapable problem: we feel something that our culture no longer gives us the vocabulary to express.

When I was talking this way not long ago to a group of scholars, one member of the audience objected that "we should not try to connect in a single concept the gas chambers of Auschwitz and a father who slaps his child." This was a wise admonition. The bloody record of Western history as one long crusade to extirpate unholiness wherever it is to be discovered (or imagined) is quite long enough as it is. One can surely do without the presumption that evil is a principle that travels on its own propulsion across time and space, lodging for a moment here or lingering there. There is, no doubt, a certain safety in the loosening of the moral categories through which such crusades were formerly organized.

But it is also true that when you discard the old words and symbols, you arrive at an unprecedented condition of inarticulate dread. This condition is variously manifest in contemporary life—in the sphere of sexuality, for instance, which used to be governed by religious prohibitions internalized as beliefs, but which is increasingly subject to legal arbitration. Young people (especially women), for whom sexual restraint was once a social norm, are now on their own in making decisions about how and when to act on their desires. Each must invent her or his own theology with respect to the body (when to have sex? with whom?), a more demanding task than the old obligation to observe (or defy) a tradition that associated unsanctified sex with sin. In the past, in other words, when a woman said no, she had a great deal of cultural authority on her side. (Satan, among his identities in the religious tradition, was a seducer and rapist.) Today she must bear the burden of her decision virtually alone. It is no wonder that many young women on American campuses, where they are free for the first time from parental oversight, take recourse to courts and councils to settle the question of whether the sexual act last night, or last week, or last month, was voluntary or coerced.

After I was admonished for drifting toward nostalgia for a world in which the category of sin was stronger and more inclusive than it is today, another member of the same audience joined the discussion and pointed out that although it may be folly to try to retrieve a notion of evil that links the slapped child with Auschwitz, we may still need a concept to connect the Nazi mentality with the father who *rapes* his child. Whatever position one takes on this question, there seems to be growing agreement that there was once such a concept as sin—broad and capacious but still meaningful—and that it has faded. The real issue is whether one should try to get it back.

Once upon a time, evil was personified. Evil was Mephistopheles or the Devil. Colorfully costumed. Almost flavorful, altogether identifiable, a clarified being from another world. But in the industrial system evil has become systematized. The production of it has become technologized, internationalized, multinationalized, and especially in times of war and high zealotry, officially rhapsodized. Just as industrialism has radically altered the ways and means of making and distributing, it has also altered the moral structure within which we live. Yet malefactors are harder to spot. They no longer boast horns and wear suits with tails, but rather three-piece suits and sometimes turtleneck sweaters of cashmere wool or magenta blouses of tailored silk.[10]

As Lionel Tiger suggests, the old language of evil has become a collection of what George Orwell called "dead" metaphors or, to borrow a phrase from Henry James's father, an "uneasy lodgment in [the] verbal memory."[11] It is at most a dormant language, of the sort one recognizes when using common words like "awful," which once expressed the fear and trembling of the puny creature full of awe before the majesty of God, but now more usually denotes a taste like spoiled milk or the irritation of sitting through a dull movie. "Bless you," one still says when somebody sneezes—a phrase that began in the Middle Ages as a prayer for the moral safety of a person who had been invaded (through the nostrils) by invisibly small demons. These words, formerly urgent, long ago became ritualistic. "New imagery ceases to be created," as Emerson puts it, and old words have subsided into rote.[12]

Even for secular liberals, it should be said, the old religious metaphors are not entirely gone. They still simmer below the level of conscious expression, and sometimes bubble back to the surface of ordinary speech, where they can be detected if one listens closely. But by and large they have been reduced to mere speech tics, as, for instance, when John Updike has one of his characters in *The Witches of Eastwick* grind a bit of spilled tea into an Oriental rug, and then remark that the "greatest thing about Orientals" is that "they don't show your sins."[13] Faced with this sort of trivialization—tea stains as sins—it is perhaps best to give up the old language entirely. It has become an embarrassment, like an incontinent old dog. The decent thing, it would seem, is to do away with it.

Yet we hesitate. If the language of evil is finally eliminated, we shall surely be left in a kind of dumbness—akin to the condition that accompanies sexual or aesthetic experiences when we let the music wash over us, or receive, without giving navigational instructions, a lover's caress. In such circumstances, one willingly gives up language for the sake of the pure exclamatory sound that is the substratum of language. This reaching beyond verbal means can be a liberation in sexual or aesthetic matters. But in the ethical life it is an imprisonment. It leaves us, in our obligatory silence, with a punishing question: "How," in the words of one literary critic, "is the imagination to compass things for which it can find no law, no aesthetic purpose or aesthetic resolution?"[14]

Let me offer one example of how this question asserts itself. Teachers of literature like myself are involved with young people who, to borrow a phrase that Frank Kermode once used to define literary criticism, are attempting to make "sense of the ways we try to make sense of our lives."[15] In my university, undergraduate students are still required to read St. Augustine's *Confessions* in order to help them with this effort. In that great book they encounter Augustine's account of his theft, when he was a member of a roving gang of boys, of a cluster of pears from a neighbor's tree. He stole them, he says, not for hunger or gain, but simply to taste them, and then, satisfied with a little skin and pulp, he flings them to the hogs. As a new member of the gang, he was, he says, "ashamed not to be shameless."[16]

When my students close their Augustine and open their *New York Times*, they read there too about gangs of boys on the streets looking for trouble (a few years ago, "wilding" was the term). Peer pressure, the sociologists say, works its mischief until, for no reason specific to any target, something gets stolen, vandalized, or someone gets mugged or worse. I suspect that most of my students, when they think about such a phenomenon (to which, as late adolescents, they may feel some intimate relation), enter the labyrinthine social universe of which their teachers try to make them aware: they think dutifully about illiteracy and poverty and fatherless families and racial tension and prurient advertising and the insidious relation of all these phenomena to violent and cruel behavior. (They may also think secretly about getting caught alone at night by victims of these deprivations.) What Augustine, on the other hand, thought about was the mystery of *his own* original sin—about a cosmos in which God chose to leave people with the burden of free will and then dangled temptation before their eyes.

Augustine was thinking about what used to be called "moral evil." Today we are likelier to use a euphemism like "antisocial behavior," a notion in which the concept of responsibility has disappeared and the human being is reconceived as a component with a stipulated function. If it fails to perform properly, it is subject to repair or disposal; but there is no real sense of blame involved—no more than with a ball bearing or a hose that has gone bad. We think in terms of adjusting the faulty part or, if it is too far gone, of putting it away.

Yet if the distance between these ways of thinking is large, and it is, a yet larger distance stretches between what used to be called "natural evil" and our degraded concept of accident. The world was once taken to be an emanation of the mind of God or an expression of the will of the gods; anything that happened in it—a war, a famine—had punitive or admonitory meaning. As late as 1912, when the opulent and "unsinkable" ocean liner *Titanic* sank on its maiden voyage, press coverage of the disaster tended to recount it as a "lesson . . . written in searing lines on ice-floe and curling wave-crest." The lesson was scriptural: "Whosoever exalteth himself shall be abased and he that humbleth himself shall be exalted."[17] But today the world for most people in the West is regarded as a place of unknown origin in which we find ourselves for an unknown reason. When the *Challenger* spacecraft blew up before the eyes of millions in 1986, one of the television anchormen, tongue-tied as the precious, sponsored seconds ticked by, groped for words. He literally had nothing to say. When at last he came up with something, it was by turning to the closest thing to metaphysical language he could find, the language of the Cold War. He looked at the hastily assembled experts who had joined him around the anchor desk, and asked, "Does this mean that the Russians are ahead?"

In this world emptied of metaphysical meaning—even the language of the Cold War has since deserted us—our insurance policies may still include clauses covering (or, more likely, exempting) "acts of God" as well as storm, fire, flood, and the like; but the fact is that such events are regarded by most people as inscrutable misfortunes. In 1993, when the Mississippi River broke over its banks and levees, washing away whole towns, farms, and factories in several states, public-opinion polls ascertained that only about 20 percent of Americans regarded the flood as a divine judgment.[18] In the face of such events, most people today are forced into gibberish or silence, a linguistic dead end that our best writers anticipated long ago. When Melville's Pip, for instance (the black cabin boy in *Moby-Dick*), falls overboard by "accident" and is left alone to bob in the empty sea, he can barely speak; he is assaulted in the endless ocean by an infinite loneliness; his self is vacuumed out. After he is rescued, again by sheer chance, he wanders about the deck of the *Pequod* uttering one refrain—"I look, you look, he looks; we look, ye look, they look"—and the crew thinks him perfectly mad. But in speaking the only language that the open ocean has left for him—a centerless conjugation—Pip talks like us.[19]

This breakup of consciousness and the fragmentation of language that follows upon it are among the chief symptoms of modernity. Taking note of this fact, one recent book on the linguistic representation of pain reports that torture chambers throughout the world are referred to, in a deliberate deformation of moral language, as "guest rooms" and "safe houses," and that part of the cruelty of relentless interrogation involves taking the subject "step-by-step backward . . . along the path by which language comes into being" until the victim is left with only a kind of prelinguistic murmur at his fear and pain.[20] This technique seems a magnified version of a more benign experience we all know as children, who like to repeat certain words again and again (most susceptible are words with repetitive sounds, like "banana," or odd and vowely words like "owl") until they lose their denotative dignity and become nonsense in the ear.

Sooner or later, however strongly one resists it, this sort of intellectual and linguistic failure afflicts us all—usually when we encounter what used to be called "natural evil" through illness and the approach of death. Nowadays this confrontation with disease commonly occurs after a few years' reprieve by antiseptics and antibiotics. In an earlier America, when medicine was virtually ignorant of the physical causes of disease, it could nevertheless draw on a rich and active language for explaining disease in *moral* terms. It could treat the body by ministrations to the soul. This was possible as long as the Bible held sway and as long as the sacramental nature of Christianity reflected its origin as a kind of amulet against death. Christ, who was once alive to many Americans in ways that he no longer is, was, after all, a miracle worker upon the body (he cured the blind and the lame) as well as upon the soul (he conferred eternal life upon all who believed in his resurrection). Milton, in *Paradise Lost*, writes of how "the earth felt the wound" when Eve sinned, and "gave a second groan" when Adam followed, as death entered the cycle of nature.

In the age of belief, natural and moral evil were closely affiliated concepts; and many people today still keep them bound together. One can still see on television some trembling evangelist place his hands on the face of a stooped invalid who has shuffled to the stage, and beseech Christ, as if he were talking to an unruly dog, to "Heal!" and then send the radiant patient back to his seat with limber step. Faith healers of this sort try to recoup the power of primitive Christianity, which expropriated the magic of old pagan remedies for its new protective rituals—consecrated unguents, holy baptismal water, the bread and wine of the eucharist. They even hark back to early Christian methods for exorcising the devil—techniques that included the priest's dabbing the ears of baptismal candidates with a dollop of spittle to show contempt for the demons within.

For most people in modern societies, however, this sort of performance seems vaguely comic. Still, even for those of us for whom the linkage of these moral and physical worlds is but a vague ancestral memory, or who descend from traditions that never made the connection strongly, the association never quite evaporates. Who has not felt, when walking into a sickroom, a need to keep apart the converging notions of vengeful providence and bad luck? We all know that only a fine line separates sympathy from contempt for the sick, and we are always crossing it. Do we blame the woman riddled with metastatic cancer for postponing her mammogram? Do we reproach the man with clotted arteries for his years of troweling on the butter and guzzling the cream? More important, do we encourage or allow them to blame themselves? I recall once visiting a friend who had suffered a traumatic brain injury. His arms were white and veiny like boiled chicken; the skin of his neck, where the tracheal tube had been inserted, throbbed with each breath, and the rattle was unnerving. I had no reason to be angry with him—on the contrary—but I felt the stirrings of anger all the same as I tried to fill the time with anecdotes and jokes and words of encouragement. My anger seemed mysterious to me, and possibly shameful, but I think it was not unusual.

This kind of anger is a feeling through which one senses a resurgence of the primitive fear of defilement, which underlies all religion—a "half-physical, half-ethical fear that clings to the representation of the impure." I wanted to find some sign of retribution in the shriveled face of my friend—a mark, or the faint trace, of a world in which some legible relation exists between justice and suffering. To sit in the sickroom (where we all know that a bed awaits us) is to slip back to "the era before . . . the dissociation of misfortune . . . and fault." If one travels back in mind to such a time, when a person's fate could be understood as having a moral appropriateness, one may feel an ominous but somehow reassuring "dread of the impure."[21] If, in other words, suffering and fault are imagined to stand in some sort of stable relation, one may discern at least a hint of order, of what some theologians used to call "excellency," in the fact of human pain. But today, if one reaches consciously for this kind of reassurance—if the nasty thought rises into consciousness that the victim deserves his fate—one feels perverse; in the patent disorder of our world the only feeling that lingers after such a regression is shame.

This shame arises from deep within our hollowness as modern beings and reminds us of what it must once have been to have "a coherent view of the world as a moral order reflecting God's purposes and physically sensitive to the moral conduct of human beings."[22] Some people still stubbornly harbor such a view—people, for instance, who believe that the victims of AIDS are being justly punished for ungodly behavior and that the disease of their bodies manifests a corruption in their souls. It is easy to dismiss such thoughts as primitive, superstitious, and inhumane —and so they are. But no matter how repugnant these thoughts may be, most people, if they are honest with themselves, will admit that they yearn for a world in which "each action of the soul becomes meaningful . . . complete in meaning—in *sense*—and complete for the senses."[23] Everyone wants to live in a world in which evil can still be recognized, have meaning, and require a response.

When this desire takes the form of an effort to get back the sense of evil in ways that have been superseded by history, it cannot succeed. Sin and sexuality, for instance, will never be reconnected as they once were, because the original linkage doubtless arose as a means of establishing social stability at a time when sex could not be separated from pregnancy. Morals do have genealogies; and, like an infertile family, a particular moral idea can reach a point where its lineage comes to an end. For most of human history, uncontrolled female sexuality was deemed sinful because it had a calculable social cost. It was incompatible with the patrilinear family and, later, with the whole social organization of bourgeois society. It was a taboo, or sin, whose rationality needed no defense. But when the technology of modern contraception broke this chain of cause and effect between sex, pregnancy, and morality, it broke it permanently. To try to get back this shattered ideal of chastity as virtue, as some well-meaning people are trying to do, is to tinker with fragments that cannot be reassembled into their old integrity. Our understanding of evil needs to be renewed, not restored.

Whether our culture can long sustain itself without *some* reinvigorated sense of sin is an open question. An answer is hinted at by the fact that Satan shows signs of coming back. He remains a presence in subjective experience even if the existence of satanic cults in the contemporary United States has not been documented as an objective fact. A growing number of "recovered memory" cases—persons who, under therapy or hypnosis, recall traumatic events from their past—have lately involved recollections of having been abused at the hands of Satan worshippers.[24] And never before have so many novels and films portrayed acts of sadism, mutilation, and terror. As we lose touch with the idea of evil, we seem to need more and more vivid representations of it—as if it were a drug whose potency diminishes with each use.

Consider a recent retail innovation on the American scene: the appearance of secondhand exchange bookstores into which customers bring used books for credit toward the purchase of someone else's dog-eared paperbacks. Like small-town public libraries, they are hubs through which books circulate, in which one browses not just through the commodities of remote publishers but through the recent experiences of one's neighbor. On the evidence of the bartered books, these experiences seem to be mainly sexual fantasies and sensations of horror and fear. Inhabited by vampires and witches, these shops are places of erotic enticement—reminders that reading still carries a faint flavor of illicit opposition to the whole tone of modern life, that it remains an act of "silent privacy, [performed] in the lair of the skull."[25] They suggest a response to our panic over the loss of a language for speaking about evil.

What are the horror books that fill these shops all about? And why are millions drawn to them? The novels typically tell the story of a protagonist (a detective, or a psychiatrist, or some unwitting witness), a classic liberal—rational, irreligious, tolerant, inclined to understand and sympathize—who finds himself face to face with a particularly brutal or serial killer.[26] The plot hinges not so much on identifying the perpetrator, who is usually known to the reader early on, as on explaining how he got to be what he is. In these books, which are not so much whodunits as psychological case studies, the hunt is less for the criminal than for his history.

More often than not, he turns out to have been an abused child who in his own way becomes a fierce believer. He attains feelings of religious intensity when he kills; and he may have a penchant for gambling—believing that through his supernatural powers he can spin the fruits of the slot machine into perfect alignment or coax the roulette ball into the chosen slot. He is, in one case, the child of a stern minister and a merciless mother, who, when she catches him masturbating, holds out his palm, slices deeply across it with a kitchen knife, and salves the wound with lipstick—a technique he later adopts as his way of marking the corpses of his victims. In another, he is a boy who by the age of eight must learn, in his father's blood-drenched butcher shop, how to skin and dress a deer carcass, while by night he submits to the sexual terror of his father's wife—who claims him as her own child only so she can torture him for being what he is in fact: the filthy excrescence of her husband's lust upon the body of a prostitute. In another, he is born with fissures in his lips and palate, "more like a leaf-nosed bat than a baby," and, after his mother abandons him, is raised by a grandmother who disciplines him by running scissors across the shaft of his penis. Grown up, he has his face sewn together and becomes a bodybuilder. He locates happy families through his job developing snapshots in a photo shop—and, in acts that look random to the gaping world, he kills and mutilates them in their snugness.[27]

These creatures conform to the ancient model of Satan as discarded, unloved son—a being once suppressed by some unappeasable authority. So when the pursuer first stalks the killer, he may feel sympathy, may even have reformist and therapeutic instincts, as if he were chasing a wounded child. (Some recent crime novels feature killers with multiple personalities—one gentle and benign, the other brutal.) The hunter is at first reluctant to condemn this pathetic victim of someone else's cruelty, but by the end he rises to a murderous rage of his own. He is a version of the bespectacled scientist of 1950s science-fiction movies—the egg-head who steps out to greet the alien monster, welcomes him, reasons with him, and begs the knee-jerk soldiers not to shoot and thereby "rob science" of the precious specimen that stands (benignly, he thinks) before them. In the old movies, this credulous fool is usually, after a perplexed pause from the creature, vaporized or bludgeoned to death. But in the new genre of horror fiction the good guy is more likely to conclude after a struggle with himself that the police mentality is right, that it is either the creature's life or his own. So in an act of almost sexual relief, he summons up his suppressed anger and blows the bastard away.

There seems, in America at the moment, to be an enormous appetite for this kind of writing. It signals a pent-up fury throughout the culture at the kind of mentality that William James, at the beginning of our century, attributed to "guileless thoroughfed thinkers explaining away evil and pain," or at what Lionel Trilling, fifty years later, called "the fatuity that does not know the evil of the world."[28] Its real theme is the liberal protagonist's conquest of his initial naïveté, which is exposed as a form of moral prudery.

This theme is certainly not confined to formulaic horror fiction. In the last few years it has been taken up by a good number of serious novelists (by no means only American ones), including John L'Heureux (*The Shrine at Altamira* [1992]), Thomas Berger (*Meeting Evil* [1992]), Ian McEwan

(*Black Dogs* [1992]), Russell Banks (*The Sweet Hereafter* [1991]), Jayne Anne Phillips (*Shelter* [1994]), and many others. Nor is fiction the only venue for this discussion. *Time* magazine recently featured a cover story on the subject of evil; *Newsweek* matched it later with a story about the loss of our capacity for shame; *Nightline* has devoted a program to exorcism; *The New Yorker* ran a two-part investigative report on satanic ritual abuse of children. Even MTV has gotten into the act, with a program on how the seven deadly sins are understood in teen culture. Several television specials have been broadcast on related issues (serial killers are all the rage), including an interesting HBO program, *Confronting Evil*, which takes the viewer into prison visiting rooms to witness confrontations between victims of violent crime and the criminals who attacked them. The question that motivates the victim, as he sits across from the man who has mutilated his life, is always the same: "Why did you do this?" The answer is invariably a version of "I don't know."

This flustered response to evil is the subject of this book. It is neatly summed up in one of the best of the recent horror novels (Thomas Harris's *The Silence of the Lambs* [1988])—in an exchange between an imprisoned madman, a psychiatrist who bites his victims to death and subsequently cannibalizes them, and a young female FBI agent who seeks his help in pursuing another serial killer. The mad doctor stands, straitjacketed, inside his Plexiglas cage and addresses the young woman outside it, who is soft-spoken, methodical, and named for a small bird:

> "Nothing happened to me, Officer Starling. *I* happened. You can't reduce me to a set of influences. You've given up good and evil for behaviorism, Officer Starling. You've got everybody in moral dignity pants—nothing is ever anybody's fault. Look at me, Officer Starling. Can you stand to say I'm evil?"[29]

These words are an epitome of modern horror—the horror of knowing that we cannot answer the monster's question.

The pages that follow are an attempt to tell the story of this reticence—how it began, how it grew, and what, if anything, may follow when it comes to an end.

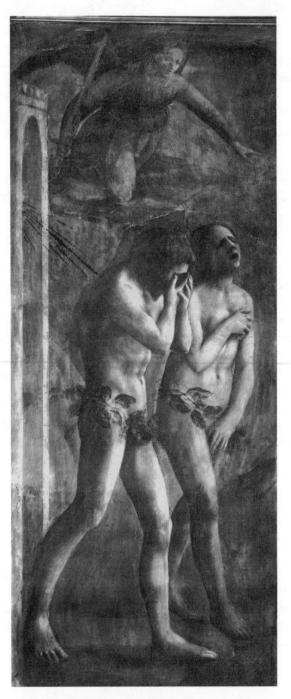

Masaccio, Expulsion from Paradise *(fresco, c. 1425)*
(BRANCACCI CHAPEL, SANTA MARIA DEL CARMINE, FLORENCE)

PART ONE

The Age of Belief

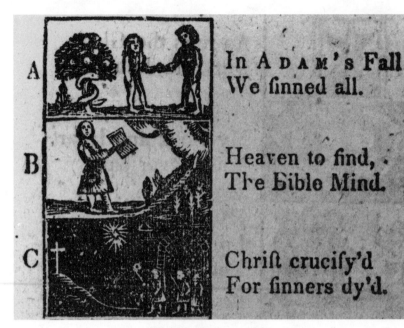

The New England Primer

ONE

The Old Enemy Comes
to the New World

[1]

Once, Satan was understood to be everywhere. But when he attacked, he gave the "fatal stab unseen," and his slyness—his very essence —was confirmed by the difficulty of recognizing him. This was always true of him, as Baudelaire made clear in his famous remark that the devil's cleverest wile is to convince us that he does not exist. One way to track the approach of modernity is to follow the devil's decline into invisibility, a process that has seemed, for centuries, as ominous as it was inevitable and that began a long time ago. "It is a policy of the Devil," remarked one Englishman in the years before the first American settlements, "to persuade us that there is no Devil."[1] As long ago as 1600, Satan had embarked on his modern project of feigning humility.

He had once been a braggart crowing in God's throne, as in the medieval mystery plays: "Aha, that I am wondrous bright . . . / All in this throne if that I were / Then should I be as wise as he." But by the time of the high Elizabethan drama of Marlowe and Shakespeare two centuries later, he has put on a disguise or stepped behind the curtain; he has become the debonair Mephistopheles and the poisonous whisperer, Iago. Yet a millennium before, in the early Christian era and into the Middle Ages, when the air was thought to be so thick with demons that a needle dropped from heaven would have to pierce one on its way down, his appearance and attributes had already been subject to fierce debate. This was in part because there was no sacred text in the Judeo-Christian tradition that exhibited him with entire clarity. "We gather not from the four gospels alone any high-raised fancies concerning this Satan," Melville remarked many centuries later, "we only know him from thence as the personification of the essence of evil."[2]

Scripture, of course, is full of images of evil—the serpent of Genesis; the Lucifer of Isaiah; Beelzebub in the Gospel of Luke; St. Paul's Belial, the "prince of the power of the air," and the devil who speaks to Christ like a pimp: "All this power will I give thee, and the glory of them: for that is delivered unto me; and to whomsoever I will I give it."[3] But the devil as a figure of identifiable aspect exists in the Bible only sporadically and in fragments that only later were assembled into a unified concept.

It took centuries for this to happen. The Christian devil emerged slowly as the amalgamation of all the scriptural elements—a process that can be followed at the linguistic as well as the doctrinal level. The Hebrew word *Satan*, which means obstructor or adversary, is given in the Book of Job to the agent of God who is sent to test Job's constancy, and to the obstacle against which David must prove his kingship in the first Book of Chronicles. This Satan, as one writer genially puts it, has "access to Heaven . . . and [is] evidently on good terms with the Almighty."[4] When the Old Testament was rendered into Greek in the third century, the Greek word *diabolos* (from *dia-bollein*, to tear apart) was chosen to translate this Hebrew Satan, and at the same time a different Greek word, *satanas*, was used in the New Testament to denote, not a tempter sent by God to test men, but an enemy of God himself. This new Satan appears most vividly in the Book of Revelation as "that old serpent, called the Devil, and Satan . . . cast out into the earth."[5] (Still another word, *daimon*, was used to signify various evil spirits from the Hebrew texts, such as the demon bride in the apocryphal Book of Tobit.) To compound the confusion, the Greek *diabolos* and *satanas* were both rendered as "Satan" in the Tudor-Stuart English translations, culminating with the standard King James version of 1604. By the later Renaissance, therefore, when the Bible had become the central vernacular text of every literate Englishman, a permanent consolidation of subtly different meanings had taken place, and Satan had reemerged as a unified contradiction, an inherently paradoxical creature.

But even before the contaminations of translation, he had already been ambiguous in the Hebrew Scriptures. In the Book of Job he has a certain independence, standing apart from the other "sons of God," and answering God's query "Whence comest thou?" with a renegade's insolence: "From going to and fro in the earth, and from walking up and down in it." When God takes up this gambit, and holds up his servant

Job as "a perfect and an upright man, one that feareth God, and escheweth evil," Satan concentrates his insolence into a specific taunt, daring God to test Job by tormenting him: "Put forth thine hand now, and touch all that [Job] hath, and he will curse thee to thy face." Thus begins the contest over Job's endurance—initiated by a cheeky, meddling Satan who doubts the possibility that a faithful man can exist in the world, and who thereby challenges his father's dominion. Show me this perfect man, he says, and I will reduce him to sputtering curses. Yet once God accepts the challenge, Satan subsides for the rest of the narrative into a mere agent of God's will, as if the master has decided to humor this upstart by agreeing to his plan at Job's expense. Everything Job has—his family, his possessions—will be fair game; only the man himself will be spared: "And the Lord said unto Satan, Behold, all that he hath is in thy power; only upon himself put not forth thine hand." After this dismissal, the story becomes a conversation between God and Job from which Satan is shut out.

With the scriptural canon still in flux, early Christian cosmology was continually redrawn and refined, and Satan's habitat, hell, was as unstable a concept as the devil himself. Some of the Apostolic Fathers considered hell as an amalgamation of the Hebrew *Sheol* and *Gehenna*—the former a place of eternal torment, the latter a kind of purgatory, a way station for souls awaiting salvation; others regarded it as a permanent prison for the damned. The distinction between God's angels of righteousness, whose office was to punish sinners, and the demons who stood watch over them in hell was also elusive. Inevitably, as one scholar puts it, "a curious question emerged: are the demons in hell keepers or inmates? Eventually they came to be both."[6]

Even the moral meaning of the events in the Garden of Eden was a matter of dispute. For the Gnostics, whose intellectual prestige peaked in the second century, the serpent was not a deceiver at all, but a giver of knowledge, the source of man's moral understanding. He was the generous creature who liberated man from the darkness imposed by a tyrannical God. (This is the beginning of a long tradition that culminates in the dark, magnetic heroes of Byron and many other romantic writers.) In cases where Scripture provided only hints of cosmic history—such as the tantalizing accounts of Christ's descent into hell ("I am he that liveth, and was dead . . . and have the keys of hell and of death")[7]—it took centuries for the doctrine to become hardened into orthodoxy. First introduced as a creed in the middle of the fourth century, the idea of

Christ's descent into hell slowly became part of the liturgy and took on the character of a violent assault—the "harrowing" (from the Old English *hergian*, to raid) of hell—as an important feature of the Last Judgment.[8]

Despite all the controversy over his nature, power, and habits, the devil, along with his subordinates and his dwelling place, has received sustained attention from only three major councils in the history of the church—in the sixth, thirteenth, and sixteenth centuries (Braga, Fourth Lateran, and Trent). A great deal of the European lore about Satan in fact derived from pagan traditions, from figures in Teutonic and Scandinavian folklore like Wotan and Loki, while the visual image of the devil had immediate sources in such predecessors as the Celtic horned god Cernunnos, the satyrs, and the Greek god Pan.

As this visual image of Satan emerged, there was still considerable disagreement over what exactly had precipitated his fall. According to Justin Martyr and Irenaeus, the fall of Satan followed the creation of man and was occasioned by his festering jealousy of Adam as a rival in the affections of God. In the fourth century a variant idea was introduced (by Lactantius): that the object of Satan's jealousy was not Adam, but Christ, who stood in the mind of the jealous angel as a kind of favored older brother. Both of these accounts had at their heart the problem of what we would call "sibling rivalry." Meanwhile other theologians, notably Origen, were convinced that Satan fell *before* the creation out of pure jealousy of God himself—a chronology that eventually became the orthodox version, as narrated, for example, in Milton's *Paradise Lost*. It is striking how close in both the "Oedipal" and the sibling-rivalry versions the ancient story of Satan's fall runs to the paradigms of modern psychoanalysis.

A great deal of early Christian writing is devoted, then, to the exposition of the nature of Satan's pride. For some writers it is a desire to supplant the father; for others it is Satan's need to believe in his own self-creation, or to govern himself without higher authority, or to achieve apotheosis without waiting for permission from God. When these ambitions are thwarted, and Satan is reduced not merely to subservience but to exile and disgrace, the plot of evil in the Christian tradition comes to center on man. The story becomes a tale of revenge, and Satan's satisfaction comes from his power to distract, inveigle, and corrupt God's new human favorite. The story of Satan's work in the world becomes the tale, in psychoanalytic terms, of the id breaking free from the superego—with the result that the ego is left broken and permanently in pain.

Despite the fluidity in early Christian thinking about Satan, there was always, along with this central idea that man's sin recapitulates Satan's pride, another constant element that unified these views into something we may call a tradition: the idea that Satan is a being without a center. This idea emerged at a time when the Christian community was small and riven, huddling in the face of persecution and—since the faith was fragile and new—intensely wary of heresy. Satan bears the marks of these stresses. He is, at bottom, a deceiver; he is falsehood, doubt, despair. He is the embodiment of fear. As a picture of his physical appearance begins to take shape (in the third and fourth centuries), he is often a creature of mingled parts—"a beast," according to Athanasius, "like to a man to the thighs but having legs and feet like those of an ass." Sometimes handsome, he is also able to disguise himself as "giants, wild beasts, and creeping things."[9]

One of his favorite haunts is the theater, where makeup and costumes and the whole spectacle of feigning are devoted to the exhibition of lies for profit or pleasure. He is an enthusiastic gambler, enticing men to mock God's providence by betting their fortunes on blind chance. Wherever he can, he subverts and inverts the structures and customs of ordinary life; he and his followers ride horses sitting backward in the saddle. Sometimes he is singular and sometimes plural—dispatching an army of demons with thin, windy voices who take on false appearances (*schemata*) and enter the bodies of their victims. Thus begins the tradition that demons are bloodless and cold, a legend invoked by women who claimed to have been raped by the devil and to have known their assailant by the coldness of his flesh. In some traditions the devil has a three-pronged penis capable of filling a woman's vagina, anus, and mouth simultaneously; he is not so much a rapist as a superequipped seducer who finds willing partners among women whose desires are beyond the competence of ordinary men. "You are the Devil's doorway," Tertullian said of Eve.[10]

All these bewildering attributes are finally reducible to one: Satan has no essence. He is the torturer and the flatterer, the usurer and the bearer of bribes, the satyrlike angel with the giant and multiple phallus, who knows the wantonness of women; but he can also transform himself into a lascivious temptress with silken skin. He is, in effect, a dark counterpart to Christ: an embodied contradiction, a spirit who chooses, at will, the form of his incarnation. As one of his most learned students, the historian Jeffrey Burton Russell, has put it in a nicely oxymoronic phrase, he is "pure—though purely corrupt—spirit."[11]

At the heart of early Christian diabolism, then, is the difficult idea of a devil who is simultaneously corporeal and inessential. He is contemptible and petty, yet if one reads about him in Patristic texts, one is struck above all by how vividly he inhabits the writers' imagination. He is a brilliant presence in the illuminated manuscripts and mosaics and oils—a semi-human creature with the features of a dog, or a half-ape, or sometimes he is a human figure with tail or horns, or simply an ordinary man with devious eyes. In all these forms he is a living actor in the world, a creature with whom men entered into contracts and pacts. (This notion proved to be a convenient basis for the persecution of Jews and others whose religious practices could be interpreted as satanic covenants.) Satan leaves his mark on the very landscape—in craters left by meteorites, in sandbars upon which ships run aground, even in odd rock formations, canyons, and gorges that seem carved out of benign nature with the purpose of malevolent distortion. One still encounters place names today that derive from a time when the devil was a mischievous wanderer at play in the world—Devil's Peak, Devil's Slide, Devil's Gorge.

[2]

When America was founded, Europe had moved to the edge of modernity, and the devil as an imaginable creature was coming under the pressure of a new skepticism. The westward movement of European civilization was, in the first instance, a triumph of empirical science and a blow to a cosmology that held the world to be flat and the oceans untraversible. Distances that could once only have been imagined could now be measured; places that could only have been surmised could now be seen. It was inevitable that this reorganization of reality would reach what Cotton Mather, at the end of the seventeenth century, called "the invisible world," the place from which the devil made his visitations.

Before the invention of the astrolabe and quadrant, by which latitude could be roughly calculated and a course plotted out of sight of land, European mariners could only dream of ocean voyages. Before these instruments came aboard Portuguese ships in the early 1400s, long-distance trade had been limited to the range of oar-driven galleys that hugged the shore, and sailors had a well-founded horror of the open sea. With their square-rigged ships and navigational cunning, first the Portuguese, then the Spanish broke out of this imprisonment, and eventually forced new continents into the European consciousness. Beyond range of the naked eye from the European mainland there had long been a watery expanse of forbidding legend—an imaginary geography interrupted only by the uninhabitable isles of the Hesperides and the Antipodes, which were thought to balance Africa on the other side of the vast, unknown ocean. There was some unconfirmed evidence of other lands to the west—garbled accounts of the hot springs of Greenland, and the occasional washing ashore of strange tree branches onto beaches in the Canaries, the Azores, and even the Hebrides. Columbus, who took the minority view that a westward voyage would lead him directly to the East Indies, did not fully realize that he had found a new continent until his fourth voyage, in 1498. Amerigo Vespucci, who remained in posthumous competition with Columbus until the United States settled on a name ("Columbia" was used interchangeably with "America" even into the nineteenth century), was convinced from the start that he had found a new world. He reported that the "Indians" were cannibals, and, in a double insult to the propriety of their women and the virility of their men, he claimed that the females were so lascivious that they enlarged the penises of their lovers by subjecting them to the bites of venomous insects.[12]

Despite such horrors and titillations, the discovery of the New World constricted the European imagination as much as it enlarged it. Driven by an appetite first for gold, then for salable commodities—fish, fur, skins, timber, spices, slaves—Europeans found that the quasi-magical world which ghosts and devils inhabited was growing smaller as the charted world grew larger; as early as the first decade of the sixteenth century a young geographer at Lorraine had added a plausible map of America to his edition of Ptolemy. The mythic ocean of the tropics—green and boiling—which had existed in the imaginations of sailors who had no means to venture south of the twenty-fifth parallel, soon disappeared, to be replaced by the hospitable South Atlantic of Magellan and da Gama. Though the Spanish and Portuguese were the first to traverse the Atlantic east to west, and to report the wealth and savories of the southern American continent, it was left to the Dutch, English, and French to devise a way to settle the more northern regions, which Jacques Cartier, as he said of Labrador in the 1530s, was "inclined to regard . . . as the [land] God gave to Cain."[13] The invention that drove this process was not a navigational instrument or new arrangements of masts and sail;

it was the idea of the joint-stock company, by which the risk of outfitting ships for ocean transport could be spread among many investors and the slim chance of gain thereby made alluring.

Not long ago, this story of the rational Western mind bringing order to the dream-chaos of an unknown country was commonly presented as a story of heroism. Now it is more usually told as the upheaving of European hypocrisy onto clean shores—the invasion of a virgin continent by a culture whose record was "deforestation, erosion, siltation, exhaustion, pollution, extermination, cruelty, destruction, and despoliation."[14] As modern historians look back on the volley of events from about 1490 to 1640, they have tended, especially in recent years, to see in them a shriveling of the reverent imagination and the onset of an instrumental attitude toward nature. And it is true that by the end of the sixteenth century the New World was already being regarded less as a wondrous park of God's profusion and more as a storehouse of commodities. If the first discoverers brought back enchanting stories of armless men and fountains of youth, those who followed later (entrepreneurs like Sir Walter Raleigh and Captain John Smith) began to look at the landscape and the natives with the cold eye of the soldier and surveyor. From our distance of time, one way to watch this process is to register the systematic extinction of one fanciful species after another in the European mind. Columbus, at the end of the fifteenth century, came from a world where centaurs, satyrs, cyclopes, and dragons were still believed to inhabit the forests of Europe, and he was sure he had found the tracks of lions and griffins on the island of Jamaica. By the beginning of the nineteenth century, when Lewis and Clark were dispatched into the Louisiana Territory by President Jefferson, the imaginary bestiary had been almost totally depleted, and their charts and inventories include no animals that we have not seen in the zoo.[15]

We have now reached the point in the career of this story where the "discovery of America" (the very phrase is now rejected as an insult to the people who had lived there before Europeans gave it a European name) is regarded as something of a pornographic joke. One consequence of this has been the discrediting of a national mythology. We have gone from what Arthur Schlesinger, Jr., has recently called "exculpatory history" to what may be called culpable history. The names of Columbus's ships, for instance, which every schoolchild used to recite as a litany of courage symbolized in three plucky little boats called *Niña*, *Pinta*, and *Santa María*, are now exposed as nicknames for Castilian whores. Columbus, in some recent assessments, has become a semi-crazed charlatan who claimed for himself the 10,000 maravedi and the silk doublet he had posted as a reward for the first man to spy land—even though a sleepless sailor in the crow's nest really deserved them.[16]

There can be no doubt that the European settlement was a violent process whose cost in human blood was concealed in the tropes of contemporary witnesses, not only in the reports of the first voyagers, and later the English and French, but also in erotic metaphors that in due course came from faraway poets, as when John Donne celebrated in the early 1600s his mistress's body—"O My America, my new-found land!"—by likening his palpating hands to roving explorers of the New World. In our own time such charming analogies have been indignantly rebuked. And in a mood that seems the cultural equivalent of death-bed confession, we now prefer to speak of the land as "widowed" rather than virgin; we know that most of its native inhabitants died from smallpox or measles even *before* the arrival of the main force of Europeans (having been infected by the first scouting parties), and many of the rest from gunfire. Once celebrated as a triumph of the adventurous European spirit, the settlement of North America now seems to us a bloody business enterprise decorated with the language of piety. In this revision of history we seem to take a kind of ghoulish pride.[17]

Despite the discomfort of having a glorious history exposed as a fraud, there is much to recommend the new story. It is, on the whole, less distorted than the old, which, in the version most directly concerned with the settlement of what would eventually become the United States, featured heroic Englishmen huddled in the snow, staying alive by the warmth of their faith and the mercy of a few exceptional Indians. The fact is that the real story, like most human experience, was a mixture of cowardice and decency, and our early historians knew this better than we do. They told it not as a monotone celebration or indictment but as a contrapuntal story, and that remains the best way to tell it. They knew, as one eighteenth-century South Carolinian, David Ramsay, put it, that at its center was "such a crowd of woes, as excites an apprehension, that the evil has outweighed the good." And in some places—such as Puritan New England, where the medieval Christian cosmology had been transported largely intact—they warned against "imputing to the Devil too much of our own sin and guilt."[18] This caution, delivered while the invisible world continued to wane and the measurable world to supplant

it, raised pressing questions for early Americans: Where was the devil to
be found? Could he survive at all in the New World of rationality? And
if so, in what form?

[3]

When the first band of English Congregationalists began assembling
along the cold shore of Massachusetts Bay in the 1620s and 1630s,
they brought with them a keen alertness for any sign that Satan had come
along as a stowaway:

> *Methinks I heare the Lambe of God thus speake*
> *Come my deare little flocke, who for my sake*
> *Have lefte your Country, dearest friends, and goods*
> *And hazarded your lives o'th raginge floods*
> *Posses this Country; free from all anoye*
> *Here I'le bee with you, heare you shall Injoye*
> *My sabbaths, sacraments, my minestrye*
> *And ordinances in their puritye*
> *But yet beware of Satans wylye baites*
> *Hee lurkes amongs yow, Cunningly hee waites . . .*[19]

This little poem, written by a man who stayed only briefly in New England, gives a glimpse of the Puritan whom we know from lore and legend. He is hardy and abstemious, with an attitude toward Satan like that
of an advance-party volunteer determined not to be ambushed. We imagine him going willingly to be admonished by his minister, who delivers
frank sermons full of warnings that the devil is lying in wait. "O foole,
O foole . . . this night thy soule may be taken from thee . . ."[20] This
popular image of the Puritan is not a bad distortion as far as it goes; it
tells us that he feared Satan lavishly, but it does not tell us what Satan
meant to him. If the poem does no better, it is because the pioneer
Puritan did not really know what the New World devil was going to look
like.

His religious education told him that Satan was a wizard of disguise.
It told him, too, that he himself had been born a child of the devil, mired
in sin, and that only unearned grace, which God dispensed or withheld
at his inscrutable pleasure, could lift him out of his filth. If he was an

indentured servant or an artisan's apprentice, he may have left England in order to save himself from joining the flow of vagabonds that was swelling the highways and towns, and from turning to begging and robbery (to "the life of a beast," as one minister called it) to stay alive.[21] If he was a clergyman or small landowner, he had to search his conscience to discover whether he had been justified in leaving his parish and neighbors in England for a land where, he hoped, one could live without moral compromise. And if he had been a man of landed wealth, he had found himself challenged in England by entrepreneurs who, without scruple, were fencing in their fields and replacing tenants with sheep. Not wanting to join such "rackers of rent" in forcing off their land families who had lived there for generations, he was nevertheless tempted by the profit opportunities in the cloth trade—and he knew that sheep and other commercial livestock were becoming more valuable than a tenant's seasonal service. He knew, in other words, that if he continued to honor the old traditions of charging his tenants nominal fees and treating them as his father and grandfather had done, he might squander his family fortune.

This emigrant to New England was likely to be a man who had wanted in conscience to honor the old customs and values, but who, in reason, knew he was living in a newly competitive world, with new rules and new opportunities. The world he left behind was a hall of mirrors from which every passageway out seemed blocked by a multiplied and distorted image of the self. And so he came to America, in part at least, to escape himself.[22]

These first emigrants to New England were modern and medieval at once, striving and static, ambitious and deeply suspicious of ambition. To and about themselves, they said that the apostolic age was their model for church, family, and community. They had objected in England to the intrusive power of a nation-state that ruled the church, and many of them had withdrawn into groups that recognized a minister's authority, not because it had been transmitted to him from bishop and king, but because it was conferred and ratified by the pious flock itself.

Yet with all their self-identification as a group of uncompromising Christians sequestered away from the hurtling world, they were also (as their enemies loudly pointed out) in the vanguard of the emerging business culture in England. Heavily represented in the ranks of lawyers and the "chattering and chaunging"[23] merchants, they insisted on regular observance of the Sabbath, which, they said, was out of devotion to the rule of God. Six days of work and one of steady worship, in which the sermon summoned them to diligence in their callings, also ensured a rhythm of living that fit the requirements of an urban tradesman's life much better than did the holy days and harvest festivals of the country. Puritan Sabbath sermons were as likely to be concerned with ethical problems posed by poor relief and creditors' obligations as with biblical doctrine. In the end, the key difference between these Puritans and their fellow Englishmen was the self-consciousness with which they lived in between a medieval world that was passing out of existence and the modern world that was coming into being. Those who chose to leave England—under pressure from the king's monopolistic taxes or the bishop's orders to conform—continued to speak of themselves as "primitive" Christians. But they came to America in modern ships, subdued the Indians with modern weapons, and sent their goods back to modern markets. Their language was simply at odds with their circumstance, and Satan was the name they gave to the contradiction.

The colonies that they established were entirely different from previous European settlements in the New World—including the earlier English colony in Virginia, which seemed to be regarded by many of its settlers as a temporary act of fortune hunting. The earlier Spanish invasion had been an affair of soldiers and priests; and the French did not at first encourage large-scale permanent migration into their own North American territories, which were regarded essentially as military and trading outposts. The English emigration to the northern colonies, by contrast, was overwhelmingly composed of families, and was conceived from the start as a permanent settlement. Like all immigrants since, these New Englanders lived in guilty equipoise between the country they had left behind (to which old friends beckoned them back, while enemies accused them of finding convenient reasons for fleeing) and the wild country they had come to. Many were younger sons with new or prospective wives, spurred by the feeling that pathways to better social status were closing in England, where a father's acreage had to be held for his heir.

However far he was willing to go to secure a new standing in a new world, this disfranchised young man was taught by his religion that the material comforts that eluded him were "but a shadow, a blast, a bubble . . . and will deceive us," while the "things that are not seen; they are eternall."[24] The imperative to look away from ephemera fitted his new life in New England, where he was likely to live, at least at first, in a

house of wattle and daub that might be swept away at any moment by
an ice storm or an undoused brand:

> *Here stood that Trunk, and there that chest;*
> *There lay that store I counted best;*
> *My pleasant things in ashes lye*[25]

And if a child went to bed with flushed cheeks, her parents knew she
might be dead in the morning.

All such sorrows were, moreover, messages from God—to be read and
"improved," as they put it, not just endured. The modern concepts of
chance and accident did not exist for these early Americans. Although
Reformation theologians had made allowance for certain social practices
such as the drawing of lots as a "casualty or casuall event purposely applied to the deciding of some doubt," it was generally agreed that "that
which we call fortune is nothing but the hand of God, working by causes
and for causes that we know not." Another theologian put it even more
clearly: "that which seems Chance to us, is as a word of God acquainting
us with his will."[26]

To be sure, some events—being "crossed oft by an Hare" during a
walk, or finding "a peece of old yron, [or] spie[ing] a covey of Partridges,
[or] hav[ing] his hat blowne of his head, and the like,"[27] were considered
too minor to merit close inspection and interpretation. Obsessive attention to such little events was the work of soothsayers and astrologers, who
construed even "meerely casuall" events as significant messages from
God. Yet the doctrine of providence maintained that *all* events, no matter
how trivial, were under God's command.

This vision of a perfectly governed world began to break down in the
later seventeenth century, when a certain franticness starts to infect the
act of reading the world for signs of God's will, as if the signs were fading.
Samuel Sewall, a Boston burgher who became one of the judges in the
Salem witchcraft trials, kept a diary well into the second decade of the
eighteenth century whose pages are filled with notations of such signs.
As the years pass, a certain desperation enters into Sewall's transcriptions
that suggests he is no longer quite sure that God remains concerned: he
makes no distinction between God's sending rain to subdue "the (otherwise) masterless flames" of the Great Boston Fire of 1676, and his own
clumsy spilling of a "whole Vinyard Cann of water just before we went
to Bed."[28]

Though it may seem preposterous when it slides into this sort of compulsiveness, this God-centered way of living continues to exercise a remarkable power over the modern imagination. Perhaps because we no longer credit the idea that "the starry roofe of this world is but the pavement of that,"[29] we can still appreciate the passion with which others once held to it. Surely it remains possible to feel the proximity of fear to ecstasy in this report of a Weymouth man who "fell into some trouble of mind, and in the night cried out, 'Art thou come, Lord Jesus?' and with that leaped out of his bed in his shirt, and, breaking from his wife, leaped out at high window into the snow, and ran about seven miles off, and being traced in the snow, was found dead next morning. They might perceive, that he had kneeled down to prayer in diverse places."[30] There is testimony here to the enormous pressure behind the imperative of faith, a pressure under which minds could and did break. One may imagine this man, with his knees numb from the snow, dying happy as he submits to his vision of a succoring God.

To meet this demand of faith without falling outside the normal life of society (and being reviled as an "enthusiast") was, in its way, an even finer torture. In leaving the Church of England, the Puritan had left behind a church that operated by what we might now call "open admissions," in which the sacraments (baptism, communion) promised salvation for all who received them—to everyone, that is, except the outright scandalous. All subjects of the king were born into this church, and baptism sealed their membership. The Puritan, however, though disapproving of those who reserved the rite of baptism for adults coming publicly into the faith (such extremists were called Anabaptists—or, later, simply Baptists), nevertheless regarded the rite as merely the symbol of a reasonable hope that the persons received would subsequently confirm by their lives that God had indeed infused them with grace. Only the mysterious transformation of the soul, wrought freely by God, could ultimately make the sinner acceptable—could "justify" him—in the eyes of God.

This miraculous transformation was the heart of Puritan religion. It was an inner spiritual event. To maintain order in the household and the street and even in the soul was human work; but it was entirely God's work to take a selfish man and make him melt at the hardship of his neighbor. "A man," as a later theologian would put it, "is as passive in his Regeneration as he is in his first Generation"; he has, in other words, as much to do with his salvation as he did with the copulation that brought him into the world in the first place. Such a transformation, which the Puritans called conversion, had nothing to do with enforcement of the law (although the law did serve to show the unaided sinner his inability to obey it by relying on his own natural abilities). Conversion, as John Winthrop, first governor of the Massachusetts Bay Colony explained, did not involve small adjustments of behavior, whether inspired by embarrassment or shame or by outward restraint or compulsion:

> As when we bid one make the clock strike, he doth not lay hand on the hammer, which is the immediate instrument of the sound, but sets on work the first mover or main wheel, knowing that will certainly produce the sound which he intends. So the way to draw men to works of mercy is not by force of argument from the goodness or necessity of the work; for though this course may enforce a rational mind to some present act of mercy, as is frequent in experience, yet it cannot work such a habit in a soul, as shall make it prompt upon all occasions to produce the same effect.[31]

At the core of the Puritan movement was a rejection of the idea that a society may be arranged according to the principles of self-interest and rationality. God demanded more. He demanded that the creature, and thus the community, be refashioned, that the hearts of men be brought into harmony with their words and acts. God effected this conversion by "framing affections of love in the heart which will natively"—not by calculation or coercion—"bring forth" acts of mercy and love.[32] For those who have undergone this experience, the world, once in fragments, becomes whole; and sin, though always lurking to reestablish itself in the transformed heart, recedes like a nightmare upon waking.

In trying to express the nature of sin, Puritan preachers commonly used metaphors of blindness, senselessness, and stupidity, because sin was understood as a kind of comprehensive ignorance, a darkness in which the sinner wanders like an abandoned child. The Puritans had left behind the medieval notion that, as the historian Roland Bainton puts it, "specific offenses could be expiated by specific penances." Puritanism furnished no catalogue of "cardinal" or "deadly" sins (medieval tradition had enumerated them as pride, envy, anger, sloth, avarice, gluttony, and lust) that could be correlated with individual acts of transgression. The Puritan believed with Martin Luther that, in Bainton's words, "sins cannot be treated singly because the very nature of man is so perverted that he needs to be drastically remade."[33] The sinner was not a man with specific deficiencies or habits that could be supplied by example or corrected by practice; he was a twisted soul, to be pitied more than scorned. Only God—not his own pitiful efforts—could save him.

Although Anglican doctrine nominally agreed that the visible church on earth had no necessary relation to the invisible church of the saints (which only God could populate), the experience of worship—in a great cathedral filled with organ music, in the presence of crimson-clad priests who held gleaming censers and wore gold-flecked surplices—carried an implicit sensory guarantee that the dutiful worshipper was saved. In old England, the rituals of the state church—kneeling before the bishop as he shook the smoke of incense from the censer; listening to the soaring chords of the organ; or, in the smaller country churches, taking communion without inhibition from the priest—had offered a pledge of God's acceptance. These rituals were promises that the penitent could be made fit in the eyes of God and, like the rites of all sacramental religions, were a way to accommodate the imperfect self to God's demand for perfection.

There arises, therefore, a series of questions that historians are still struggling to answer: Why did these Puritan dissenters abandon their apparently generous church? Why were they dissatisfied? Who, in their souls, were these people who turned away from the comfortable house of the Church of England, and preached against its ceremonies, its surpliced bishops, and its whole hierarchy of ancient arrangements?

One way to approach an answer to these questions is to recognize that these were people who found in a church of open sacraments a cheapening of God's promise of salvation. Do not think that you shall be saved, they insisted, simply because you are the children of Christian parents. For the Puritan, each human soul is on its own—solitary, exposed, dependent on the unpredictable will of God. Even if your parents were among those in whom "Christ was Form'd, and visibly legible,"[34] as one preacher put it, it says nothing of you; it is blasphemous to imagine that grace can be transmitted through the loins. In this respect, Puritan theology was a kind of mirror of social reality: grace was no more inheritable than social standing at a time when even eldest sons born into substantial families found that their patrimony was not enough to ensure a status equal to that of their father.

But if grace could not be inherited (to believe that would be to revert to a tribal notion of God's people), neither could it be earned. To believe in grace as a reward for human righteousness would be to return to the covenant of works, which Adam had broken in Eden, and which (in the Puritan view) the Papists had turned into a system by which supplicants were invited to bribe a church that promised something it could not deliver. In fact, the Puritans argued, God had modified the original covenant of works when he renewed it for the Jews through Abraham:

> . . . it was a great mercy to [Abraham], to expresse thus much to him, *I am Al-Sufficient*, I am able to helpe thee, *I am thy exceeding great reward*, I am able to be a Sunne and a Shield unto thee, to fill thee with all comfort, and to deliver thee from all evill: but yet this which is heere added, is a mercy of a much higher nature, (saith the *Lord*) *I will make my Covenant betweene mee and thee;* that is, I will not onely tell thee what I am able to doe, I will not onely expresse to thee in generall, that I will deale well with thee, that I have a willingnesse and ability to recompence thee, if thou walke before mee, and serve mee, and be perfect; but I am willing to enter into Covenant with thee, that is, I will binde my selfe, I will ingage my selfe, I will enter into bond, as it were, I will not bee at liberty any more, but I am willing even to make a Covenant, a compact and agreement with thee.[35]

According to Christian myth, the Jews responded only fitfully to this unspeakable generosity, and, as St. Paul explained, God, through the sacrifice of Christ, then extended his covenant with "the house of Israel" yet further. He promised to all believers that "I will put my laws into their mind, and write them in their hearts . . . I will be merciful to their unrighteousnesse, and their sins and their iniquities will I remember no more."[36] This new and miraculously relenting covenant—the covenant of grace—was held out to the new "Israelites," and said simply, "Believe in me and you shall be saved." In this new age, the day of the inheritable covenant was over. Each person was now privileged or guilty not according to membership in a nation, but according to the sincerity of one's belief. A gospel minister might mediate between man and God, by offering doctrinal instruction and pastoral guidance, but in the last analysis the transaction was carried out entirely outside any human institution. It came into being through faith alone, and out of it emerged a new person.

Most of the crabbed tracts of the Puritans (who still identified strongly with the Old Testament Jews, in both their chosenness and their backsliding) were concerned with the problem of what this belief entailed, and how one could know its authenticity. How could you know if God had inscribed true faith in *your* heart? The temptation was to regard good social standing—Christian "carriage"—as evidence of the soul's reputation with God. This, according to these stringent Protestants, was a deadly mistake. A diligent churchgoer might look trim or stately and still be a vessel of Satan; and a poor servant in rags might glow with grace. Despite its severity, Puritanism was in essence a religion of comfort to the dispossessed—to the younger children of the gentry, to wage laborers who took up the radical cause during the English revolution, to women who "cleanse their children from their filth . . . sweep sincks, and scum pots."[37] Whoever its hottest adherents might have been in any particular time or place, at its heart was the belief that the things of this world are no more significant than the play of shadow upon a wall. Puritanism taught that the affections must be weaned from palpable things, and that the mind must concentrate on the exquisite hope of receiving the uncoerced lightnings of God—and that this hope could be realized for any man or woman chosen by God, regardless of his or her standing in the world.

These are among the reasons that, two hundred years after the first settlements, Nathaniel Hawthorne aimed his withering gaze at his New England forebears and charged them with hypocrisy. He took their ideals seriously. He was therefore offended by how far they fell short of them in the New World. He had them, in his great novel *The Scarlet Letter* (still the best commentary we have on early New England), wear gloves and ruffles embroidered by a woman whom they have condemned for her illicit love. He had them live in houses with bits of colored glass embedded in the stucco even as they preached against pride and ostentation. Hawthorne was very hard on his ancestors, as, he imagined, they would have been on him. He did not concede to them what we may more readily allow—that their demand to "live in the world, but not of it" was virtually impossible to honor. The great mass of the Puritan community surrendered early to the deepest contradiction in their contradictory religion: to the incessant paradox that God had no use for the tiny achievements of men and yet the only way to know one's standing in the mind of God was to take stock of one's worldly achievement. This need to exhibit the orderliness of the soul and its creations (to the self and to the community) was, as Max Weber argued in *The Protestant Ethic and the Spirit of Capitalism*, a force that transformed Europe, and it was transported to America near its height. In its most typical form it was an imperative to keep a clean and tidy home and business as the best assurance that God might be pleased with the way one groomed one's soul.

Puritanism, despite its fervent desire to return to the burning piety of the Apostolic age, helped to carry Europe, and the new child of Europe called America, into the modern world.

[4]

In this culture of spiritual cleanliness, it was tempting to reimagine Satan as the opposite of a fastidious Puritan saint, as an exemplar of the slovenly. If the primary virtues of medieval Catholicism had been poverty and chastity, over a period of centuries these were replaced by prosperity and the regulation of an orderly life. At the same time a coordinated shift took place in the conceptualization of sin by which some of the old deadly sins—especially sloth and lust—became deadlier. Laziness, alcoholism, and lewdness became stock elements in the reformers' satire of the Catholic clergy, and the Puritans who came to America brought such images of vice with them. They warned against keeping "froathy Company and Companions," against "Carnall Gentlemen and base refuse people" who "turn away from . . . a plain searching truth . . . but if any man will tell them some fine stories, Oh, this pleaseth them admirably."[38] There is the nervousness of the middling man in these proscriptions—a need to steer between the tavern hounds below and the indolent fops above. When these emigrants spoke of the "suburbs," they had in mind a semi-civilized place on the edge of the city where unkempt drifters lived; when they hunted for a witch, they were likely to find a stringy-haired widow mumbling to herself and living on the public dole. As such images accumulated, they became the foundation of American Protestant moralism, which surges up periodically into the outbursts of reform that punctuate American history—in, for example, the abolitionists' revulsion for the dissipated Southern dandy, or in the progressives' urgency to clean up the unhygienic immigrant.

Yet the origins of this tradition, in which sin is a synonym for the disreputable, are to be found less in early New England than in the South. Unlike New England, the South was settled at first by an all-male vanguard of soldiers and craftsmen who were comfortable within the established church and whose social origins tended to be low. There were debtors just out of or on the verge of prison, and young men without a calling or even a portion of an estate, leaders who, advertising themselves as fit for controlling any unruly crew, had spent their youth mysteriously wandering. In the South, the fear of degeneration seemed urgent from the start, as starvation, Indian ambush, and, later, sexual profligacy with defenseless slave women became regular observable features of life. The earliest emigrants to Virginia believed, as the future King James had written in the 1590s, that witchcraft was "most common in . . . [the] wild partes of the world," which was, after all, where they were going. The Indians, they thought, presented a spectacle of "tiranny chayned under the bonde of Deathe unto the Divell."[39] The Indians' complex polytheistic religion, to the extent that the newcomers paid any attention to it, struck them as just so much devil worship, or black magic. They thought of themselves as going to the devil's country for the purpose of raiding it and sending its plenty—and eventually themselves—home.

The more stringent Protestants of New England also brought with them a tradition that claimed the New World wilderness had been reserved as "Satan's hunting park" until their own arrival. But most of them were committed from the first to staying on. Some of them believed that

> when the devil was put out of his throne in the other parts of the world, and . . . the mouth of all his oracles was stopped in Europe, Asia, and Africa, he seduced a company of silly wretches to follow his conduct into this unknown part of the world, where he might lie hid and not be disturbed in the idolatrous and abominable, or rather diabolical service he expected from . . . his followers; for here are no footsteps of any religion before the English came, but merely diabolical.[40]

But in New England "this Antick Fancy of *America's* being Hell"[41] never really took hold. (The Puritan community included a number of serious students of the Indians' religion, who found in the natural piety of the wandering tribes no evidence of Satanism, but a resemblance to the ancient Hebrews and even a mirror of themselves.) It was chiefly in the South that the devil seemed a savage stalker outside the stockade rather than a master of disguise who was infiltrating the English community. By the mid-seventeenth century, when black slave labor began to be imported to work the tobacco plantations, speculation was revived in Virginia that "the Devil . . . has infused prodigious Idolatry into [the] hearts [of the blacks], enough to rellish his pallat and aggrandize their tortures when he gets power to fry their souls, as the raging Sun has already scorcht their cole-black carcasses."[42]

Unfortunately, the early Southern devil can only be glimpsed here and there, because there was nothing in the South like the systematic tradition of theological writing of New England. But surviving fragments suggest that the Southern devil was initially conceived as a creature who had slipped out of civilization; he had none of the regal arrogance of Milton's Satan, but was closer to Dante's—drooling and clawing like a child or an incontinent old man, blinded by his own tears of embarrassment. He was a devil of indolence and indulgence, a grotesque exaggeration of what was to become the Southern version of the classical ideal of *otium*. Trafficking in fraudulence and quackery, he was a charlatan dancing for rain, a demon well suited for people who "detested work more than famine."[43] A devil who embodied what they feared they might become, he was a progenitor of Huck Finn's Pap, snarling at those who had risen above him and full of bile against their hopes.

In New England, by contrast, a more subtle and morally demanding diabolism can be followed from the start, which was in many respects continuous with the medieval tradition. The New England devil was not an outsider; he was invasive, internal. The Puritans imagined a prideful Satan who, rather than anticipating what they might become, mocked them with an image of what they already were. This Satan may have been handed down to them over centuries from the Church Fathers through the medieval scholastics and the continental reformers, but in him they recognized, above all, a portrait—horrifying in its familiar pride—of themselves.

Perhaps the most conspicuous fact about the postmedieval world in which these early Americans lived was its human mobility. Moving in unprecedented numbers "outward from their original centers of habitation," people were finding themselves less firmly consigned than they had ever been to the status in which they were born.[44] With both physical and social mobility on the rise, it became, rather suddenly, a problem to fix proper proportions between acumen and greed. In such a world, in which the stabilities of feudal life were breaking down, certain questions became newly urgent: What was a fair return on an investment and what was excessive? What, in a hard winter, was one's obligation to one's neighbor? These sorts of questions occupied the minds of the early leaders of Massachusetts Bay. "What rule," they asked of themselves, "must we observe in lending" and in the "forgiving" of unpaid loans? "What rule must we observe and walk by in cause of community of peril?"[45] One reason they had come to America was to find a world where answers to such questions would be clear and consensual, where one loaned money not to a good credit risk but to a neighbor who needed it, where men of means might not be consigned to a personal hell of ethical uncertainty, as more than a few of them had felt themselves to be in England.

But even after the long ocean journey, these devilish questions followed them. As the New England English emerged in the middle of the century from their first small settlements—as from "an *Hive*, overstock'd with *Bees*"[46]—and pushed out into the Connecticut River valley, then to the Hudson River and beyond, church attendance fell, laws of compulsory attendance were passed, and tithes were levied. Merchants who sold dear were prosecuted by magistrates who appealed to the medieval idea of a "just price"—that is, a price that was voluntarily restrained by the seller in times of scarcity. In other words, the first New Englanders lived in a culture that was pushing in two directions at once: outward over the wilderness, with an irrepressible zeal for acquisition and gain (among the most active land speculators were the ministers themselves, who nevertheless decried the new country for being, as one put it, "full of healthful bodies, but sick souls"); and inward into the soul with a message of restraint and moderation.[47]

The ethical message was at odds with the social reality. Leading investors fell almost immediately to squabbling among themselves over land rights and, in times of famine, over the proper balance between charity and the prudent hoarding of grain. Relations among the several congregations and towns became uneasy, and struggles ensued over issues of church membership and the right understanding of difficult doctrines, especially the connection between justification and "sanctification," or the visible attributes of a justified Christian.

The concept of Satan was not exempt from these disturbances. He had been brought to New England as a central figure in the Puritans' dogma, but he quickly became a symbol adrift. One reason for this was that the changeable Satan of medieval tradition had a good many of the characteristics of the competent businessman. Traditionally a figure of anathema, he now became intertwined with a figure of aspiration. As the Genesis story confirmed, he had charm at the ready; he had the ability to inspire confidence in even the riskiest ventures (as Milton dramatized in *Paradise Lost*); he was restless within the world as it was delivered to him. And he had the glint of thwarted ambition in his eye. With all these ominous attributes, he gave up the futile quest for equality with God, and turned to the conscription of man.

This problematic Satan was an immensely important figure in early America because it was a culture saturated with the consciousness of sin. There is no body of writing before or since the Puritans that has issued more precise maps of the intricate soul; ministers took exquisite, almost competitive, pains in laying out the traps and dodges of Satan as he wound his way into the hearts of unwary men. Yet Satan is almost never pictured vividly. A concordance of Puritan writings, if ever such a volume could be compiled, would list many entries for "devil" and not a few for "Satan," but if one turns to the cited page in the hope of finding a noxious creature with fire in his nostrils, or eyes in his buttocks, or even a horned silhouette, one will be disappointed. The Puritans' Satan was much more an abstract idea than a representable creature or thing; exorcism was a discredited Papist ritual, a "foul superstition and gross magic," and sin itself tended to be represented as a kidnapping of the soul by a captor less brutal than maddeningly elusive. The rhetorical power of the Puritan preacher lay in his ability to evoke sin as something both overwhelming and insidiously slight: "like winde when it gets into the veines, it will have vent, and a troublesome one: and so will sin, if it gets into the soule."[48] Its deadly silence accorded with Christ's teaching that unspoken thoughts are as blameworthy as actions:

> Do ye not perceive, that whatsoever thing from without entereth into the man, *it* cannot defile him; because it entereth not into his heart, but into the belly, and goeth out in the draught, purging all meats? . . . That which cometh out of the man, that defileth the man . . . evil thoughts, . . . covetousness, wickedness, deceit.[49]

So a sinner might be externally indistinguishable from a godly man; he might smile and speak sugared words, but the difference was known by God. "This people draweth nigh unto me with their mouth," Christ is reported to have said in the Gospel of Matthew, "and honoureth me with *their* lips; but their heart is far from me"—a hypocrisy known to the sinner himself through the torment of guilt. "The Lord," the Puritan preacher reminded his congregation, "will *search Jerusalem with candles* . . . the Lord seeth all the pranks of the adulterer in the darkest night."[50]

[5]

To understand the origins of this paradoxical idea of sin as both obscure and intensely visible, we must turn back to a countertradition within Christianity that posed a challenge to diabolism itself. This tradition, to which Puritanism tried to belong, opposed the temptation to give the devil a fixed habitation and a name and thereby to formalize belief in what a later theologian termed "a principle or force of evil antecedent to any evil human action."[51] It heeded a countervailing impulse, which was to suppress the devil's actuality, to mute and restrain him. From the Apostolic Fathers through the Reformation and beyond, this division within Christian thought reflected a conflict that many interpreters see as perennial, between

> alternative modes of explanation for the generally miserable character of human life: one, the mythological mode, ascribed evil to the activities of an independent cosmic principle loose in creation—Satan, or the devil; the other, the historical mode, set sin before evil and spoke constantly, in the prophetic tradition, of a falling away from the human obligations of the covenant—a failure not of the cosmos as such, but of the human response.[52]

The second way of talking about evil, the "historical mode," is really a way of conceptualizing evil without relying on an embodied evil spirit which, as one modern psychologist puts it, proves "unsatisfactory because it projects the power [of evil] outside the self."[53] Within the Judeo-Christian tradition the alternative to this externalization of evil has been a pure monism, a vision of the universe as a receptacle that has been filling ever since creation with the emanations of God, who is thereby exempted from the charge of having anything to do with the production of evil. Here is a typical Enlightenment formulation of the idea:

> Virtue is a real Ens [a real entity], diffused through all the habits and acts of moral agents which are fit and right; and conveying to them all such qualities as the grand standard requires. The other is only the privation, the want, or absence of that positive nature: hence 'tis called *anomy*: or, want of conformity to the law. This want is defect. And the production of defects, cannot be the object of power.[54]

The only disfigurement in this vision is darkness, where God is not.

This tradition runs from Eusebius through the millenarian reformers to Hegel and Marx, and it celebrates the continuous infusion of the spirit of God into the workings of history or, in a variant that derives principally from St. Augustine, it looks beyond history to the obliteration of the temporal world at some future apocalyptic moment when truth will overcome darkness. In neither of these views is there any need to explain evil by resorting to a malevolent actor; there is, instead, an overwhelming parchedness for God. Evil is understood as a state of estrangement from the divine, a deprivation that can be transcended by the succoring vision of God's incarnation. For some, this vision has been already realized in history (in Christ, or in the socialist state), while for others it is a more abstract or distant prospect (associated with the Messiah's second coming, the fulfillment of his martyrdom), to be awaited with humility and serenity—and always with joy.

Focused on this imminent or distant coming of divinity, the monist claims that all apprehensions of evil along the way are fallible constructs of the human mind by which we confuse fleeting pains with the ultimate, unfolding reality of God's perfection. Since the only true reality is the consciousness of God, this belief requires, if it is to have any appeal for the sufferer, some way of achieving a sense of participation in the divine consciousness as the means to escape the partiality of the self. "When these waves of God flow into me," says Emerson (who belongs emphatically to this tradition), "I no longer reckon lost time."[55]

The difficulty with monism in any form, whether it is the refined philosophy of Spinoza or the crude "mind-cure" of Mary Baker Eddy, is that it is extraordinarily demanding. Requiring a suspension of the self's urgent need to know, it demands an acknowledgment that "our view of things is limited to an infinitesimal area of space and time," and that "we cannot at present understand what the function of seemingly disproportionate or gratuitous evil may be."[56] Its truest believers display a kind of self-crucifixion that reckons only, as Paul Ricoeur (quoting the Gospel of John) has beautifully put it, with "the fear of not loving enough."

> [This] is the purest and worst of fears. It is the fear that the saints know, the fear that love itself begets. And because man never loves enough, it is not possible that the fear of not being loved enough in return should be abolished. Only *perfect* love casts out fear.[57]

Such an exigent way of apprehending the world as a place in which unloveliness is to be loved is profoundly faithful to the Scriptures' representation of evil as an abstraction. It began to be elaborated in Christian form in the second century by Clement of Alexandria, who, drawing on the Platonic tradition, conceptualized evil as nonbeing. For Clement the universe was a hierarchy (a "great chain") of being in which only God may be said to possess absolute existence, and in which all the rest of creation can be imagined as a descending order, each stage of which is more remote from the primary emanation of divinity. In this spatial model of creation, the lower levels are distinct from the higher according to the degree of their deprivation. For such an imagination the devil can be understood as a metaphor for ultimate nonbeing, or what Calvin was much later to call (also with an astronomical image) "the sphere of atrocity and horror under the name of a person."[58]

This vision of evil as literally nothing, a metaphoric representation of absence, is a difficult idea that reached its grandest expression in the fourth century in the writings of St. Augustine, who comes closer than any writer in the Christian tradition to expressing the subjective horror of evil while denying it objective reality. The immense power of Augustine's *Confessions*, which reverberates through every subsequent account of conversion in the Western tradition (the Puritans called him their patron "St. Austin"), has to do first and foremost with the dramatic reversal he himself experienced in his conception of evil. As a young man, he reports, he was persuaded by the Manicheans to regard the universe as a collision-ground of "two masses, contrary to one another, both unbounded, but the evil narrower, the good more expansive." The young Augustine had an appetite for women; he liked to gamble and to attend the theater; and he took pride in his own elegant rhetorical performances. A dualistic cosmology—a view of the universe as a battleground between contending forces—therefore accorded with his sense of warfare within himself. "I believed," he writes of his days under the spell of the Manicheans, "Evil . . . to be some such kind of substance, and to have its own foul and hideous bulk; whether gross, which they called earth, or thin and subtile (like the body of the air), which they imagine to be some malignant mind, creeping through that earth."[59]

The beauty of Augustine's *Confessions* is its account of how he turned away from this idea of a corporeal, unitary evil locked in struggle with the good. As his faith grows, Augustine finds that the devil simply falls out of his cosmology. And so his conversion becomes, among other things, a masterful treatment of the difficult *literary* problem of representing evil as a negation rather than an entity. "Nothing can be liker the very actions of devils," he writes as he recalls his days in thrall to the satiric pleasures of a debating group called the Subverters, who "wantonly persecuted the modesty of strangers, which they disturbed by a gratuitous jeering, feeding thereon their malicious birth." These young verbal sportsmen are full of lethal contempt, "themselves subverted and altogether perverted first, the deceiving spirits secretly deriding and seducing them, wherein themselves delight to jeer at and deceive others."[60] Satan and his minions slip quietly, anonymously, into this sentence as "the deceiving spirits" who entangle their victims in pride and disdain; there is no bestial, fleshy devil here, only a life-killing spirit that Augustine calls perversity. This is his key concept: the idea of an intelligence turned in upon itself, self-consuming, ironic, caught in a syndrome of mockery that is the disbeliever's envy of the believer, ultimately a form of self-hatred.

One of Augustine's metaphors for this sinful condition is the image of the knot, which allows him to speak of the complexity and intransigence of evil without granting it any essence of its own. A distortion of something whose essence precedes its disfigurement, evil is in the twistedness, not in the rope. Here, again, is his famous remembrance of his theft of some pears from a neighbor's vineyard, of which he and a gang of boys "took huge loads, not for our eating, but to fling to the very hogs, having only tasted them":

> my pleasure was not in those pears, it was in the offence itself . . . What then was this feeling? . . . But yet what was it? . . . thou incomprehensible inveigler of the soul, thou greediness to do mischief out of mirth and wantonness, thou thirst of others' loss, without lust of my own gain or revenge: but when it is said, "Let's go, let's do it," we are ashamed not to be shameless.
>
> Who can disentangle that twisted and intricate knottiness? Foul is it: I hate to think on it, to look on it. . . . I sank away from Thee, and I wandered, O my God, too much astray from Thee my stay, in these days of my youth, and I became to myself a barren land.[61]

The only visualization of evil here is the fleeting image of a nervous boy, the juice of stolen pears on his lips, breaking the skins of the fruit and then flinging them away. The force of the writing is its flustered confusion before the insubstantiality of sin, before the mystery of a nameless desire somehow stronger than shame. Augustine remembers himself as a strayed boy, sunken away, "barren"—not filled, as the Manicheans would have it, with rank corruption. In the metaphor of "twisted and intricate knottiness" Augustine has found a way to imagine evil as misshapenness, a prideful embroidering of God's spun yarn.

There is a forecast here of a certain suspicion of the decorative that reached high pitch more than a thousand years later during the Reformation. In its most extreme form in England, it led to the vandalizing of stained-glass windows and the defacing of gilded crucifixes as idolatrous displays of human artfulness. In New England it found expression in chill and unadorned meetinghouses from which organs and choirs were banished; in translations of the Psalms that followed the Hebrew syntax slavishly (resulting in unscannable English lines) because, as the preface to the Bay Psalm Book put it, "God's altar needs not our pollishings." This aesthetic stringency found a permanent place in American life, beginning with the Augustinian pietists of Puritan New England and running through Shaker and Moravian artifacts and certain forms of literary romanticism driven by a quest for the undistorted original forms of nature. More generally, when we encounter this kind of laconic piety, we simply call it "puritan." To be a Puritan, at any historical moment, has been to think of the baroque as the style of Satan.

For the modern mind, one of the mysterious features of this severe and seemingly joyless piety is its apparently contradictory idea that evil can be both insubstantial and real. Augustine posited a world in which human conflict is a shadow play; in which human interventions against God's providence—what St. Paul had called our "kicks against the pricks"—are a child's pathetic flailing against the giant's grip. Human life is a squabble in a dark corner of the playground between children whose voices disappear in the first wind. Augustine writes with disgust not only of quarrelsome children but also of infants who rage when they are not satisfied and for whom there is nothing in the world beyond their own guts and sucking lips. To read Augustine on evil is to encounter an imagination that is both struck by the triviality of sin and stunned by its infinite depth and range and ugliness. Like the sorrows that flow from it, sin is both an illusion and an actuality. According to this purest Christian imagination, the world is a charnel house in which nothing real is consumed.

This extraordinary idea of sin as privation has proven to be almost inaccessible to the modern mind, in part because we think that without materiality there can be no existence. We tend to confuse a privative conception of evil, which should imply no reduction of its hideousness and virulence, with our own attenuated versions of evil as a concept that has disappeared into relativism. Carl Jung, for instance, reeling from the horrific events of the 1940s, insisted that evil must "no longer be minimized by the euphemism of the *privatio boni* . . . no longer . . . dismissed from the world by a circumlocution."[62] One of our theologically best-informed writers, John Updike, has recently led a pontifical character into the same confusion of mistaking privation for diminution: Evil "is not a word we like to use," says one of his "witches" of Eastwick, ". . . we prefer to say 'unfortunate' or 'lacking' or 'misguided' or 'disadvantaged.' We prefer to think of evil as the absence of good, a momentary relenting of its sunshine, a shadow, a weakening."[63] Augustine would grant the truth that "shadow" is a better metaphor for evil than "Satan." But he shivered in the shadow, and would not dare to regard its darkness as a lesser terror than the presence of some unitary devil separable from himself.

[6]

This peculiarly calm self-loathing—a hatred of the self continuous with an unresentful love of God—which has been called "the Augustinian strain of piety," was the opening mood of American civilization. To the degree that Puritanism did acknowledge Satan as an active, independent force—that is, to the degree that Puritanism was a dualistic religion—its devil was never a brute, but a tempter. Men remained free to repudiate him, and thereby responsible if they were seduced. Satan was the temptation to overcharge a needy neighbor; he was faintness of heart when self-sacrifice might solace a friend. When the more systematic New England theologians narrated the original fall of man, they told the story virtually without an embodied devil and with no effort to deflect responsibility upon God: "the Law was altogether blameless," like "the rock which the steersman foolishly runs against." It was man's waywardness that constituted his original sin; " 'tis the commendation of the rock to shiver in pieces the vessel that dasheth against it."[64]

This modified kind of dualism, a picture of mankind wandering in a world befogged, required a very delicate portrayal of the tempter devil —something that has historically been extremely difficult to accomplish.

The devil, once he is visualized and given voice (as he is by Milton), tends to run away with the show. He becomes a figure of riveting power, ubiquitous and irresistible. He commandeers the imagination and fills the mind with an almost pleasurable horror—pleasurable in the way that postponed sleep can be. Even in his most masculine role, the devil has something of Circe's and Delilah's charm. Sinuous, at ease in the body of the serpent, he enfolds his victim like a woman and penetrates like a man, until the boundary between possessor and possessed is erased:

> The divell casts wicked thoughts into their hearts and carries them into the commission of those evils which formerly he had suggested; the Divell rules in them; he speaks their tongues, and works by their hands, and thinks and desires by their minds, and walks by their feete.[65]

This devil is a marionette master who has practiced the art of manipulation ever since he "managed the serpent to speak, and reason, and plead, which was altogether preternatural to that creature"; and his simultaneous mastery and dependence on a submissive victim is inherent in his very name: "the Latin and Greek *Diabolus* signifies an *Overthrower*, or one who darts through another."[66] There is the backstage quality of a secret agent in this devil; he is the spectral ancestor of the fifth columnist who moves among people unaware of his operations. But he is also, by turns, openly insolent. He has harbored a festering resentment since before his own fall, when he had begun to feel "degraded, in being employed [by God] to minister for man," until he found "the consummation of [his] transgression" by communicating his pride to man.[67]

Milton put this devil at the center of a great poem, *Paradise Lost*, and almost from the beginning some of its most appreciative readers began to side with him against God. This is because the constituents of sin can seem to be virtues. Independent, disobedient, and solitary, the Puritan devil was a creature who lived, as did the Puritans themselves, on the dividing line between cultures—between what Puritanism had been (a religion of self-effacement before an angry God) and what it was becoming (a religion of individuals striving under the gaze of a parentally proud God).

If Satan was scattered and fragmentary in the New England mind, it was in part because of this dividedness. It was also because his Old World representatives (chiefly "the pestilentious . . . Bishop of Rome"[68]) and their New World substitutes (whooping Indians and heretics within the

Puritan community) were too distant or scarce to serve as convincing models. There was a certain amount of alarmist talk in early New England about the Romish Whore of Babylon sending legions across the sea, just as there was residual talk about the Nip and Hun sending saboteurs to American cities in the years after World War II. But, fundamentally, Satan in early New England was an unmoored symbol, as elusive to these Calvinists as he had been to the Church Fathers; his image had to be coaxed out of the Scriptures, where, "though he be not named in the history of man's doleful fall . . . yet he is plainly intimated."[69] He was even available as a phantom player in college high jinks; on a spring night in the 1650s President Henry Dunster had to rush back to Harvard in order to dispatch with a gunshot a prankster who was impersonating the devil in Harvard Yard.[70]

There is some evidence that to less educated people Satan was a more fearful reality. He appeared in primers and was sometimes pictured in broadsides as the figure of the Pope stamping on the Bible. He was the object of curses, and when a child had given up its last breath or an unharvested crop was killed by an autumn snow, he could be the occasion of desperate prayers. He incited children to "roar, and howl, and shriek, and hollow, to drown the voice of the devotions" during services, and was sometimes represented as a battlefield coward who had been "ranked foremost in the visible Creation, but he broke his Rank, deserted his Place, flew from his Colours."[71] Yet the metaphors are always shifting and unsettled; he never becomes a fixed image, no more in the popular imagination than in formal theology, where he remained, as he always had been, doctrinally unstable. For Milton, whom New Englanders read with devotion, he had fallen long before the creation of man, and received the news of "puny" man's creation with a lust for revenge—to ". . . drive [him] as we were driven, / . . . or if not drive, / [then to] Seduce them to our Party . . ." For the New England author of *A Compleat Body of Divinity*, however, the angels "all stood right 'till after man was made,"[72] and it was the advent of man that was their downfall, not an opportunity to avenge an apostasy already suffered. This theologian complained that "the scripture seems to speak something darkly about . . . the ground of [his] Apostacy, or that wherein [he] fell," and others spoke of devils in the plural, as "that great number of apostate and rebellious angels, which through pride and blasphemy against God, and malice against man, became liars and murderers."[73]

The function of Satan in the early American imagination was ultimately inconsistent with too much specificity. "Wheresoever the streame of the brimstone of God's wrath seizeth," wrote one Puritan minister, "there is Hell," thus agreeing with Milton that "the mind is its own place, and in itself / Can make a Heav'n of Hell, a Hell of Heav'n." Yet even as Milton rendered hell as a movable state of mind, he also pictured it vividly as a "Lake with liquid fire," and "A Dungeon Horrible, on all sides round / As one great Furnace flam'd, yet from those flames / No light, but rather darkness visible." At the center of hell, Satan was, like his medieval prototype, still a breathing paradox, the one creature fit, in the wonderfully twisted phrases of Milton's Beelzebub, to traverse the "palpable obscure," and carry himself over the "vast abrupt."[74]

Within the range of these doctrinal disagreements, sometimes held simultaneously by the same writer, a recognizable Satan does emerge. Common to all these versions is his inextinguishable *pride*, and according to Milton, his carnal ambition always ran close to despair: "Which way I fly is Hell; myself am Hell." At the heart of him is self-feeding anguish. The devil can mimic faith: "Satan . . . may transform himself into an Angel of Light . . . but [he] cannot pacifie the conscience, much less purifie it, himself being an unclean spirit."[75] Damned in the sense that he can never escape himself, the devil is finally "unclean" because he is a tortured soul who needs to make other souls dance to the music of his own despair. He invades his prey, as Milton tells it, by a rape so delicate that the victim sleeps through the violation:

> *Fearless, unfear'd [the serpent] slept: in at his Mouth*
> *The Devil Enter'd, and his brutal sense,*
> *In heart or head, possessing soon inspir'd*
> *With act Intelligential . . .*

This nighttime burrowing into bodies was a measure of his power, but it was also his limitation. According to every school of Christian eschatology, the devil knows that he will ultimately be defeated by being driven out of his playground world, and so he is desperate to frolic while he can. In his *danse macabre* he is terrifically adroit, almost dainty. When man "was in all his integrity" before the fall, Satan had "applied himself to our first Parents visibly and audibly . . . because he could in no other way than offer them a Temptation," but now he has no need for the gross vessel of the serpent. There is "a nearer and more secret commerce [now] that Angels can have with our spirits, than by the outward senses," and with "all our powers tainted with sin," he "can insinuate his suggestions into the *fancy* or *imagination* of fallen man." He does not need the serpent, but works directly through human instruments, and we "readily receive the impression."[76] He has shed his body and become a wisp, a shudder, a muffled knock on the door that can be confused with the rattle of the wind. He will never be spotted with a spyglass or by any sentry peering afar, because he is the contents of our minds. Yet few people in early America doubted that his elusiveness was anything but craft and stealth, and no one raised the appalling possibility that the difficulty of detecting him might mean that he was not there.

A witch kissing the devil beneath his tail (c. 1626, Guazzo, Compendium Maleficarum*)*
(MARY EVANS PICTURE GALLERY, LONDON)

The Devil in the Age
of Reason

Although Satan continued to live furtively in the American mind, and retained his ability "to insinuate his suggestions . . . into the *fancy* or *imagination* of fallen man," he was, by 1700, hedged and vulnerable. In the premodern world, when the great mass of people lived in small agricultural units (families, villages, towns) that required cooperative labor, and under the rule of hierarchies that demanded subjection, self-interest had been a sin and Satan was its necessary symbol. He was the name for vanity and avarice. He was the name for the resentment that wells up when pride is thwarted. But as the outlines of a new world began to emerge—dynamic, commercial, driven by market forces—and ambition and entrepreneurship became recognized as talents and even virtues, Satan made less and less sense as a metaphor of the overweening self. He began to be an anachronism.

In the days when he had been an abstraction—a spirit working surreptitiously within human motives and desires—he did not really lend himself to visible manifestation, and the Puritans, who talked of sin in sermons, not images, had rarely pictured him. It was only when the concept of evil as pride began to break down that the devil became a vivid presence as a dispatcher of witches and demons. By 1700 he was a symbol from which the moral content was being drained; and soon, all that was left of him were his external attributes—rank smell, reedy voice, scales.

These spectacular features are what we now remember of him. But they had no moral content. And soon they, too, became vulnerable to a new skepticism. As Satan lost his significance as a moral symbol and his plausibility as a physical being, the terms by which he was described became hybrid: the old Christian vocabulary ("fallen man") persisted, but it now had to compete with a new science of mind that no longer described human consciousness as a soul susceptible to invasion by a supernatural devil, but portrayed it as a kind of machine that was liable to disorder. In speaking of the old idea of the devil, even conservative theologians had to accommodate themselves to the requirements of an emerging rationalism that ultimately left no room for him.

This dissociation of the devil from the self marked the beginning of his end as a significant cultural symbol. The process went forward in two ways simultaneously: belief in embodied spirits was reduced to a superstition; and pride was rehabilitated as a defensible emotion. By the early eighteenth century, Satan was no longer physically or morally credible, and the problem for his survivors was how to find a way to speak of evil without him.

[I]

The first hints of what was happening came in the form of a basic change in the idea of the imagination. What was this mental faculty by which people saw things invisible to others? How did it receive such "suggestions" as half-bestial creatures with hoofs and manes and the power of human speech, or shrieking crones who fly by night to the beds of young girls and lure them to dance naked in the woods? In the last decade of the seventeenth century, New England culture nearly split apart over this issue of how such irrational ideas could enter a rational mind. Were such prodigies, whose existence was confirmed by reputable persons, really dispatched by the devil? Or were they—in a word that now began to establish its modern meaning—"fantasies"?[1]

In the winter of 1691–92, when erratic behavior was first noticed among several girls in the Cape Ann village of Salem, these questions became matters not only of general debate but of a local dispute in which the life and death of the disputants were soon at stake. The trouble at Salem, which has become one of the most infamous occasions in American history, began when the eleven-year-old daughter of the local minister, along with an older cousin, began to behave in ways similar to the girls in a case of possession that had taken place in Boston four years earlier:

Sometimes they would be Deaf, sometimes Dumb, and sometimes Blind, and often, all this at once. One while their Tongues would be drawn down their Throats; another while they would be pull'd out upon their Chins, to a prodigious length. They would have their Mouths opened to such a Wideness, that their Jaws went out of joint; and anon they would clap together again with a Force like that of a strong Spring-Lock.[2]

When these facial gymnastics failed to subside into the usual impudent grimaces of adolescence, witchcraft was murmured as an explanation. Natural causes could not be found, and by late winter, legal authorities from outside Salem were brought in to examine three women who had been detained on charges of entertaining Satan. New Englanders had a long tradition to draw on when they suspected the presence of witches; they had scriptural sanction for acting severely ("Thou shalt not suffer a witch to live," God says to Moses in the Book of Exodus) and centuries of legal and medical precedent. One of the first suspects, a slave from the West Indies named Tituba, confessed to mixing potions with young girls and reveling in the woods at night with the devil himself, whom she described as an apelike creature of distorted human feature. Another was an old woman who flouted the laws of compulsory church attendance, and still another a "destitute, wizened, pipe-smoking hag."[3] These accused women were typical of many throughout the century who were charged with witchcraft, or "entertaining Satan." Rarely young or respectably married, they tended to be spinsters or widows or discarded old wrecks who dirtied themselves and talked to themselves and wandered about spreading profanities and a bad smell—magnified versions of the stock folklore shrew whose touch could ruin a young girl just as she was becoming a woman. When social conditions were right, certain marginal women slipped easily into conformity with such images, a slippage that meant at least shame and at most death.

The outburst of witch-hunting at Salem has been explained by historians in many ways—as a particularly vicious expression of Puritan misogyny; as a device by which economically stressed families struck back at those who were adapting well to the expansion of entrepreneurial opportunities or were profiting from formerly disreputable trades like tavern-keeping[4]—and has become an emblem of religious fanaticism. Yet in the larger context of early American history, the most remarkable aspects of the Salem episode are its rarity and its brevity. The potential for what we now call witch-hunting, inherently large in a religious culture alert to the omnipresence of Satan, had been generally kept in check by established evidentiary tests. There had been occasional incidents of what was considered satanic misuse of the bodies of women, as in the notorious case in the 1630s of a deformed child delivered stillborn to a woman suspected of heresy and sedition:

> When it died in the mother's body, (which was about two hours before the birth,) the bed whereon the mother lay did shake, and withal there was such a noisome savor, as most of the women were taken with extreme vomiting and purging, so as they were forced to depart; and others of them their children were taken with convulsions, (which they never had before nor after,) and so were sent for home, so as by these occasions it came to be concealed.[5]

Gossip about this kind of thing, rife with old rumors about Satan's acrid smell and his terrible effect on persons near him, was not uncommon; but formal charges of witchcraft required that certain specific anatomical features in the accused be confirmed. Witchcraft lore claimed that a witch had a "preternatural excrescence of flesh" in some secret place on her body (usually near the vagina or between the breasts) for suckling her "familiar spirit." The "familiar" was a kind of demonic mascot who served and accompanied her on her errands of conscription for her master; it could take the "Shape of a Man, Woman, Boy, Dog, Cat, Foal, Hare, Rat, Toad, &c,"[6] and the teat from which it sucked, sometimes called the "Devil's Mark," was distinctive for not bleeding if pricked. With this familiar in tow, witches were said to congregate into groups of nighttime revelers in order to satisfy their real hunger—for intercourse with Satan himself. There they initiated new conscripts by sending forth their "specters" (ghostly images of themselves visible only to the targeted person) to invite or cajole younger women with promises of pleasure and luxury, or, if the candidates resisted, with threats of harm or death. In some cases the witch's specter, or even Satan in his person, would actually enter the body of a resistant victim; this was the dreaded possibility of possession, which could be known to observers by the victim's thrashings or moanings. What it amounted to was a dramatically visible and audible battle for a young woman's soul—deliciously akin to sexual excitement. For the men who intervened, it carried the tantalizing prospect that the perpetrator of her struggle could be named, apprehended, and rendered impotent. Conspirators could be unmasked and unfaithful wives revealed.

Naming witches was, in part, a means by which men dealt with their deep fear when confronted with transgression in women and children; it was a way to deal with the problem of transmitting authority to unreceptive youth, or to take retribution against a haughty neighbor. Most of all, it was an explanation—and sometimes a remedy—for private and public disorder.

Given the psychic rewards that successful witch-hunting promised, it is remarkable how seldom New Englanders resorted to it. Even the outbreak at Salem, during which eighteen women (as well as two dogs and a man) were executed, was a relatively slight tremor in early America; it has been reasonably said that "the intellectual history of New England up to 1720 can be written as if no such thing ever happened."[7] Few formal accusations of witchcraft were recorded in the first twenty-five years of the Massachusetts Bay Colony, and only a handful thereafter before Salem, after which the executions permanently stopped. Why, then, does Salem persist in seeming a watershed in our history? There must be more here than the exotic appeal of moonlit covens or young girls' erotic wishes channeled into hate.

The significance of Salem became apparent when, in the fall of 1692, the blood-sated juries began to waver at the judges' call for more convictions. The most prestigious of the Boston ministers, Increase Mather, who had at first endorsed the proceedings, now composed and circulated in manuscript a work called *Cases of Conscience* calling for a halt to the trials. Varieties of circumstantial and physical evidence had been adduced in the investigations; witches, for example, were sometimes identified by the "fact" that corpses bled at their touch. But the court was depending excessively, Mather argued, on spectral evidence—that is, on the victim's claim that he or she had been visited by the specter of the accused or of someone recently dead, who identified the defendant as an ally of Satan. Although Scripture taught that two concurring witnesses were sufficient for a sentence of death, the court, Mather now thought, had been too quick to reach its judgments; it had drawn "too resolute conclusions" that Satan could only take the form of a guilty person's specter and could not impersonate the innocent. To believe this, Mather now argued, was to commit "bold usurpations upon [the] spotless *Sovereignty*"[8] of God, who has framed the cosmos in such a way that a madly resourceful devil, more inventive than anyone could imagine, is loose within it. The problem with the judicial procedures at Salem was not that men had imagined

Satan where he was not, but that they had underestimated his capacity to be everywhere. They were forgetting the fundamental fact about him—his ubiquity. And they forgot to look for him in their own motives.

Much later, when some of the judges realized this, they tried to explain themselves by saying Satan had tricked them. Five years after the executions, and twelve years before the General Court of Massachusetts authorized reparations to the families of the victims, one of the judges, Samuel Sewall, posted a recantation on the door of the Old South Church in Boston in which, "asking pardon of Men, And especially desiring prayers that God . . . would pardon that Sin and all other his Sins," he reported himself "sensible of the reiterated strokes of God upon himself and family; and . . . sensible . . . as to the Guilt contracted, upon the opening of the late Commission of Oyer and Terminer at Salem," and ready to "take the Blame and Shame of it."[9]

Behind Sewall's repentance lay a genuinely embarrassed sense that he had been a hasty and credulous judge, that he had swallowed too many slanderous stories whole, and that he had brought insufficient skepticism to his office. All these self-indictments were strong and sincere; Sewall felt stooped and battered by providence, and suspected he was guilty of many retributable sins. But the cosmology that he had held at Salem— the picture of the world into which a satanic plot involving female deputies had neatly fit—was unmodified by his consciousness of having erred.

Sewall and his peers never flinched from the conviction that the devil had been present at Salem. They fought back their incipient doubt that the swooning girls might not, in fact, have been pierced by the eye glances of tormentors invisible to everyone except themselves; the judges had, after all, seen with their own eyes sober men in the courtroom swing clubs at phantom bodies and flinch at their resistance, as if the club had slammed into some invisible mass. When Sewall posted his recantation, he threw himself on the mercy of God not because he had lost confidence in the devil's strength, but because he felt Satan to be a more formidable enemy than he had before imagined.

In some respects, then, Satan emerged from Salem more cunning than before—ubiquitous and utterly unpredictable. This new Puritan Satan was an external enemy, all the more dangerous for his mastery of surprise. Cotton Mather, Increase's zealous son, exulted in this realization and celebrated the devil's power as a sign that the last great battle between God and Satan was at hand:

the devil is now making one attempt more upon us; an attempt more difficult, more surprising, more snarled with unintelligible circumstances than any that we have hitherto encountered; an attempt so critical that if we get well through we shall soon enjoy halcyon days with all the vultures of hell trodden under our feet.[10]

There is, however, a certain plaintiveness in such celebrations as the Salem prosecutors acquired a touch of the ridiculous, first in private whispering, then in public lampoon. Around the edges of the events—from men who wrote privately to curious friends, or who published from the safety of presses far outside Boston—openly skeptical, even contemptuous, voices began to be heard. When, in the fall of 1693, both Mathers rushed to the bedside of a Boston girl who was showing symptoms of "possession," a cool and doubtful merchant named Robert Calef was on hand to witness their examination. "She was in a fit," he reported later, "and [Cotton] . . . rubbed her breast, etc. . . . and put his hand upon her breast and belly, viz. on the clothes over her, and felt a living thing, as he said, which moved the father also to feel, and some others." Watching with amazement as two dignified men publicly handled the body of the reclining girl, Calef concluded that the real victims of Salem were the accused witches whose bodies had been "dragged" for burial "to a Hole, or Grave, between the rocks." In a brave reversal, even Increase Mather himself soon conceded that it was the false accusers, not the convicted witches, who were the true "Daemoniacks" and servants of the "Father of Lyes."[11]

So as the implacable Salem authorities appeared to grow comic and even lewd in their diligence, their devil-hunting became the subject of satire, and New Englanders began to divide over questions that had previously been uncontroversial—whether, for instance, the "wonders of the invisible world" (Cotton Mather's phrase) might not be delusions, and whether those who believed them were not dupes. One outraged commentator referred to the judges mockingly as the "Salem gentlemen," and ridiculed them for failing to grasp the distinction between a cause-and-effect relation and a mere coincidence. A witch's spell is communicated through the eyes to the victim, and so

the justices order the apprehended to look upon the said children, which accordingly they do; and at the time of that look, (I dare not say *by* that look, as the Salem gentlemen do), the afflicted are cast into a fit. The apprehended are then blinded, and ordered to touch the afflicted; and at that touch, though not *by* the touch, (as above), the afflicted ordinarily do come out of their fits.[12]

Fixing the blindfolded witch's hand upon the body of the bewitched, the theory said, makes the effluvia flow out of the possessed back into the sorcerer as if by completing the circuit, and the spell is broken. But critics (under the sway of Descartes's *Discourse on Method*) were quick to point out that "a touch of any hand, and process of time, will work the cure . . . as experience teaches"[13]—a demurral that comes from a new temperament for which experience overrules authority and theory is suspect if it is strained by observable facts. For the first time it was becoming respectable in New England to believe that only physically measurable and experimentally testable phenomena were real in any intelligible sense. To such a mind the lore of Satan was becoming a kind of primitive poetry.

What had happened was this: First Satan had been turned from an attribute of the self into a visible being outside the self. Then, in his new variety of fantastic forms, he had been dismissed. In other words, the devil was being reduced to something that educated men could not believe in. This was the beginning of the end of the devil as a meaningful symbol of evil. Cotton Mather was right in a way he did not intend: the old Christian devil *had* entered his death throes at Salem, which turned out to be the site of his last New England campaign. But this was not because the promises of Revelation were being fulfilled there—"And the beast was taken, and with him the false prophet that wrought miracles before him, with which he deceived them that had received the mark of the beast . . . [and] both were cast alive into a lake of fire burning with brimstone." It was because the devil, like an old actor whose declamatory style has become comic, was losing his audience.

[2]

At the core of the new rationalism was a vision of the human mind as a machine liable, like any other, to malfunction. Since the Greeks, Western psychology had taken account of the effect upon the mind of bodily events—illness, inebriation, sexual excitement—and had recognized that the imagination "produces not only art . . . but also fantasies and monstrous untruths."[14] But explanatory analogies, like this one from Thomas Hobbes's *Leviathan* (1651), now became more insistently physical than ever before:

> As we see in the water, though the wind cease, the waves give not over rowling for a long time after; so also it happeneth in that motion, which is made in the internall parts of a man, then, when he Sees, Dreams, &c. For after the object is removed, or the eye shut, we still retain an image of the thing seen, though more obscure than when we see it.[15]

As Hobbes's metaphor for memory suggests, the process by which objects are apprehended by the sensory organs of the body—eye, ear, skin, nose, tongue—was understood as a physical event: as "matter which presseth our organs," and though the "insensible particles" that moved from object to perceiver might be invisible, their operations could be surmised by analogy with the effects of things seen or heard. "As pressing, rubbing, or striking the Eye, makes us fancy a light; and pressing the Eare, produceth a dinne; so do the bodies also we see, or hear, produce the same by their strong, though unobserved action."[16] Just as a finger on the eye or ear can produce the effect of light or sound, so distant objects are perceived through the impact of particles whose collision with the sensory organ results in a sound or image. Perception is construed as a physical event; and imagination, which had been understood since the ancients as a subcategory of memory, came to be defined as the residue of such an event, the echo of a bombardment. Imagination, as Hobbes put it, is "nothing but *decaying sense*," the slowly dissipated impact of a past sensation. Products of the imagination are like the outer rings of a ripple, an idea that Hobbes elaborated in the following beautiful image:

> The decay of Sense in men waking, is not the decay of the motion made in sense; but an obscuring of it, in such manner, as the light of the Sun obscureth the light of the Starres; which starrs do no less exercise their vertue by which they are visible, in the day, than in the night. But because amongst many stroaks, which our eyes, eares, and other organs receive from externall bodies, the predominant onely is sensible; therefore the light of the Sun being predominant, we are not affected with the action of the starrs. And any object being removed from our eyes, though the impression it made in us remain; yet other objects more present succeeding, and working on us, the Imagination of

the past is obscured, and made weak; as the voyce of a man is in the noyse of the day.[17]

The mind here is a filing system, a packet of discrete sheets on which sensations have been stamped. Old ones are shuffled to the back of the pile, where, with time, their imprinted images fade and ultimately disappear, leaving the sheets blank. In this process of obliteration (death is, in effect, the final shedding of our memories) each new sensory experience pushes the last one further toward the rear, whence it will ultimately be lost. But the process is reversible through the power of imagination, by which old images are brought suddenly forward, recalled by an association that carries them over the many intervening experiences into an affiliation with something recent. A fall from a horse onto rocky ground twenty years ago might merge with today's stumble in the mud, and the two images coalesce until the specific terrain and pain associated with each event become fused into an idea vividly real to the mind but corresponding to no external event that can be said actually to have happened. Such ideas appear to the mind by means of the "compound imagination," which stores images in the memory and combines them into unified images of multiple parts. These composite "fictions of the mind" are what John Locke, whose psychology was becoming standard in American textbooks by the mid-eighteenth century, called "fantastical" ideas,

> made up of such collections of simple *ideas* as were really never united, never were found together in any substance: v.g. a rational creature, consisting of a horse's head, joined to a body of human shape, or such as the *centaurs* are described; or a body yellow, very malleable, fusible, and fixed, but lighter than common water; or an uniform, unorganized body, consisting, as to sense, all of similar parts, with perception and voluntary motion joined to it.[18]

This associative power of imagination could readily explain the dreams of a girl who sees, floating above her bed, the image of a cackling hag who yesterday had slapped her hand from the handle of the town pump.

It seems a long way from this mechanistic conception of the mind to the modern idea of the unconscious as a roiling nest from which symbols, unmanaged by reason, are continuously spilling into consciousness. Already by the early nineteenth century the associationist model began to seem inadequate, and long before the Freudian revolution of our own century, descriptions of consciousness were becoming less static and were moving toward a proto-cinematic conception of the mind as a screen upon which images are superimposed in continuous projection. In America, this transformation was most strikingly expressed in William James's famous phrase the "stream of consciousness," which recasts time itself as a tumbling jumble of memory fragments rather than a neat succession of discrete moments. Late-nineteenth-century pragmatists like James, and before them the Romantics, did alter substantially the representation of consciousness, and carried it well beyond the formulation that for nearly two hundred years had held pretty much as Locke and Hobbes had asserted it. Yet the basic idea of the human imagination as a factory of inventions had been established before the end of the seventeenth century, when intellectual life first acquired its modern skeptical tone and made it imperative for educated people to keep watch over the unruly ardor of their minds.

What this meant for theology—and therefore for the fate of the devil —was that by 1700, when English-speaking people had been in North America for only three generations, educated persons believed themselves well equipped to explain the visions that for centuries had been construed as interventions by God or his agents in the mental life of individuals. "Ghosts," as one scholar explains, "were not exorcised—only internalized and reinterpreted as hallucinatory thoughts."[19] It was, of course, hardly an original discovery that the human mind had a capacity to "see" things that were not physically present. Two thousand years before Locke, Aristotle had known perfectly well that "visions appear to us even when our eyes are shut";[20] and the scholastic revival of the Middle Ages had preserved the classical idea of the imagination as the mind's capacity to store and combine sense-images into new conceptions. But Aristotle's attention to the imagination in the *De Anima* had been relatively slight, if not cursory; and he had treated it as a secondary function, without the vividness and power of actual sense-impressions: "when we merely imagine we remain as unaffected as persons who are looking at a painting of some dreadful or encouraging scene."[21] The new rationalists of the late seventeenth century, however, were urgently aware—after decades of religious strife in which enthusiasts of all sorts played an incendiary part—that people could be animated and driven by inner visions. In this context the telltale word "hallucination" comes into English usage as a way of discounting the claims of believers like George Fox, founder of the Quaker sect, who, in 1694, described his religious conversion in visceral, physical terms: "Now was I come up in spirit, through the flaming sword, into the paradise of God. All things were new, and all the creation gave another smell unto me than before . . ."[22]

Later, when associationist theory offered a technically satisfactory explanation of such experiences, it was, again, not strictly new, but it was received and disseminated under genuinely new conditions. Britain had embarked on its transformation from a feudally organized agricultural country into a modern nation-state with international seaports, the beginnings of heavy industry, and a growing class of merchants and lawyers. Neighborly barter by handshake was giving way to complex exchanges of goods for credit, of which personal memory simply could not keep track; and bookkeeping was becoming a requisite skill. At the same time, the microscope and telescope were bringing into focus large parts of formerly invisible worlds. Under pressure from such emerging realities— created and discovered—the general awareness of both the limits and the capacities of the human mind became widespread and more refined. Both the fallibility and the creativity of the mind were disclosed with a new candor, and one result was the peculiar mix of skepticism and confidence that characterizes the tone and style of Enlightenment thought. Eighteenth-century writers—Voltaire, Johnson, Pope—invented a new style of writing authoritatively about their own ignorance.

Despite all this new rationalism, many people continued to see with perfect clarity their personal demons and ghosts, and to report them to the doubting world. In the turbulent period from the 1760s through the 1790s, there was a spurt of publication in England's American colonies about ghostly visitations and magical events—often stories of terror, but also sometimes tales of avuncular spirits bringing good advice in hard times. Reading through this literature, one becomes aware of what we would call a "backlash"—a half-articulate nostalgia for an invisible world in which it was no longer quite proper to believe. A brisk-selling pamphlet in Philadelphia, for instance, published in the year of the Stamp Act (1765), reported on a Silesian count who "tormented his Subjects in an unmercyfull way" until "it came to pass, that his Body was Transformed into a Dog, all but the Head, which remained as a human Head"—an event of which, "if the Lord of Hosts would send his just Judgement upon every Blasphemer . . . we would see daily Examples in *Philadelphia*."[23] Ten years later, when the imperial crisis had broken out into open warfare, a New England printer issued a story about the devil bursting into the bedchamber of a Boston Tory and tutoring him in the infernal plots of Parliament against the citizens of Massachusetts. And ten years after that, when cries of Jacobinism were being heard throughout the new American republic, a shaken Yale man published a memoir in which the ghost of a former classmate, four years dead, comes to rebuke him for his pleasure-seeking and his secular ambition: "how would you long to be absent from the body," the spectral collegian intones, "that you might be present with the Lord."[24] In all these stories, visitors from the spirit world come to condemn modern life; they are a gallery of mischievous old-timers who remind the unfortunate living of a time when morals and allegiances were clear.

American newspapers, too, furnished stories to meet the public appetite for messages from the spectral world:

> Last Wednesday Morning, one Mr. Willard, at Braintree, being delirious (and his Watchers going to Sleep) he untied himself, and got out of Doors, took an Ax which he found, and Struck himself on his Head, but it happened to slide off on one side, and did not hurt him very much; afterwards he held the Edge of it upwards, knocked his Neck on it, and jam'd, and cut it terribly. He says the *Devil* told him to eat an Apple, which he did, by which Time the People happened to find him, or 'tis thought he would have killed himself. He said that Mr. *Devil* shall not serve him so again.[25]

The devil was becoming a prankster invented by disturbed minds. As such, he was a creature disdained by literate people as a superstition of the unlettered. Retrieved for literary purposes from a once-living tradition, he was used to entertain an audience that no longer had any intimate relation with him. In the illustrations that accompanied the tales of his activities, he was drawn in the outlines of caricature, with the inner detail of his malice washed out; squat and inelegant, this new devil was closer to a dybbuk or leprechaun than to the old grandmaster of hell.

Occasionally, one still encounters an eighteenth-century Satan who retains something of the self-shriveling rage that for Milton and the Church Fathers had been his essence. For instance, a pious Philadelphia churchgoer named Jane Cish, after meeting three angels of justice and mercy in a dream, notices that they are flanked by "a fourth form [who] appeared black and maugre; he stood at a distance from the other forms, with his looks distorted, full of envy, hatred and rage."[26] In the context of the believe-it-or-not stories that poured from the presses in this period, this brooding Lucifer stands out. For a moment, Cish finds words to convey the old visceral power of the doctrine of original sin: "I beheld Adam and Eve walking in the garden . . . yea, they swam in pleasure . . . as a fish doth in the waters of the ocean. I saw also the disposition and rectitude of their soules, for their bodies were no hindrance to my sight." After they fall at Satan's urging, they are, she says with compassionate fright, "chilled with horror," and she is "ashamed of the abomination and wickedness I beheld in the heart of man, and felt a willingness to suffer any punishment, seeing myself so worthy of wrath."[27] This woman *feels*, as Augustine had felt, her estrangement from God. Her Satan is unusual because he is more than a cartoon.

[3]

Even before his entanglement with the events at Salem, Increase Mather, who died just as the skeptical Enlightenment was taking root in America, had become aware that "the Sadducees of these dayes say that there are no spirits, and that all stories concerning them are either fabulous or to be ascribed unto natural causes."[28] By the turn of the century, Mather knew that the first reaction of educated people to dreams and visions like that of Jane Cish was no longer a shudder that God was sending a decipherable message but, more likely, a determination to find some physiological—and spiritually meaningless—explanation. The world into which Mather was born, in 1639, was regarded as a text inscribed and continually revised by God, not far removed from the world in which Joseph in Egypt was summoned to interpret Pharaoh's dream as a prophecy imperative to be known. But by the time of Mather's death in 1723, the world had moved immensely closer to our own, in which dreams are regarded as shocks in the mind set off by physical events taking place somewhere deep within the circuits of the brain. A process had begun that by our own time has almost reached completion: the distinction between brain and mind was breaking down.

The loss of this distinction was tantamount to losing the idea of the soul, a process to which there was brave resistance. One senses it, for example, in the titles of popular pamphlets about crime, which tried to preserve a consoling distinction between the victim's mutilated body and her intact soul: *The Life and Dying Speech of the Negro Arthur . . . who was executed . . . for a rape committed on the body of one Deborah Metcalfe* (1768); *A Most Bloody and Cruel Murder Committed on the Body of Mrs. Elizabeth Wood by her own son* (1793).[29] But such efforts to preserve some sense of personhood apart from the material body were largely unavailing. Until the 1820s and 1830s, when the idea of imagination (to which Hobbes and Locke had attributed so much mental mischief) began to be substituted for the antiquated idea of soul, the process continued unabated. Human beings were being reconceived as machines, and machines have no soul.

In the growing number of texts on mental disorders—physicians' handbooks, dissertations, popular guides—the conception of mind as a conduit to God continued to retreat before the idea of the brain as a storage device for sense-impressions. Madness, as opposed to melancholia or fleeting episodes of "phrenitis," was commonly defined as "*false perception* of objects, depending on morbid sensation." This definition—here proposed by a Columbia University medical student in 1796—entailed the idea that the madman believed "in the truth of the suggestions of the senses, and in consequence of this," was susceptible to "extraordinary and irregular efforts to attain some imaginary good or avoid some evil." This typical account of mental symptoms was really a restatement of associationist theory, in which the regulatory mechanism of the mind has failed, and a "morbid or unusual association of ideas" is filling the brain with demons and angels whom the madman may assault or embrace.[30]

When eighteenth-century physicians turned to the question of how to treat such conditions, they could appeal to little more than hearsay about what therapies worked. Traditional remedies—bathing in mineral waters, gentle massage, removal of the sufferer from too much stimulus—were the best they could do, and they explained the occasional efficacy of such treatments (physical disorders like the "twisting of the guts" were still treated by forcing the patient to swallow lead bullets) by a crudely mechanical theory of causation. "The organs of sense," not the brain, were thought to be "the seats of thought," because it was these organs—the retina of the eye, receptors in the outer layers of the skin—that were directly excited when phantasms approached from external objects, as in "the erection of the papillae of the tongue, at the approach of a sapid body."[31] Removing these organs from exposure to stimulus could give them a chance to recuperate, in the same way as splinting a sprained finger or limb.

In explaining how madness arises, physicians often used an implicit analogy to the phases of excitement and relaxation in the sexual organs, and to the varying intensities of sexual feeling for different persons. The *"irregular association of ideas"* was compared to "the spastic contractions of other muscles," which, "according to the sensorial power distributed to different people" leave some sane and satisfied, while reducing others to "a state of stupidity."[32] Early psychiatric texts are a lively reminder of how sheer assertion (that, for example, "the pulpy expansion of the *retina* is composed of muscular fibres") tends to convey a sense of mastery though it is based on nothing remotely like knowledge.

So even as it reached for prestige as an empirical science, psychiatry was really nothing more than a rudimentary program of hygienics. It inherited the traditional restraining function of religion, and in describing the qualities of madness, physicians found themselves employing a degraded religious vocabulary. Pride, for instance—once the queen of sins and the festering center of Satan himself—was now dispassionately described as "too exalted [an] opinion of one's own merit," which, "inasmuch as it subjects us to more frequent disappointments, may be considered as a remote cause of mania." This "science" was still based on the classical premise that, as the Columbia medical student recited it, "the medium between enthusiasm and apathy is the most suitable for human nature."[33] It insisted that extreme mental excitement was a disease, and thereby set itself against a long Christian tradition, beginning with the account of the Apostles speaking in tongues in the second chapter of Acts, that "a man must be besides himself, or else hee cannot live to God."[34]

Yet the residual idea of the mystic still lingered within the new understanding of madness:

> [madmen] fly from human society; they ramble with wonderful rapidity from one object to another, with shouting, singing, and laughing; some, while they roam through the lofty regions of fancy, count the stars, and mark in their imagination, the revolution of the planetary system . . . while others are spreading their vent'rous wings and flying to different parts of the earth, and from earth to heaven.[35]

There is something touchingly archaic about this sort of "scientific" writing. It has the flavor of certain literary doctors of our own time who are loath to consign madness to the category of disease. Eighteenth-century physicians had not lost all their awe before the surprises of the soul. They were aware that mental disorders could be precipitated by evanescent phenomena like words or sights or sounds: "At the time of the South Sea bubble," wrote one young physician in the 1790s, the doctor in charge of an important English "lunatic hospital, found that the greatest number of his patients were those who had suddenly acquired fortunes"; and the author of the first full-scale American textbook on diseases of the mind, the eminent Dr. Benjamin Rush, noted that *"tristimania"* often follows good news such as succeeding to an estate or winning the lottery. "When no air has blown across my affairs," he quotes one melancholic patient, "and no shade obscured my sun, then am I most miserable." Yet even as the medical profession moved toward purely psychological accounts of depression, the only known interventions for treating the disease remained physical—stimulating blood vessels in the head, for instance, so that the blood supply to the brain may be increased. This seemed a promising therapy since some patients had been known to recover spontaneously from depression after attacks of the itch, presumably because of the circulatory benefits of vigorous scratching.[36]

We see, then, that as the Enlightenment established itself in America in the course of the eighteenth century, it effected a sweeping reorganization of reality with which we still live: the dispossession of the invisible world as a legitimate object of knowledge. Lunatics were no longer possessed, but sick. Madness, which had been "linked to the presence of imaginary transcendences," was becoming a clinical and sometimes a penal problem.[37] The first recorded order by a New England court for mental examination of a plaintiff in a witchcraft trial came in 1724—another sign that the world of spirit was being lost. Most cases of possession by transcendent spirits were now regularly exposed as frauds. In England, where the Jacobean statute upon which the colonial codes were based had been repealed in the 1730s (long after it had ceased to be enforced), the new Hanoverian law reduced the punishment for "witchcraft" from death to one year's imprisonment, and the crime itself was redefined as the *pretense* of "witchcraft, sorcery, [or] inchantment."[38] One could no longer *be* a witch; one could only *pretend* to be one or delude oneself into thinking so.

In the colonies as well (although as late as 1730 Rhode Island passed an act reiterating that witchcraft was a capital felony), the old statutes had fallen mostly into disuse, and throughout the century the cry of witchcraft turns up in the public record mainly when accused persons initiate suits for slander. A few sporadic exceptions can be documented after 1700: one full-scale witchcraft trial in Virginia in 1706; a Massachusetts man—apparently a fed-up colonial Portnoy—who accused his mother of witchcraft in 1718; a "Cart Loade of Old Dutch People" seized as witches by a New York constable in the 1740s.[39]

On those occasions when the cry of witchcraft did still arise, it was likely to be quickly muffled, as if it were a night regression that would embarrass everyone—even those who participated in the hue and cry— when they woke to reason in the morning. In 1770, for example, a Massachusetts girl exhibited all the traditional fits and trances that a century earlier would have warranted interrogation of those she accused; but her minister, though a believer in "spirits, an invisible world, and particularly the agency of Satan," cautioned that "many things have been . . . called the works of the devil, which were nothing more than the contrivance of . . . children."[40] A few years earlier, a Boston broadside had turned the torment of a Simsbury girl into doggerel:

Sometimes she'll jump and dance the room about;
And like one craz'd she'll make a fearful rout;
Sometimes she'll jump and climb the chair,
And there she'll be, tho' no one's near.

Sometimes she sees black cats and crows that fly,
And other frightful sights just by;
Sometimes she's bit & scratch'd by hands unknown,
Which makes this child to sigh and groan.

But alas! alas! to tell you all,
That doth unto this child befall,
Would take more lines than two or three,
Therefore I pray you to quit me.

The weary versifier stays with his subject just long enough to offer some advice to the girl's parents:

And now to you her parents dear,
Pray, unto God, now lend an ear;
And do not think to ease the smart,
By conjure or by foolish art.[41]

This diminution of witchcraft (which, unlike sorcery or necromancy, involved personal commerce with the devil) into a domestic farce was one among many signs that Satan was no longer taken seriously as an invisible contender for human souls. It marked the final passing of the quasi-medieval world of the seventeenth century, in which the way to knowledge had still been mainly explosive, and one man's sudden advent into wisdom gave no advantage to his successor. The new spirit of Enlightenment was entirely different. It was accretive and progressive; its characteristic projects became collective—encyclopedias, circulating libraries, philosophical societies—and one of its novelties was the notion that the dissemination of knowledge could save posterity from the work of rediscovering what was already known. These conceptions of progress effected by human rather than divine means were fundamentally different from the old vision of a cosmos directed by a God who gave—or withheld—the grace that no man could pass on to another.

This contest in colonial America between belief and knowledge left its effects everywhere. It was registered in small moments—as in 1774 when a Princeton-educated clergyman stormed out of the drawing room after another man cast doubt on the devil's existence—and more largely, in the fissure that was opening up between those who assented to the new spirit of reason and those who resisted it. As the ancient belief in a God-drenched world broke down under the pressure of rationalism, science tried to move into the breach. It displayed impressive explanatory power, but it offered little means of modifying the world that God and the devil had abandoned. Americans found themselves, in short, in a situation not unlike what the historian Keith Thomas has memorably described for the citizens of early modern England, who "renounce[d] the magical solutions offered by the medieval Church before they had devised any technical remedies to put in their place."[42] As physicians abandoned the vocabulary of "divine phrenzie" and moved toward a materialist understanding of the mind, mental excitement was no longer attributed to the activity of transcendent forces but became, instead, a physical disease. It was, however, a disease that physicians had no idea how to treat.

This situation left many people in a state of extreme spiritual need, because there are few experiences more disturbing than the discovery of an irremediable problem. To name the disease while withholding the cure is a kind of torture ("This is the greatest miserie of all," as one Puritan minister had put it more than a century before, "to see meat and not to eat it . . ."), and so it is not surprising that with the self-conscious impotence of early modern science came a surge of popular anxiety. God and the devil were in retreat, which meant that prayer and penitence were losing their force as ways of affecting one's life. With nothing of comparable power to take their place, people turned to alternative comforts: to astrology, for instance, which seemed to offer a way of observing the world complete with techniques for propitiating the spirits that govern it. Many nominal Christians in eighteenth-century America still believed that to get a female foal one must bring the stallion to the mare after the full moon; or that chestnut wood, if cut under the waxing moon, would throw off sparks in the fire; or that timber cut under the waning moon in certain months of the year would stay permanently free of worms.[43] These kinds of belief make men suitors, and compel them, like pagans, to try tricks and charms to coax favor from Mistress Fortune. There is nostalgia here for a vanished world governed by spirits—sometimes hostile, sometimes benevolent, but always responsive to man.

[4]

So at the time of its war with England and its Declaration of Independence, American society was dividing into skeptics and seekers. One can still feel the pressure that was opening up this division by looking into the texture of the language itself, whose lingering religious elements were now being pushed down into a fossil layer where they would no longer be part of living speech. Words that had once designated transcendent principles were now functioning as the names of symptoms and conveniences. The word "evil," for example, begins in the second half of the eighteenth century to be used as a synonym for dyspepsia and diarrhea, and turns up in advertisements for "antiscorbutic drops," guaranteed effective against "scurvy, leprosy, ulcers, the evil, fistula, [and] Piles."[44] Benjamin Franklin eliminated entirely from his *Autobiography* the word "sin" and, borrowing a term from the print shop, substituted "erratum" whenever he spoke of betrayal or other actions that he wished to excise from the public record of his life. The result was a classic instance of what the twentieth-century theologian Reinhold Niebuhr has called "a definition of sin as error rather than as evil."[45]

The most directly imperiled vocabulary was that of the Bible, especially of its prophetic books, with their airborne thrones, seas of glass, the moon turned to blood, beasts with many eyes. The now conventional theory of association argued that reading too much in such a book carried risks, and a growing literature of scandal developed around the careers of pious criminals—often semi-literate men gone wild with jealousy, or women driven to despair by illegitimate pregnancy—who had heard and heeded the voices of spirits who told them, in scriptural language, to kill. Horrified by such true believers, rationalists warned that an overheated imagination was a threat to morals, and that, if it were not subdued and confined, it would propagate a race of lunatics.

Here, in brief, is the career of one of these colonial sons of Sam—a thirty-three-year-old farmer named John Lewis, who, on a June morning in 1760, in Bucks County, Pennsylvania, watched his wife prepare her daily bath. She was pregnant, the baby two weeks overdue, and Lewis feared that "in the Condition she was in, she could not stand over the Wash-Tub."[46] Ann, his wife of seventeen years, refused assistance, and shooed him out of the house until he went "to prepare some Stuff to make a Plow," at which he continued until dinner. "After Dinner," he reports, "I desired her to lye down with me on the Bed," which she refused, saying "she must finish her Washing," and a little later, after another spate of field work, he "desired her again to lye down on the Bed, which she did." Lewis explains what happened next:

> She had not been long thereon before I jumped on her in a furious Manner, with my two Knees on her Belly, and seized her with my two Hands by the Neck, and with my two Thumbs did throatle her! — She cried out, "Johnny . . . don't kill me." — I made no Reply, but Proceeded in my bloody Work; and she again cry'd out (as well as she was able), "My Life! my Life!" — I still kept my wicked Purpose untill she expired under my murdering Hands! . . . I then resolved to commit another murder, viz. on the Body of one of my Children, about two Years old, the rest being all out of Doors . . . But recollecting that it was a-sleep, I concluded there was no Danger from its surviving; so it pleased God to prevent my taking its Life.

The point of Lewis's confession, which was first published as an exemplary preface to a tract entitled *A Plain Address to Quakers, Moravians, Separatists, Separate-Baptists, Rogerenes, and other Enthusiasts* (1762), was that, acting under the delusion of divine sanction, he had heard "a call from the Almighty . . . to kill my Wife and unborn babe." The colonies seemed to be coming alive with such self-proclaimed fulfillers of prophecy; and it was plain, according to those who were sounding the alarm, that "Satan [could still] meddle with Scripture" so that simpletons like Lewis believed it had been written for them.[47]

This tense situation within American religious life was a symptom of a major cultural schism. If the "subtilty of Satan" had once been to subvert belief, either "wholly [to] destroy the truth . . . [or] deface it what he may,"[48] it was now—according to the rationalist view—becoming Satan's business to foster the illusion of truth, to paint alluringly another world from which needy believers might receive directives. If "the model of madness" had "for preceding centuries . . . been to deny God," the madman was now the person who believed too intensely in God, who was (as Bronson Alcott later put it, describing the ecstatic poet Jones Very) "insane with God—diswitted in the contemplation of the holiness of Divinity."[49] To be possessed meant to be a believer—someone in whose dreams God and Satan remained intensely real.

America was dividing, in other words, between those who clung to the old gallery of demons and devils and those who shook them off as tricks of the mind. Farmer Lewis was of the first sort. He was a spiritually needy believer, representative of those for whom "enlightenment" was a form of cruelty. Tortured by his wife's real or imagined infidelity, he leapt at what he thought was a communication from a personal God who condescended to speak to him. Here is the passage from Revelation which he received with gratitude:

Notwithstanding, I have a few things against thee, because thou sufferest that woman Jezable, which calleth herself a prophetess, to teach and seduce my servants to commit fornication, and to eat things sacrificed unto idols. And I gave her space to repent of her fornication, and she repented not. Behold, I will cast her into a bed, and them that commit adultery with her into great tribulation, except they repent of their deeds. And I will kill her children with death and the churches shall know that I am he which searcheth the reins and hearts: and I will give unto every one of you according to your works.[50]

Conservative clergy stood aghast at the licentious reading by common folk of such passages, and held up their crimes as examples of where untutored reading of Scripture might lead.

This kind of admonitory sensationalism became part of the clergy's campaign to reassert their authority over the interpretation of Scripture. There is no better way to gauge the distance that religion had traveled between the seventeenth and eighteenth centuries than to observe the new rejection of the old Puritan injunction to "go home and consider whether the things that have been taught were true or no." In the shadow of the Enlightenment, the new imperative was to beware of "*Impulses* or Impressions as a Rule of Conduct," even when they appear to derive from "a Text of Scripture," and to rely instead on a schooled minister who could keep things under control by showing exactly what the Bible does—and does not—mean.[51]

One of the bitterest controversies of this struggle began now to form itself over a seemingly trivial question: whether a seminary degree had any bearing on a man's ability to preach with heart-knowledge as opposed to a merely "notional" understanding of the gospel. Partisans of what became known as the Great Awakening, who sensed the spiritual need of ordinary people, were not interested in a minister's academic credentials. They were only interested to know if he had a true sight of sin and was infused with grace. Pietist groups proliferated throughout the colonies, as people with intense religious hunger gathered not only in small immigrant sects like the Mennonites, Dunkers, and Schwenkfelders of the Middle Colonies but also in larger numbers as New Light Presbyterians in the North and Methodists in the South, and were led out of established churches by ministers with reputable degrees and intellectual sophistication.

Despite this denominational variety, the disputes of the Great Awakening ultimately boiled down to one long argument about the legitimacy of strong feeling in religious experience. One camp derided it, while the other held to it as proof that God had not abandoned his human children in the post-Apostolic age. Some believed that though the soul was subject to fantasies and delusions, it was a trainable instrument of reason; others insisted that it remained the battleground between Christ and the devil. For the former—the anti-Awakeners—the essence of religion could be adequately expressed in the institutional life of a church; and violent sensory experiences were suspect. For the latter, the world of observances was dispensable, but a person's life could and *must* be radically changed upon the apprehension of what one scholar of the period calls "an order of being other than that walled and hemmed-in existence in which a stale institutional religion . . . [was] content to dwell."[52]

In the words of James Davenport, a passionate advocate of the Awakening, who was expelled from Connecticut in 1742 by the colony's General Assembly (for his "supposition and pretence of *extraordinary intercourse with heaven*"), the moment of conversion comes when the "joyful Voice" of Christ suddenly sounds within the souls of tortured sinners, and turns their "Sighs . . . into Songs." For the rationalists, who tended to avoid such musical metaphors, grace was better described as a kind of personal housecleaning:

> Light is put into the understanding; the will made pliant and ductile; the affections are placed on their proper objects; the passions calm and quiet; the conscience serene and placid; and the life uniform and regular . . .[53]

Grace, in this formulation, has become a psychological tidiness; the furnishings of the mind are in their proper places, the colors muted; the house of consciousness a kind of sanitarium.

History never conforms fully to such neat oppositional paradigms, it should be said; most Americans probably felt both the pietist and rationalist impulses at work within themselves, and heard from their ministers some mixture of the two. Only from the articulate few do we hear purified versions of either. But there can be no doubt that a gap was opening between the bookish religion of the elites and those who experienced religion primarily as an upheaval in their souls. At issue were the most urgent questions of the moral life. The rationalists envisioned man essentially alone, free and responsible only to himself, in a universe governed from afar by an increasingly remote God. From the Awakeners, who tried to save the idea of a personal God from the assault of reason, they demanded to know how such an omnipotent divinity—foreseeing all, controlling all—could be consistent with the moral responsibility of man. It fell to the leading intellectual among the Awakeners, Jonathan Edwards, to answer the question:

> The common people don't ascend up in their reflections and abstractions, to the metaphysical sources, relations and dependences of things, in order to form their notion of faultiness or blameworthiness. They don't wait till they have decided by their refinings, what first determines the will; whether it be determined by something extrinsic, or intrinsic; whether volition determines volition, or whether the understanding determines the will; whether there be any such thing as metaphysicians

mean by contingence (if they have any meaning); . . . They don't take any part of their notion of fault or blame from the resolution of any such questions. If this were the case, there are multitudes, yea, the far greater part of mankind, nine hundred and ninety-nine out of a thousand would live and die without having any such notion as that of fault ever entering into their heads, or without so much as once having any conception that anybody was to be either blamed or commended for anything.[54]

This forecast of modernity leads into the disputed heart of eighteenth-century American culture. It was Edwards who recognized that the principal doctrine of the Christian faith—the doctrine of original sin—was not being assimilated by the Enlightenment mind, that it was disappearing along with the vivid creature—Satan—who had once symbolized it. And if the devil was being discredited, it was becoming equally difficult, if not impossible, for an educated, "self-made" person to worship an omnipotent God who possesses perfect foreknowledge of every human disposition and action, who equips the first man with the curiosity and vanity that leave him open to sin, then imputes that sin to all humankind and justly blames them. This was a doctrine unlikely to prosper as the world turned modern. Here is Benjamin Franklin, spokesman for the rationalists, proposing a more suitable scheme:

> If the Creature is thus limited in his Actions, being able to do only such Things as God would have him to do, and not being able to refuse doing what God would have done; then he can have no such Thing as Liberty, Free-Will or Power to do or refrain an Action. . . . [And] if there is no such Thing as Free-Will in Creatures, there can be neither Merit nor Demerit in Creatures.[55]

Franklin's conclusion (which is precisely what Edwards judged an absurdity) that moral judgments are vitiated by the Old Calvinist cosmology has a touch of Swiftian glee; all his life he showed little capacity to blame himself for anything, and had difficulty with a God who damns some persons for what they cannot help doing, and saves others at his inscrutable pleasure. To believe in such a God, and then to condemn the sinful acts that he countenances, seemed to Franklin (and many others) to be, in the deepest sense of the word, irrational.

Franklin was the future. It was a future poised between the alternatives of licentiousness and self-discipline, but without any transcendent standard by which to make the choice. Franklin seems a near neighbor of ours because he was a divided personality in the modern sense, a diligent servant of his own compulsions. Edwards, on the other hand, seems remote and aloof. He understood that the older narrative of grace and damnation remained close to the lives of a great many people who were witnessing, more than hastening, the advent of Franklin's new world. Most people, he believed, do not restrain themselves from judging their neighbor because some feature or failure of his life—economic (poverty), biological (madness), temperamental (drunkenness)—has driven him to beat his wife or defraud his townsman. A lascivious man who cannot control his lust is, to Edwards, simply blameworthy, despite the incontrovertible facts of the urging body into which he was born and the presence of other compliant bodies within his sight and reach. He cannot, when he falls into concupiscence, plead an extenuating circumstance called God, or (in a subsequent vocabulary) fate, or (in our own idiom) hormonal surges. He is, in the strict Edwardsian view, responsible for himself.

These two great opposites—Franklin and Edwards—articulated the two poles of feeling between which American culture was now reorganizing itself. Franklin's is our first genuinely modern public voice; and it was the prescience of Edwards to anticipate the breakage between experience and moral ideas that it expressed—to see that the forces of the culture were increasingly arrayed against the demands of religion, not out of some general hostility, but in the specific sense that the twin concepts of personal responsibility and a determining God were becoming incompatible. Eighteenth-century culture was, in other words, showing the telltale signs of modernity, of its penchant for explanation rather than confession, and of its conviction that circumstance mitigates crime.

As the figure of the devil and the doctrine of original sin receded ever further into myth, intellectuals became interested, for example, in the issue of why childhood friends or siblings (even twins) may diverge in their moral development after periods of shared nurture. By the 1770s the search was on to pin down *circumstantial* causes for spiritual difference: "Two children" take a walk with their tutor; "one busies himself in plucking flowers or running after butterflies, the other walks in the hand of their conductor . . ."[56] Was this difference in temperament inborn and destined to play itself out in their lives? Or could the wandering child be reined in by a rebuke from the instructor? The rationalists (in this case, an Englishman, the influential reformer William Godwin) were increasingly committed to the nurture side of this ancient nature-nurture debate. In the process, they formulated a fundamental premise of modern liberal culture: that a person's moral being can be fashioned by managing the circumstances around him. The self was coming to be understood not as a created entity with a distinct soul, but as an unformed substance that would attain a certain shape and character through the impact upon it of external influences. A human being was a kind of accident, and, as such, he was an entity not quite responsible for himself.

Edwards's preemptive response to this modern idea was to sweep away the whole issue as wrongly formulated, to say that freedom of the will consists not in some idealized state of insulation from influence, in which the will might somehow determine itself, but solely and entirely in the freedom *"to do as we will"* in the world as it is. This has nothing to do with

> the cause or original of that choice; or [with] how the person came to have such a volition; or [with the question of] whether it was caused by some external motive, or internal habitual bias; whether it was determined by some internal antecedent volition, or whether it happened without a cause; whether it was necessarily connected with something foregoing, or not connected. Let the person come by his volition or choice how he will, yet, if he is able, and there is nothing in the way to hinder his pursuing and executing his will, the man is fully and perfectly free, according to the primary and common notion of freedom.[57]

The question of what precedes an act of will is of no moral consequence for Edwards. "We do not predicate the sinfulness of volition," explained one of his disciples, "on the agency of the cause, but on the volition itself; on our own agency." (Having been abused as a child—to take a currently prevalent example—is no excuse for abusing one's own child.) Mankind possesses all the freedom of will necessary to be morally responsible; one is not a tree, which may not be praised or condemned if "it oftener happens to be lit upon by a swan or nightingale; or a rock [which may not be called] more vicious than other rocks, because rattlesnakes have happened oftener to crawl over it."[58] Man is a free and rational creature, and foisting off responsibility for his errors or evils onto some antecedent cause is nothing more than an evasion.

Edwards knew—and this is what gives him his quality of tragic prophecy—that it was an increasingly common evasion. If he had lived to read Godwin's account of the promenading children, he would have granted that one child may be enchanted by the fragrance of a flower while the other stumbles in pain over a hidden root, but he would have insisted that both are responsible for what they become. If one grows to love and bless the world and the other to hate and pollute it, neither of them may explain or excuse himself because of a formative childhood walk in the garden. God, in arranging what seem the accidents of our lives, bears no responsibility for what we become. This is our burden, and ours alone.

[5]

The question we must ask about these debates is why in the eighteenth century this concept of human responsibility suddenly became so problematic. The world may have seemed more full of accident than before; families may have been more likely to raise children whose social status would differ widely, with one son remaining in the shrinking world of subsistence farming, for example, while another set off for the bustling city. But fortune and accident had always been busy in people's lives, and despite the hints that can be gleaned from church and town records, there is no firm correlation between evangelical religious feeling and social standing.

If religious divisions did not conform very well to fault lines of class or gender or age, there is nevertheless some evidence that the colonies were undergoing a transformation similar to what had happened in England a century earlier. Land grants were drying up as local populations outgrew the original limits of the towns. A general psychic problem, especially acute for young men, arose from this situation—in part because the modern ethic of mobility and self-reliance, which might have sanctioned or encouraged dreams of escape from the depleted towns, had not yet fully taken form. Younger sons led ever more crimped lives (the statistics show smaller land inheritances, later marrying ages, and a widening gap between rich and poor), and found themselves in what amounted to extended adolescence. Unable to marry at the age of peak sexual appetite, shut out from their patrimony by older siblings, they were expected to show undiminished filial obedience even as the traditional rewards of inheritance grew uncertain. It was, as the historian Patricia Tracy has said, "a particularly bad time to be an adolescent,"[59] and it is not surprising that those who were required to linger in celibate filial roles, even as they knew that their best prospects lay beyond the boundaries of home, were drawn to a version of religious experience that stressed self-doubt and even self-hatred as signs of imminent grace. The evangelicals talked about experience in ways that young people could readily understand; they described the soul in turmoil, as a battleground between desire and obligation, while for the rationalists, the soul was unconflicted and serene.

Another way to understand this division is to recognize that evangelical piety in the Enlightenment years was a way of resisting the estrangement of responsibility from providence. Evangelical religion has always appealed to those who feel caught by the paradox of what Reinhold Niebuhr, two hundred years after Edwards, called "responsibility despite inevitability"—the experience of living with a sense that one's life is determined and yet that one is held responsible for it.

This kind of faith has always been a religious style of special power for adolescents, who are filled with conflict between desire and guilt, and for blacks, who have struggled throughout their history in America against feeling both helpless and blameworthy. It has also been a religious style of powerful appeal to women. Among its most revealing texts are the execution sermons (usually accompanied by transcribed confessions of the condemned) delivered before the hangings of infanticide mothers—unmarried young women who, in acts redolent with helplessness and guilt, smothered their babies rather than allow themselves to be revealed to the world as fallen. The confessions of these wretched girls are among the purest acknowledgments in our literature of soul-killing shame. "Oh! I can truly say," said one young woman just before being hanged in 1700, "I loath my self for my sins, I abhor my self, and if I were to live a thousand years in this world, it should be in the hatred of all Evil."[60]

By the end of the eighteenth century, however, one finds clergymen complaining that "instead of looking for criminality in that which is criminal, we seek for it in a cause; and, by this means, place it at such a distance from ourselves as to feel very easy and unconcerned about it." This comment is apposite for our own time—of which E. L. Doctorow has recently remarked that "we shunt off our evil, embody it in . . . our defendants and turn away."[61] Composed on the edge of modernity, it is a prediction of a culture (our culture) in which most social acts are mediated by invisible transactions whose human consequences are obscure, and one commonly feels "easy and unconcerned" at the ways in which our lives impinge on people we do not see. (The Marxist tradition has, accordingly, built a theory around the concepts of "reification" and "alienation" to explain how this process permeates modern life—how commodities, even when produced at great human cost, take on a life of their own while the human beings who produce them disappear into anonymity.) Two hundred years ago, when social and economic life still proceeded largely through exchanges of services and goods between people who knew each other well, this development was not yet clear, and vocabularies for describing or concealing it were not in much demand. Yet Jonathan Edwards and his followers understood that it was becoming more and more a psychological imperative to divert responsibility for the effects of one's actions onto something, or somebody, else.

Here is one minister, Samuel Whitman, writing in 1797 about the source of evil:

> If there was no other way to account for the origin of evil, than on the supposition of its flowing from God as its fontal cause, we should then be under the necessity of adopting the *manichean* principle; and, therefore conclude that there must be two Gods; the one the fountain of good, and the other the fountain of evil.[62]

This conclusion, says Whitman, is blasphemy. But what is the other way that can save God from being revealed as the fountain of sin and pain? It is to appeal, with the kind of bland equanimity that Voltaire mocked in *Candide* (1759), in which a blithering philosopher goes about proclaiming this "the best of all possible worlds," to an order that stands beyond the reach of rationality:

> Providence may see harmony, where to us discord reigns. The pride of man may object against the government of God, on account of those events which infinite wisdom sees to be necessary, in order to the accomplishment of the most important purposes.[63]

What seems evil, in other words—death, suffering, unfulfilled wants —is really good. The trouble is that just saying it does not make it *feel* so. Simply invoking an order invisible to myopic man cannot, in the end, restore anything like the lost power of faith. Such a theology is theoretical, bloodless, drained of the juice of belief. Its language ("fontal cause") is legalistic, technical; it might excuse God from responsibility for the invention of sin in some technical sense, but it cannot possibly bring any comfort to someone in pain. It may lead to the recognition, as William James put it a hundred years later, that "certain evils minister to ulterior goods, that the bitter makes the cocktail better"; it may recommend "the doctrine that all the evil in the universe is but instrumental to its greater perfection." But it can never overcome the fact that "the scale of evil actually in sight defies all human tolerance." It is a species of "transcendental idealism [that] brings us no farther than the Book of Job," and leads instead to the unbearable concession that "God's ways are not our ways, so let us put our hands upon our mouth."[64]

This is the inevitable outcome of the sort of pure rationalism that was taking hold of the American mind in the eighteenth century. It leaves people starved for faith. Edwards, almost alone, seemed to know this— to recognize in advance the modern despair of those who "renounce the higher harmony altogether . . . [as] not worth the tears of . . . one tortured child."[65] Though Edwards is best known for his fire-and-brimstone sermons, he was actually a compassionate preacher searching for a way to preserve the consolatory power of the Augustinian vision in an age when God and the devil had become abstractions. Sin, for him, remained nothing more or less than blindness, dullness, closedness in the face of "the beauty of the Godhead, and the divinity of Divinity . . . without which God himself (if that were possible to be) would be an infinite evil: without which, we ourselves had better never have been; and without which there had better have been no being."[66] As this beautiful phrasing attests, Edwards still felt to the core of his soul the horror of evil as estrangement from God. And he knew that since the traditional way for people to escape this horror—by apprehending transcendent harmony through ecstatic religious insight—had been proscribed as a kind of mystic madness, the whole structure of theodicy had come to depend on reason alone.

Edwards saw the coming disaster of modernity—that in the face of evil, human beings would be left spiritually helpless:

To be a creature, and as such obeying the laws of its Creator, and yet to be also a freely acting being . . . to be responsible, and yet to consider one's actions as the operations of a Superior Being—the unity between these two sets of concepts is a unity which we must postulate in the idea of a world that would be the highest good. But it is a unity which can be understood only by the one who has obtained a knowledge of the super-sensible (intelligible) world and has seen how this world lies at the basis of the world of experience. On this knowledge only can be based the proof of the moral wisdom of the Creator of the world—no mortal man however can attain to this knowledge.[67]

This summary of the paradoxical nature of theodicy comes not from Edwards, but from the most powerful philosopher of the European Enlightenment, Immanuel Kant. It recapitulates the whole debate which American thinkers, however provincially, had joined. Reason, says Kant, must always fall short in the project of reconciling the idea of God with the experience of evil because neither can be comprehended by reason alone. "No theodicy [can keep] its promise; none has managed to justify the moral wisdom at work in the government of the world against the doubts which arise out of our experience of the world."[68]

Kant's simple but devastating point is a eulogy for eighteenth-century metaphysics; it rises to eloquence when he, too, turns to the biblical tale of Job—a good man whose acceptance of affliction is contrasted with the droning explanations he is offered by his friends:

Job spoke as he thought, as he felt, and as every man in his position would feel. His friends, however, spoke as if they were overheard by the Almighty whose behaviour they were judging, and as if they cared more for winning his favours by passing the right judgement than for saying the truth.

The babble of reason in the face of suffering is a kind of sycophancy to God, a flattery unworthy of the God who "honoured Job by showing him the wisdom of his creation and its unfathomable nature . . . [who] let him see the beautiful side of creation . . . but . . . also showed the horrible side, by naming the products of his might." "Theodicy," Kant concludes, "is not a task of science but is a matter of faith."[69]

By the end of the eighteenth century, most American theologians were talking like Job's friends. Outside the evangelical churches, Protestantism had become bleached and brittle; the heart was gone out of it. It was neither genuinely dualist, with a vibrant devil contending for the world against God, nor was it able to rekindle the Augustinian idea of a universe in which evil may be understood as metaphysically nothing. Religion no longer offered a viscerally satisfying account of the evil which people still felt around and within themselves.

In earlier times, descriptions of moral experience had been dominated by a fascinating seducer let loose by God, whose victims, both goaded and guilty, nevertheless felt responsible for themselves. This devil had now entered his death throes. He had once been, along with the God who unleashed him, an immensely powerful symbol for the compatibility of responsibility and predestination—a unity which many people still felt in the depths of their experience, but of which they were no longer able to speak.

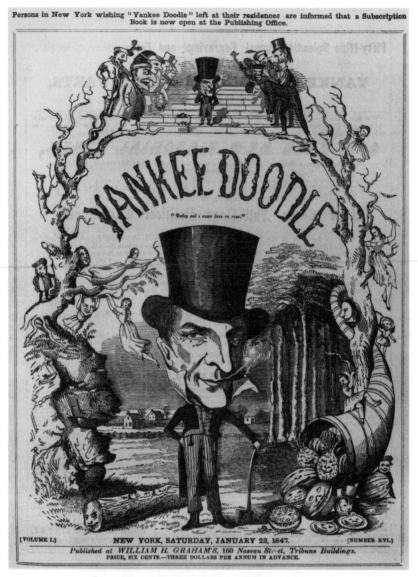

Cover illustration from Yankee Doodle *(1847)*
(COLUMBIA UNIVERSITY LIBRARY)

THREE

The Birth of the Self

If one reads along through American literature headed toward our own time, a moment comes when one realizes that the writings have become modern. To tour the religious and political landscape of the colonies is to travel by night through terrain that feels foreign and unmapped; one overhears talk of grace and damnation and other categories that have, for us, receded into sentimentality or sheer unintelligibility. But near 1800 we turn a corner and see that the neighborhood is becoming familiar even if we cannot name the exact address. The structures and pathways and signs are arranged according to conventions we recognize—and the fatigue that accompanies the work of navigation is lifted. We proceed by memory and instinct again.

One reason for this dawning sense of familiarity is that the literature becomes suspicious, even contemptuous toward what people believed in the past. It begins to regard, as we do, all preceding products of the human imagination as exploitable resources embedded in a history that has an irreducible *pastness*. It relinquishes the typological structure of history, which had prevailed in variant forms from the Church Fathers through the Puritans to the founders of the American republic and which saw history as one elaborated instant in the mind of God; and embraces instead a sense of the past as an aggregate of phenomena whose source and coherence are obscure. History becomes inert rather than prophetic, and can be animated only by the controversial work of the retrospective imagination.

[1]

Among the relics of the overturned world where metaphysics and facts had once seemed connected was the entire machinery of Christian symbolism for evil. After the blows he had sustained during the Enlightenment, Satan begins to conduct himself in the late 1700s like a superannuated athlete who has hit the banquet circuit. As if to satisfy admirers who still treasure his memory, he comes back for a last hurrah in the patriot rhetoric that inflamed the Revolution, whose partisans (borrowing from the British tradition of republican dissent) tended to think of the world as a battleground between infernal imperial forces and besieged citizens. The king's counselors are a "conspiratorial cabal" that not only pours poison into his gullible Majesty's ear, but was already plotting to control him when he was an impressionable child. Like Satan flattering Eve, a "clique around the Princess Dowager" inspires "arbitrary principles into her son [the future George III] and . . . instructs him how to . . . establish a despotism." And when this boy comes of age, he is surrounded day and night by "serpentine" advisers who prod him into dispersing their agents throughout the British empire, which is held together not by reverence but by sycophancy and bribery, the linkages of their greed.[1]

To read these accounts of the fall of imperial Britain is to encounter a world in which every legitimate transaction turns into an opportunity for abuse. Satan was a useful metaphor to the patriots, whose incendiary writings had what today would be called a "paranoid" tinge, and who needed a symbol to represent the source of all the world's evil. In the patriot story, the English king sends his customs agents to his colonies across the Atlantic, where they hover lasciviously over citizens trying to carry on an honest trade. When they swoop in for the kill, they do it with demonic ardor. We may think today of the patriot manifestos—Tom Paine's *Common Sense*, Thomas Jefferson's Declaration of Independence —as careful, reasonable arguments built on an Enlightenment concept of natural rights; but they were also tirades that vilified the king and the Tories in the old way, as minions of Satan. The Revolution was, in this sense, only half secular; the other half came straight out, afire, of the Bible:

A Tempter and Tormentor, is the Character of the Devil. — Hutchinson, Oliver, and others of their Circle, who for their own Ends of Ambition and Avarice, have procured, promoted, encouraged, councilled, aided and abetted the Taxation of America, have been the real Tempters of their Countrymen and Women, into all the Vices, sins, Crimes and follies which that Taxation has occasioned: And now by [them]selves and their Friends, Dependents, and Votaries, they a[re] reproaching those very Men and Women, with those Vices and follies, Sins and Crimes.[2]

With the advent of this sacred war, the devil acquired a series of new countenances as British generals succeeded one another as symbols of cruelty. One patriot poet likened Satan to Lord Cornwallis, in whom "Nature . . . disgrac'd the form divine," and "mistook . . . him for a— swine: / That eye his forehead to her shame adorns; / Blush! nature, blush—bestow him tail and horns!"[3] And after independence, the devil's currency as a symbol of perfidy was further enhanced when *Paradise Lost* returned to literary fashion. Milton's poem became a favorite text especially for New Englanders like John Adams, who worried that greed and ambition might be uncontainable in a kingless republic. Yet despite his persistent value as a moral symbol, the devil's return was brief. Arrested by the Revolution, his decline resumed, and he continued to devolve into a mere source for analogy. He became a convenience for moralists and writers of political satire.

In the aftermath of war—always a tonic for the devil's career—this diminished Satan remained available for inclusion in programs for which he was now little more than an adornment. In a poem entitled "The Triumph of Infidelity" (1788), the pious president of Yale, Timothy Dwight (who was Jonathan Edwards's grandson), presented him as a Jacobin brat scheming, in rhymed couplets, "to plunge the New World in the gulph of sin." But within a few years his new loss of stature (after each recovery he ends up weaker than he had been before the setback) was broadly reflected in the titles of popular books: a British play, *The Devil Among the Taylors*, had wide appeal in the 1780s and was published in the United States in 1805; eventually comic devils became the norm —*The Devil in Love* (1830), *The Devil Turned Doctor* (1831), *The Devil's Comical Almanac* (1837). Such entertainments were among the natural consequences of the accelerating retreat from Calvinist suspicion of the unregenerate self. The ancient symbol that had dramatized how a tempter plants his promises among human desires was now totally cut off from the idea—original sin—that had initially required it.

It is therefore not surprising to find an irreverent Federalist poet telling the story of the fall itself (in a poem entitled "The Origin of Evil") as a dirty joke in which the devil plays no part at all:

> *Innocent of nuptial blisses,*
> *   Unknown to him the balm of life;*
> *With unmeaning, wild caresses,*
> *   Adam teaz'd his virgin wife.*
>
> *As her arm Eve held him hard in,*
> *   And toy'd him with her roving hand,*
> *In the middle of Love's Garden,*
> *   She saw the Tree of Knowledge stand.*
> .   .   .   .
> *Her soft hand then half embrac'd it,*
> *   Her heaving breasts to his inclin'd,*
> *She op'd her coral lips to taste it,*
> *   But first she peel'd its russet rind.*
> .   .   .   .
> *But when its nectar'd juice she tasted,*
> *   Dissolving Eve could only sigh;*
> *"I feel—I feel, my life is wasted,*
> *   This hour I eat, and now I die."*
>
> *But when she saw the tree so lofty,*
> *   Sapless and shrunk in size so small;*
> *Pointing she whisper'd Adam softly:*
> *   "See! there is DEATH! and there's the FALL!"*[4]

Though not yet banished from more seemly theological disputes, the devil eventually brought this kind of farce with him wherever he went. Employed by the temperance movement as a champion of drink, he turned up in folk tales as a bright-eyed boozer for whom "a mug of flip, hissing hot, slipped down his throat, as though he was used to it," then as the lead actor in a hugely popular temperance story, *Deacon Giles's Distillery* (1835), the tale of a greedy purveyor of rum whose laborers walk out in protest over his disregard for the Sabbath and are succeeded by a group of demon volunteers. Happy to work near the open flame and among the boiling pots of the distillery, the new crew refuses the offer of complimentary grog on the ground that "they [have] had enough of hot things where they came from."[5]

On those occasions when this freelance devil still showed up in fearsome rather than comic form, he was likely to be revealed as a fraud. Here is a remarkable passage from the memoir of a Virginia gambler written in the 1820s:

> [My mother] would fit her admonitions to my capacity, by telling me not to steal any thing, nor never to tell a *lie*, nor swear, for if I did there was a great black ugly clubfooted man called the Devil, that would take me and all bad boys and put them in hell, and burn them up; but if I was a good boy, I would be taken up to heaven with God, where my little brothers and sisters were gone, and she would go with me, where we would all live together forever. . . . I paid strict attention to this command, till one day my eldest sister ordered me to go to the spring with a little piggen and bring some water; which command I refused, and told her to go herself; she struck me, and I cursed her; upon which she told my mother, who gave me a severe whipping, and made me go to the spring quickly: I cried very much, and on the way I thought the sky opened, and I saw the heavens; I saw that good man; I fell on the ground, and thought I heard something say, you shan't come here if you are a bad boy, you must go to hell! The heavens closed, and I saw what I always shall remember; a great black something in the shape of a man, with horns on his head; and with a loud voice saying "I will catch you." I screamed, hallooed and cried, and instantly returned without the water. My mother was going to whip me again; I fell on my knees and begged if she would go with me, I would shew her and sister. They both went with me, but we saw nothing. It was just about sun set; my mother and sister both said they would forgive me—that it was the effect of some fright that had been revived in my imagination upon reflecting that I had done something wrong.[6]

This exemplary passage stands on the threshold of modernity. It stresses the fragility of the suggestible child, for whose moral teachers the devil has become a myth tailored to little minds that must be trained under the aspect of fear. Satan has been reduced to a pedagogical convenience; the danger in this story is the danger not of unbelief, but of excessive belief—of what we would call credulity. The child has slipped into a kind of quaking primitivism, and so his merciful mother clasps him up and gives up her privilege to be fearsome. She reveals the myth to be myth, and, in an act of what may be called modern love, she disabuses the boy of his fear by revealing its source to be a phantom of his imagination. By our lights, he has been saved; but by an earlier, half-remembered standard, he has taken a first long step toward damnation.

Still, the old forms of belief were not quite swept away. In Morristown, New Jersey, as late as the 1820s, "if a woman had any deformity, or had lived until her face became wrinkled, she could not escape the appellation of a witch. If a horse had the colic, or if any beast was in agony of pain, and behaved in an uncommon manner, the general opinion was that the creature was bewitched." "Naturalized under the nickname of Old Scratch," Satan still remained alive in folklore, where he turns up as a gambler's ally—in one version revealing himself as the owner of an ebony horse that breathes smoke while thundering down the straightaway; in another fulfilling the boast of a man who, upon entering his horse in a Sunday race, dismisses the Sabbatarian objections of his churchgoing neighbors with the boast that "I'll ride, though I ride to Hell." The animal throws and tramples him, then gallops off leaving hoofprints that stay fresh no matter how often they are covered with new dirt.[7]

Satan also stayed alive as a fun-house attraction. In the mid-1850s, the most popular exhibit at New York's Peale's Museum was the "Infernal Regions," where Beelzebub, Cerberus, Python, and Lucifer himself could be seen escorting the damned into a pit of fire. Barkers dared the crowds to enter, whereupon one visitor reported being "plunged into pithy darkness, whilst he is surrounded by the mournful shrieks of condemned spirits. The clashing of chains, and uproar of devils and imps complete the scene of horrors."[8]

The relegation of Satan to the status of road-show entertainer was complete by mid-century. In former times, when poets had written about the self as a collection of "Cursed Dregs, / Green, Yellow, Blew streakt Poyson hellish, ranck, / Bubs hatcht in natures nest on Serpents Eggs,"[9] the old prideful devil had flourished, because he had explained the horrors of the unregulated self. But now, with desire and ambition and even defiance becoming hallmarks of virtue, a felt need was rising for some new conception of evil. All the qualities of Satan—his resourcefulness, resilience, his knack for persuasion—were contemporary marks of pride.

In other words, it had become unconvincing to evoke the devil from pulpits and soapboxes as the embodiment of "unchecked self-interest" because America was now all about the glory of self-interest.[10] Those who would sustain his authority as the model of evil had to do so now in a context of trivialization and outright mockery. John Greenleaf Whittier, quoting Coleridge in the 1840s, put it best:

> Dimmer and dimmer, as the generations pass away, this tremendous Terror—this all-pervading espionage of Evil—this well-nigh infinite Haunter and Tempter—this active incarnation of motiveless malignity, —presents itself to the imagination.[11]

Yet even Whittier could not have predicted that twenty years later a dashing Union general would charm his fellow guests at a masquerade ball by dressing in

> Cape and coat, black velvet with gold lace. Pants the same, reaching only to the thighs. Red silk tights with not even drawers underneath. Red velvet cape with two upright red feathers, for horns. Black shoes with pointed toes upturned. Handsome belt. Mask, black silk.[12]

It is hard to exaggerate the cultural change signaled by this little fact that in 1865 George Armstrong Custer could use the devil as a pretext for dancing without underwear in a leotard.

[2]

All these disavowals of the old Satan—in literature, folklore, theology, and normative behavior—completed a long process. By the mid-1850s, as one writer put it, the "personal existence of Satan" was "so feebly realized, and so superficially regarded . . . [that] the fact of his existence, and influence upon the minds of the people, is virtually disbelieved."[13] Yet the death of Satan was not, by and large, greeted cheerfully. On the contrary, it showed that the conditions for a crisis, unmitigated by its auguries, were at hand: the disintegration of the culture's symbolic coherence. The death of the devil was a leading, but by no means the only, manifestation of this crisis.

Many alert people at the time, and virtually every historian in search of some scheme of periodization, have agreed that in the first half of the nineteenth century fundamentally new forces swept through all ranks of American life, effecting changes more profound than those brought on by the political upheaval of the Revolution itself. Naming these changes has been a more contentious matter, and can degenerate into a contest for primacy among them. One may begin with the influx of immigrants: some 200,000 Irish arrived in the 1830s; nearly 800,000, driven by the terrible potato famine, in the 1840s; close to a million in the 1850s,[14] introducing into the United States for the first time a significant number of Roman Catholics, many of whom took up residence in a new American locale—urban slums. Bolstered by the consequent supply of cheap labor, full-scale industrialization now got under way and delivered a range of shocks to a society that had been fairly stable for two centuries. Women, whose household handicraft had now to compete with factory-finished goods, began to go to work in significant numbers outside the home,[15] while others in better circumstances took maidservants from the newly stocked serving class and embarked on what we would recognize as the life of middle-class leisure. All these changes inevitably affected the ways Americans thought about their obligations to one another—about what was good and what was evil in the realm of human relations.

No region was untouched. As towns were transformed, so was the countryside. Western farmers began to ship their goods in quantity to the swelling Eastern cities (the Erie Canal was completed in 1825), and agriculture became a business on a new scale. New Englanders who had lived for generations according to rhythms of subsistence and barter found themselves raising specialized crops for sale, or mortgaging their lands to the Boston banks, or even—when competitive pressures became unmanageable—migrating to the Western Reserve, where they sometimes discovered within themselves a biting resentment toward something that began to be known as big Eastern money.[16]

Changes in the South were less various but more portentous. The cash-crop imperative was coming to dominate agriculture, as cotton production grew with technological innovation and economies of scale were made possible by an enslaved labor force. Capital went mainly into the acquisition and maintenance of slaves, so industrial development stalled and the South became a kind of agricultural colony—first of Britain, then of the Northern states. Dependent on the cotton trade for most finished goods, machinery, and even food, Southern society remained quasi-feudal, with a small landowning class perched more and more resolutely on the backs of its black laborers. (Melville, in *Moby-Dick*, offers an image of this hierarchy transposed to the world of whaling, where one of the *Pequod*'s officers literally stands "like a snowflake . . . mounted upon [the] gigantic" shoulders of his coal-black harpooner.) Wherever one looked in this novel America, the prosperity of one man, or faction, or region, had visibly cruel consequences for another.

It is not surprising that the language of public morality changed to accommodate the realities of this new economic order. As plantation magnates established cooperative relations with financiers in Boston and New York, for example, Southern intellectuals who had once been mute about their inherited embarrassment, slavery, now began to articulate a complex rationale in its defense. It became a "positive good" rather than a lamentable necessity—a tendency of thought that led eventually to the perverse claim that slavery was actually "the corner stone of civil liberty."[17] For the first time one could read in the leading Southern journals (*Russell's Magazine, The Southern Quarterly, De Bow's Review*) systematic claims for white racial superiority, along with critiques of the Northern factory system as cruelly exploitative. Critics both within and outside the South judged this intellectualism to be nothing more than hypocrisy mandated by greed.

In short, America was becoming a business culture through and through, North and South, each side blaming the other for installing the dollar as king. Here is a mathematics problem from a textbook compiled in the 1850s by a professor at Davidson College in North Carolina:

A Yankee mixes a certain number of wooden nutmegs, which cost him ¼ cent apiece, with a quantity of real nutmegs, worth 4 cents apiece and sells the whole assortment for $44; and gains $3.75 by the fraud. How many wooden nutmegs were there?[18]

Even as the Davidson students puzzled over this teaser, their own putative culture of honor was being exposed in the Northern press as a flesh market in which black women were stripped naked and evaluated for their breeding potential and black men examined like horses for sound teeth and limbs.

The growing rancor between North and South was, according to some, a belated outburst of disgust that took the safe form of attacking greed only in distant places. Southerners saw themselves as guardians of civilization against Yankee barbarians whose animus toward slavery was simply opportunistic. And for all their reformist zeal, the New England moralists (who emerged directly out of the attenuated Puritan tradition) were themselves so attuned to hypocrisy and self-deception that they regarded all political activists with suspicion, and generally kept aloof from causes. Before he was shocked into engagement by Daniel Webster's support of the Fugitive Slave Law in 1850, Emerson, for example, spoke of the abolitionist's "incredible tenderness for black folk a thousand miles off," charging that "thy love afar is spite at home."[19]

Underlying this disgust with public moralism was a paralyzing sense that the rule of the marketplace had become total. "Every bee in the hive," reported one English visitor in 1832, "is actively employed in search of that honey of Hybla, vulgarly called money."[20] America seemed to be a carnival of greed, and its literature was more and more populated with tricksters and thieves—from the scavenger in *Walden* who pockets stray nails left behind by Thoreau as he builds his hut to the charlatan Duke and Dauphin in *Huckleberry Finn*, who travel from town to town purveying their phony brand of Shakespeare. In town and country, people invented new words like "strumpetocracy" and "whorearchy" to describe the growing population of prostitutes—actual and metaphoric—that seemed to be taking over public life. One hears incipient versions of Satchel Paige's dictum, "Don't look back; someone may be gaining on you," as in one journalist's view of the speculative frenzy that broke out in Mississippi and Alabama in the 1830s, where "swindling was raised to the dignity of the fine arts" and "he who does not go ahead is run over and trodden down."[21]

In this circus of greed, confidence men came in many forms. Visitors to New York noted that one should expect the street-corner grocer to water his milk and doctor his weights and measures.[22] In literature (as in Edgar Allan Poe's story "The Devil in the Belfry" [1839], about a stranger who deranges the life of a village by making the town clock strike thirteen), the confidence man sometimes possessed gigantic sexual features reminiscent of the old Satan—a "long hooked nose," a fiddle "nearly five times as big as himself." But this modern-day devil was reduced from a brutal rapist to a quick-fingered groper en route to his next victim even before he finished fiddling with the last. He was, in

Poe's nicely colloquial term, a "diddler." The trouble was that if he were to be caught and run out of town, there would be nobody left: antebellum America was a place where everyone was trying to diddle everyone else.

To escape this world of distrust and deceit ("Nature hates calculators," declared Emerson[23]) was a motive for going West, or to sea—where the principle of cleanliness was a kind of sacred rite. Melville reports that he had seen a deck swept in a gale; and he offers this portrait of the kind of human pollutant who was contaminating the world ashore and whose stench could only be overcome by the salt wind of the sea:

> He was an abominable looking old fellow, with cold, fat, jelly-like eyes; and avarice, heartlessness, and sensuality stamped all over him. He seemed all the time going through some process of mental arithmetic; doing sums with dollars and cents: his very mouth, wrinkled and drawn up at the corners, looked like a purse.[24]

This man is not merely disfigured with creases or furrows—misplaced crow's-feet—about the mouth. His anus has been transposed to his face. He exhibits a modern version of an ancient feature of the devil, whose buttocks were sometimes equipped with eyes, and who, if one lifted his tail, revealed a mouth complete with tongue and teeth. "When he dies," Melville suggested, "his skull ought to be turned into a savings' box, with the till-hole between his teeth."[25]

In other words, the devil is universally familiar, with nothing alien or even grotesque about him. He appears in Hawthorne's fiction as a cold voyeur of "thin visage, and . . . deformity of figure," from whose eyes there glimmered "a light . . . blue and ominous"; in *Moby-Dick* he is the rodentlike Peleg (a contraction of Pegleg), half man, half thing, who grows damp with excitement when some new prospect for making money draws near. By the time of Louisa May Alcott's *A Modern Mephistopheles* (1877), he is a stock figure with "a pair of eyes, intensely black, and so large they seemed to burden the thin face."[26] In all these guises he is priapic, engorged with the desire to hoard other people's lives and fortunes for his own use. Yet he is also one's neighbor, one's colleague, oneself.

In 1850 Emerson wrote in *Representative Men* that for many Americans the cost of thinking about themselves was becoming intolerably high:

> We live in a market, where is only so much wheat, or wool, or land; and
> if I have so much more, every other must have so much less. . . . Nobody
> is glad in the gladness of another, and our system is one of war, of an
> injurious superiority. . . . a man comes to measure his greatness by the
> regrets, envies and hatreds of his competitors.[27]

Revulsion was the keynote among commentators in every region, and the
tone of antebellum America makes an uncanny harmony with our own
time. One feels peculiarly at home with this literature: the whole nation,
then as lately, seemed afflicted with a fever of speculation that "made
the talismanic word 'land' more interesting . . . than it ever was to the
shipwrecked mariner."[28] The American imagination seemed everywhere
bent on transforming natural objects into tools.

This was the first great age of the "developer," the man who gazes
upon today's mountain range and sees tomorrow's mining camp. Utility
and property were bywords of the times, which oscillated between periods of boom and bust; the first national depression struck in 1819; the
crash of 1837 brought on "hard times; men breaking who ought not to
break; banks bullied into the bolstering of desperate speculators; all the
newspapers a chorus of owls . . . loud cracks in the social edifice."[29] A
few dissident voices protested that the real problem was not want but
plenty, that "property proves too much for the man . . . that nothing is
so vulgar as a great warehouse of rooms full of furniture and trumpery;
that, in the circumstances, the best wisdom were an auction or a fire."[30]
Such circumstances were, of course, still the envy of those who did not
suffer from them.

When Charles Dickens made his first visit to the United States, a country in which everyone seemed to think himself on the verge of prosperity
even if he had just skirted disaster, he noted that the people's representatives were inveterate chewers of tobacco who used the Senate floor as
a public spittoon. In a country that seemed awash in brown saliva, he
warned unwary visitors not to pick up anything with an ungloved hand.
But the Americans had an answer. Here is Emerson:

> In England, every man is a castle. When I get into our first class cars
> on the Fitchburg Road, & see sweltering men in their shirt sleeves take
> their seats with some well drest men & women, & see really the very
> little difference of level that is between them all, and then imagine the

astonishment that would strike the polished inmates of English first class carriages, if such masters should enter & sit beside them, I see that it is not fit to tell Englishmen that America is like England. No, this is the Paradise of the third class; here every thing is cheap; here every thing is for the poor. England is the Paradise of the first class; it is essentially aristocratic, and the humbler classes have made up their minds to this, & do contentedly enter into the system. In England, every man you meet is some man's son; in America, he may be some man's father.[31]

This passage from Emerson's *Journals* is a pure expression of the emerging American ideology, on behalf of which Emerson almost overcame his customary distaste for the jostle of bodies, and which still compels at least our theoretical allegiance. "What . . . is this American system?" asked his contemporary Orestes Brownson. "Is it not the abolition of all artificial distinctions founded on birth or any other accident, and leaving every man to stand on his own two feet . . . What else is it that we are constantly throwing in the face of the old world?"[32] Visitors from that Old World have been struck ever since by how Americans, upon first meeting, tend to call each other by their first names—not just to deny discrepancies of class, but because surnames are signs of a descent that has no currency in the affairs of the present, which is the only dimension in which Americans want to live—in "time . . . [as] expressed in the gerund . . . rising and falling, going and coming, making it or not making it."[33]

This impatience with the contingencies bequeathed by history—whether advantageous or inhibiting—first coalesced into an ideology in these antebellum years, and amounted to a religion of the undetermined present. America was a country of frantic *nowness*. Leading "the massive subjective turn of modern culture,"[34] it installed the individual at the center of life, and its citizens expressed horror at any state or government encroachment on the prerogatives of the self. A politician like Andrew Jackson earned his authority precisely because he trumpeted the right of the people to take it away.

Yet this democratic ebullience, for which Tocqueville, visiting in 1831, coined the term "individualism," was tempered by what he called a "strange melancholy which often haunts the inhabitants of democratic countries in the midst of their abundance."[35] Here is Margaret Fuller at

Niagara Falls (already in 1843 a favorite spot for tourists to enjoy the endangered sublimity of nature), describing the implacable American spirit of making *use* of creation:

What I liked best was to sit on Table Rock, close to the great fall. There all power of observing details, all separate consciousness, was quite lost.

Once, just as I had seated myself there, a man came to take his first look. He walked close up to the fall, and, after looking at it a moment, with an air as if thinking how he could best appropriate it to his own use, he spat into it.

This trait seemed wholly worthy of an age whose love of *utility* is such that the Prince [Pückler-Muskau] suggests the probability of men coming to put the bodies of their dead parents in the fields to fertilize them, and of a country such as Dickens has described . . .[36]

Fuller understood that the American spirit was expressing itself as possessive contempt for the uncultivated world. Others put it more charitably: "European travellers who passed through America noticed that everywhere, in the White House at Washington and in log-cabins beyond the Alleghanies, except for a few Federalists, every American, from Jefferson and Gallatin down to the poorest squatter, seemed to nourish an idea that he was doing what he could to overthrow the tyranny which the past had fastened on the human mind." This idea was more than a pretty decoration pasted on greed. It animated the entrepreneur, the migrant settler, and the immigrant alike in a land where "a plane, a chisel, and two dollars a day make a carpenter." It encouraged the "penniless and homeless Scotch or Irish immigrant" to believe that "every stroke of the axe and the hoe made him a capitalist, and made gentlemen of his children."[37]

It was not just talk and dreams. Well before mid-century, even the intrinsically conservative legal system began to shift from protecting antecedent property rights to removing obstacles to development. The capitalist entrepreneur who assembled investors in order to divert a stream or build a bridge that might cost another man his livelihood began to find that the law was likelier to be on his side than against him.[38] And under the aspect of world history (which politicians, in this oratorical age, routinely invoked as the dark backdrop to the bright foreground of American liberty), he could even think of himself as a progressive exercising the rights that the despots of Europe would deny him. The self was first; the self was all.

In our own time we have come to disbelieve this religion of upward mobility. We think it a sham. We see it obstructed and mocked all around us; our own politicians appeal to it in the most cynical terms, but mostly do nothing to foster it. Our best historians—who justly point out that the banks and railroads were the real profiteers in the westward rush, not the scrappy entrepreneur of our myths and movies—teach us about the illusions that this notion of upward mobility peddled to ordinary people in the early years of the Republic. And certainly for every dreamer there was a cheat—an auctioneer who "find[s] men of straw to lead the first bids . . . and . . . stand[s] by, while the poor artizan, the journeyman mechanic, the stranger who had brought his little all to buy government land to bring up his young family upon, staked their poor means on strips of land which were at that moment a foot under water."[39]

Yet despite the inevitable spiritual tax imposed on both winners and losers in America's unbridled market economy ("the cost of a thing," Thoreau remarked, "is the amount of what I will call life which is required to be exchanged for it"[40]), the country was teeming with undiscouraged dreamers, and their hopes animated the careers of leaders who rose from the poor—leaders like Jackson and, thirty years later, Abraham Lincoln:

> The prudent, penniless beginner in the world, labors for wages awhile, saves a surplus with which to buy tools or land, for himself; then labors on his own account another while, and at length hires another new beginner to help him. This . . . is *free* labor—the just and generous, and prosperous system, which opens the way for all . . .[41]

With these words, which became a refrain in his election campaigns, Lincoln extended the meaning of Emerson's *mot* that in America "every man . . . may be some man's father." In Lincoln's America the rewards of free labor did not need to await the next generation: every man might father an improved version of himself.

This installation of ambition as the one common good was the great transformation of nineteenth-century American life. By 1850, Americans found themselves both liberated and imprisoned by the enormously compelling idea—once decried as pride—of the striving self. There could be no place for the old devil in this new world, whose religion was pride of self. And the institutions that tried to preserve the old morality were failing. "I think," said Emerson, that "no man can go with his thoughts about him into one of our churches, without feeling that what hold the public worship had on men is gone, or going. It has lost its grasp on the affection of the good and the fear of the bad."[42]

There is no period in our history that shows more vividly how a whole people responds when their old moral guidelines become obsolete. As the old Christian concept of Satan entered the final stage of its collapse, every region and class hurried to nominate some diminished substitute. The Jacksonians had their Monster Bank, which withheld credit or extorted excessive interest from the common man; the slavemaster had his self-righteous Yankee, who extended the right of self-ownership to blacks and thereby cut away the foundations of his prosperity; the native urban worker, struggling to command a decent wage, now had a drunken "paddy," who was willing to work for a pittance; the indebted farmer had the foreclosing creditor; the creditor had his paper-money mob. These devils came from all classes and with many accents, but they were all alike in one respect. They were agents of containment; they were enemies of *ME*.

Pride of self, once the mark of the devil, was now not just a legitimate emotion but America's uncontested god. And since everyone had his own self, everyone had his own god. Opposition to pride as a legitimate emotion was now condemned as the reaction of entrenched privilege, and a concept of "un-Americanness" began to take form. To be deferential was to be alien and strange. Primogeniture had been terminated long before in all the states, a change that Tocqueville judged the single most important in American history, and that hastened the reduction of "the prejudice that [had once] stigmatized labor." So candidates of all parties could now claim lowly origins as a political asset, and rapid social rise was proof of one's mettle. In the election of 1840, in order not to cede the moral high ground to their Democratic opponents, Whigs actually called themselves Democratic Whigs and organized parades that featured log cabins on wheels, from which they served cider to prospective voters. A half-century after Jefferson had shocked the Federalist establishment at his inauguration by climbing the steps of the Capitol in "yarn stockings

[and] slippers down at the heel," there was virtually no candid social conservatism left on the political scene.[43]

Genuine social conservatism, the kind that actually questions whether democracy is a self-evident good, went underground in these years, and it has pretty much remained there ever since. In the United States, as Lionel Trilling put it at a later moment when conservatism was again trying to retrieve its intellectual dignity, "the conservative impulse and the reactionary impulse do not, with some isolated and some ecclesiastical exceptions, express themselves in ideas but only in action or in irritable mental gestures which seek to resemble ideas."[44] By 1850 America had almost achieved its liberal consensus. The holdout was the South.

[3]

The liberal individualism that assumed its modern form in these years was built on a moral and psychological contradiction. It sanctified the rights of the self and charged malice to any obstructor of those rights; but even in a nation with enlarging frontiers and expanding markets, the aspiring self was bound, sooner or later, to collide with another whose aspirations were equally legitimate. In the new world of the acquisitive self one man's good was likely to be another man's evil.

The presence of this conundrum in timeless clichés—"one man's meat is another's poison," "your loss is my gain"—gives a hint of how conventional it has become to regard life as what we nowadays call a "zero-sum game." But in fact this paradox invaded the lives of Americans for the first time on a large scale only in the antebellum years, when men and women first encountered—and created—the fearful symmetry of life in a market culture. The ugly proportion between rich and poor in the "free" states was pointed out by slaveholders in the South, and events provided confirmation of their critique: financial panics grew more frequent and severe; strife increased between factory owners and workers. Sooner or later in such a culture, one discovers the seesaw rhythm whereby one life goes down (or up) as another goes up (or down)—an inverse relation of human fortunes that became a steady theme in American literature before the Civil War. "In this republican country, amid the fluctuating waves of our social life," as Hawthorne put it, "there is always somebody at the drowning point,"[45] and the same idea later found expression in Twain's *Huckleberry Finn*, when Pap speaks explicitly of how his meager sense of self, his buoyancy, depends on the degradation of niggers. On the principle of the pulley, the rise of one person means the descent of another.

The most obvious expression of this social truth—despite the canny efforts of Southern apologists to expose the "free labor" lie—was slavery itself. It was an unblinkable fact that at the heart of America's putatively free society lay a barbarous institution that made one person into the instrument of another person's will. "With all its 'safe-guards' and 'necessary legislation,' " it was "the greatest crime on the largest scale known in modern history; taking into account the time it has occupied, the territory it covers, the number of its subjects, and the civilization of its criminals."[46] By promising infinitely expanding production and consumption, the new capitalist order in the North may have swept away the old mercantilist idea that if one individual enriched himself, then "others must be poorer, in an exact proportion to his Gains."[47] But in the South, the old proportion held. While whites—at least some whites—prospered, blacks suffered: and no one seemed to notice the contradiction between this state of affairs and the ideology of liberty and freedom of which Americans were boisterously proud.

For a long time, it seemed that in order to see the contradiction clearly, one had to be a foreigner. "How is it," the English moralist Samuel Johnson had asked already during the Revolution, "that we hear the loudest yelps for liberty from the drivers of Negroes?"[48] Some years earlier, a French emigrant traveling in South Carolina had made a personal journey into America's heart of darkness:

I was not long since invited to dine with a planter who lived three miles from ———, where he then resided. In order to avoid the heat of the sun, I resolved to go on foot, sheltered in a small path, leading through a pleasant wood. I was leisurely travelling along, attentively examining some peculiar plants which I had collected, when all at once I felt the air strongly agitated, though the day was perfectly calm and sultry. I immediately cast my eyes toward the cleared ground, from which I was but at a small distance, in order to see whether it was not occasioned by a sudden shower; when at that instant a sound resembling a deep rough voice, uttered, as I thought, a few inarticulate monosyllables. Alarmed and surprised, I precipitately looked all round, when I perceived at about six rods distance something resembling a cage, suspended to the limbs of a tree; all the branches of which appeared covered with large birds of prey, fluttering about, and anxiously endeavouring to perch on the cage. Actuated by an involuntary motion of my hands, more than by any design of my mind, I fired at them; they all flew to a short distance, with a most hideous noise: when, horrid to think and painful to repeat, I perceived a negro, suspended in the cage, and left there to expire! I shudder when I recollect that the birds had already picked out his eyes, his cheek bones were bare; his arms had been attacked in several places, and his body seemed covered with a multitude of wounds. From the edges of the hollow sockets and from the lacerations with which he was disfigured, the blood slowly dropped, and tinged the ground beneath. No sooner were the birds flown, than swarms of insects covered the whole body of this unfortunate wretch, eager to feed on his mangled flesh and to drink his blood. I found myself suddenly arrested by the power of affright and terror; my nerves were convulsed; I trembled, I stood motionless, involuntarily contemplating the fate of this negro, in all its dismal latitude.[49]

Americans did their best to keep their caged victims concealed not only from foreigners but from themselves. But it was impossible to keep them indefinitely out of sight.

One can feel the rising pressure over slavery by following what amounted to a series of rehearsals in earlier public debates. One early-warning alarm that broke the delusive silence over the "dismal latitude" of the oppressed came in the form of a national debate over the Indian removals of the 1820s and 1830s, as whites pushed ever deeper into the Mississippi River valley. In 1831 the Supreme Court, still headed by its first Chief Justice, John Marshall, disallowed a petition from the Cherokee nation for protection of their lands from the claims of the Georgia state government. The petition was denied on the ground that the Cherokees were a "domestic dependent nation" without the legal privileges of an autonomous state. In handing down the decision, however, Justice Marshall confessed that "if the courts were permitted to indulge their sympathies, a case better calculated to excite them can scarcely be imagined." It was as if he were speaking for the nation in recognizing that some evils had to remain concealed, because if they were acknowledged, the whole American system might disintegrate from the shock. A year later, Marshall backed away from his own decision and ruled that state law "has no force" in Indian affairs, which were to be left to the federal government. Andrew Jackson, who had fought alongside Cherokee warriors against the Creeks and Seminoles in the War of 1812, now declared himself afflicted by the same division between head and heart: "The regard which I cherished for [your fathers]," he wrote to the aggrieved Cherokees, "has caused me to feel great solicitude for your situation." But the public Jackson, *President* Jackson, did nothing to defend them against the state of Georgia, and made his notorious remark that "John Marshall has made his decision. Now let him enforce it."[50]

Such professions from powerful public figures of their pain at their own impotence seem lip service now. But they were more than formulaic, and less than hypocrisy. They were acknowledgments of a new dissonance between moral feeling and legal authority from men who spoke from opposite ends of the American political spectrum, but who felt equally the grip of history as what Hawthorne, in his story "Wakefield" (1835), called "an iron tissue of necessity." They felt themselves, despite their ample arrogance, to be small actors. In their protestations there was both an echo of past scruples ("I tremble for my country," Jefferson had written about slavery in 1787, "when I reflect that God is just, [and] that his justice does not sleep forever") and a forecast of the coming storm over slavery, the issue that, more than any other, drove a wedge between private morality and public law.[51]

These men were modern in the sense that they felt increasingly restive in the grip of what Emerson called the "strict platforms, and sad offices" that turned the self into an instrument of some untraceable collective will. In this respect they anticipated Lincoln, who thirty years later expressed a sense of chastened thanksgiving ("I claim not to have controlled events, but confess plainly that events have controlled me") as military necessity backed him slowly into emancipation, an idea he had long resisted as politically impossible. When it finally proved expedient, it closed up for him a terrible cleavage that had divided his mind from his conscience: "I hate," he wrote to a friend in 1855, "to see the poor creatures hunted down, and caught, and carried back to their stripes; but I bite my lip and keep quiet."[52] What Lincoln did for his country was to force it to confront the evil it had tried for so long to suppress, and he could only do it because he acknowledged the same long-standing evasion in himself.

In the years of prelude to the Civil War, Southerners continued to try to deflect attention from the contradiction within their claims to civilization based on liberty. "All competition," declared one Southern critic of the Northern business culture, "is but the effort to enslave others without being encumbered with their support," until "the rich, the professional, the trading and skillful part of society have become masters of the laboring masses, whose condition, already intolerable, is daily becoming worse."[53] These charges rang true in a time when more than half the nation's wealth was falling into the hands of the upper 5 percent of families. In the cities, disparities were growing even starker, and a mobile population in the North drifted among mill towns and construction sites for railroads and canals, yielding a flow of "chronic failures and castoffs" that filled the urban slums. The airless tenements and stinking latrines that we associate with modern urban poverty came into being for the first time; in 1849 New York City's police chief spoke of "the constantly increasing number of vagrants, [and the] idle and vicious children of both sexes, who infest our public thoroughfares" as "a deplorable and growing evil."[54]

Yet captive to the cognate dreams of equality and progress, Northerners still clung to the belief that the necessary symmetry of poverty and prosperity was a thing of the past, and they aimed all their outrage at the South, where the rich lived not just off the poor but off the enslaved. For them, the very idea of slavery was the intolerable defect in the American scene, and there was little cost in acknowledging it because it was far away. It violated the axiom that degradation and social failure were self-wrought punishments. If you were at the bottom of the ladder, the American civil religion (the religion of the self) said you had gotten yourself there, and slavery, as an inherited and racially determined condition, was fundamentally at odds with this principle. Slaves, by definition, had to remain in the circumstances into which they were born, and this flagrantly violated the most basic tenets of democracy.

The only way one could save slavery from this indictment was by systematically demonstrating that blacks were actually unfit for the natural rights granted to all other persons. And so an argument along these lines began to emerge. Blacks, the slavery apologists said, had an "animal insensitivity" that made them immune to the hardships of sun and whip; they suffered from such clinical conditions as "drapetomania" (running away) and "rascality," not to mention their notoriously uncontrollable sexual desires. Finally, the case against their equal rights was raised (or lowered) to a new level with the introduction of the theory of "polygenesis"—the idea that the several recognized human races had distinct and separate origins rather than a common ancestry. This point was "proven" by such techniques as comparing the skull size of living black persons with ancient African skeletons, from which so-called scientists inferred "the separate creation of the races within the areas that they now principally inhabited, and maintained that the races constituted distinct species of *genus homo* and not simply varieties of the same species." By 1860, visitors to Barnum's Museum in New York were lining up to see "a most disgusting object—supposed to be the link between the Negro & Monkey."[55]

To make this idea of blacks as a distinct species stick, its proponents had to contend with several embarrassments. For one thing, it ran counter to the biblical claim of common human ancestry in Adam. For another, prevailing biological theory declared that hybrids were sterile. Mulattos, according to the emerging theory of polygenesis, were hybrids, and yet no one could deny their capacity to reproduce. (Indeed, a light-skinned woman was often the most sexually desired inmate in the household of the slavemaster, whose own carnal depravity was confirmed by the lighter-skinned children she bore him.) But none of these counterarguments proved decisive. Biblical objections were generally evaded by a quiet concession that racial difference might have its origins in environmental factors, and the theory of hybrid sterility was simply modified: it took a few generations, it was said, for the fertility of mulattos to dry up.

This debate over slavery was propelled by essentially academic arguments. And yet all their squabbling about natural attributes and racial origin was finally beside the point. Slavery was a *scandal* in the root sense of the word—a moral trap, a snare. It became the sole manifestation of evil upon which a majority of Americans could agree. Even those who defended it were aware of its power to contaminate both its victims and its masters. Literate slaves who wrote about their experience made clear how corrupting it was—how it robbed them of their sense of family, how it inflamed the master's lust by its aphrodisiac mix of sex and power, and how it reduced young girls to choosing between protecting their virtue and saving their lives. Long before the political crises of the 1850s, the literature of the South demonstrated, in spite of itself, that slavery was a moral poison. Here is a published account from the 1820s that conveys, with what was supposed to be light humor, just how depraved the master-slave relation could be:

A celebrated Physician had a black boy, uncommonly tractable, whose name was Tom; Tom was kept behind the counter employed in pounding medicine, &c. He was a fine boy in his sphere of business, but Tom took it into his head that he must be a doctor, and accordingly applied to his master to learn him the profession. Oh masser, I make such a good doctor; I earn you plenty of money. Well Tom you must go with me, learn how to administer medicine, feel the pulse, know the situation of the body, &c. Yes masser. The doctor was at that time attending a poor woman in the neighbourhood; he observed to her, Madam, my boy Tom wants to become a doctor, he is a fine boy, and very useful to me in his place, and I wish to put out of his head the idea of becoming a doctor, will you be so good as to assist me in my stratagem? I will come here to-morrow morning precisely at twelve o'clock and bring Tom with me; you take care to have the chamberpot nicely washed, and when you see us coming, put into it a hot custard pudding, let there be plenty of eggs, and let it be smoking hot, and instead of asking you the situation of your body, or how you are in your bowels, whether costive or not, I will simply ask you, after going through other formalities, how are you to day madam? let me look at your tongue, let me feel your pulse, &c. then madam I will say, where is the chamberpot, have you had an evacuation to day? you must then produce the pot with the custard pudding in it; I will then ask for a spoon, and eat it before Tom, and say madam you are clear of fever, your evacuation is very good, I must eat it all; you will soon get well; I will send Tom to visit you to-morrow. Tom squinted his eyes, amazed, that his master should eat that which he took to be something else. Tom get the horses. Yes masser. Whilst Tom was out, Now madam, time this thing well for me to-morrow, I will send Tom positively at twelve o'clock, and have in the pot, procured from yourself or some one of the family, something hot, about the size of the custard pudding that you gave me. The next day Tom arrives to visit his patient, at the appointed time, with all the pomposity and consequence of an Empyric, or that self-conceit could inspire. Well misses, how you do to day? Oh Tom, I think I am getting worse. O no misses, don't you be scared, I cure you. Let me feel your pulse misses; let me see your tongue misses; why misses you are perfectly clear of fever; misses where is your stool? She said under the bed Tom. Tom called to the servant; Water, you black rascal fetch me a spoon. The water obeyed, all up to the trick but poor Tom. He stuck the spoon into the contents of the pot, and then into his mouth; he spit a part out and exclaimed, Oh my dear misses, I fear you die. I think a mortification has taken place since yesterday; this smell and taste very bad; not possible to eat all this. Masser eat all yesterday. Yes Tom, said the lady, and you must eat it all or I will die. Well please God, my dear misses, I will try; and he forced all down, and returned home to his master. Well Tom, how did you leave the lady? Why masser pulse feel pretty well, the tongue seem clear of fever, but the stool very bad; I frade masser mortification take place since yesterday; masser please you go next time, and for God sake don't let me be doctor any more. Thus was poor Tom's mind put at rest, he became reconciled to his situation, and never aspired to any thing above the mortar and pestle.[56]

This revolting story is an early version (1822) of a genre that has since thrived in many forms—in the Uncle Remus stories of Joel Chandler Harris, in the mockeries that Huck Finn performs at the expense of Nigger Jim, in the Hollywood representation of blacks as mindless Stepin Fetchit creatures, and in many bitter confirmations by blacks themselves that self-degradation and sport are two of the services they are expected to provide for the master's infernal fun.

No one can read or hear such stories without sensing their cruelty. But cruelty is an element of comedy as well as of horror. While some shudder, others laugh. These stories have the pretense of gentility and are full of euphemism. The master eats "that which [Tom] took to be something else"; the narrator speaks only of "the contents of the pot," and is too well-mannered to say that the thrill of the event is to make a nigger eat shit. There is a touch of prurience: the lady gives her body and its most intimate excretions to the medical man, and takes her own pleasure in forcing the black to degrade himself by feeding on the contents of the chamber pot that she hides, steaming, beneath her bed. All the unspeakable hypocrisy of the man who exercises power over another man is here—the debonair smile, the affability, the appropriation of the charmed lady for pulling off the scheme. But finally it is a sting, a scam, a dis, a con (the vocabulary of the con game is always monosyllabic and harsh, like words for sex acts). It is a cadenza on the theme of cruelty, an answer to the question "When charmed by the beauty of that viper, did it never occur to you to change personalities with him? to feel what it was to be a snake? to glide unsuspected in grass? to sting, to kill at a touch; your whole beautiful body one iridescent scabbard of death? In short, did the wish never occur to you to feel yourself exempt from knowledge, and conscience, and revel for a while in the care-free, joyous life of a perfectly instinctive, unscrupulous, and irresponsible creature?"[57] This kind of story, which turns a human being into a dismissible clown, was the lingering music of Satan—and everyone, whether outside or inside the slave system, knew it.

[4]

The saving—and killing—paradox was that despite the depth of racism in North and South, there was an antipathy to slavery ("sympathies in the bosoms of the southern people," as Abraham Lincoln put it, that "manifest . . . their sense of the wrong of slavery") in the very constitution of the American self:

> I want every man to have the chance—and I believe a black man is entitled to it—in which he *can* better his condition—when he may look forward and hope to be a hired laborer this year and the next, work for himself afterward, and finally to hire men to work for him![58]

Even as Lincoln reiterated this devout idea that private ambition could become public good, and even as the "most imperious necessity" of Americans was "that of not sinking in the world,"[59] a certain innocent indignation remained in the tone of politics and public discussion. It was as if Americans needed to believe there were still land and space enough to support a costless prosperity for everyone. Casualties were little acknowledged. These illusions were maintained, as we now know, by rendering invisible the dislocated peoples who paid with blood and sweat and dignity. Most obviously these included the blacks who were shut out of the dream of collective progress, but also the Indians who were driven from their tribal lands, the Asian laborers who helped build the transcontinental railroad and then were shipped back across the Pacific, and even the poor shopgirls who turned, out of need, to prostitution when solicitous customers offered to pay for more than store-stocked goods.

Until Lincoln made outrage at slavery the basis of a national candidacy, the very concept of human exploitation was fantastically scarce in America's dialogue with itself. The cost of confronting it seemed impossibly high until Lincoln demanded it be paid. Although fringe voices like those of the abolitionists had been raised in protest since the 1830s, the Republican Party was bred in the 1850s out of a mixture of nativist and anti-Negro sentiment, and it condemned slavery more as a threat in the labor market than as a moral offense. It has been aptly said that the conspicuous "shame of American literature [was] the degree to which our authors of the 1830s and 1840s kept silent" about the great evil of their age.[60] Before Lincoln no President had gone on record as being personally opposed to slavery!

And so it is not surprising to find in the major writers a reluctant recognition of the uselessness of authorities. Hawthorne, for instance, was obsessed with ministerial figures—Mr. Hooper in "The Minister's Black Veil" (1835), Dimmesdale in *The Scarlet Letter* (1850)—who resort to spectacular visual displays (Hooper shrouds his face in crepe; Dimmesdale reveals a branded *A* burned into his flesh) in order to reclaim the strayed attention of those for whom the church has become mainly a venue for gossip. These stories, among the most politically urgent ever composed by an American writer, are about the panic of moral teachers who recognize that the symbolic vocabulary that had been intact for their fathers is disintegrating. In his 1850 masterpiece, *The Scarlet Letter*, Hawthorne presents a young minister who has committed the sin of adultery, but whose every effort to convince his congregation that he has sinned—including public self-abasement—is unavailing. His flock simply cannot see the evil he has exposed in himself. When he stands before them and declares, "People of New England . . . ye, that have loved me!—ye, that have deemed me holy!—behold me here, the one sinner of the world!" they think he is speaking euphemistically. They cannot believe that he means it intimately and personally, just as he says.

This sense that the world was sinking into a moral darkness in which evil could not be discerned was felt in the literature of the 1830s, and it grew continually stronger until the clarifying possibility of civil war arrived two decades later. In this sense, the discovery of slavery as the devil's work was a spiritual liberation. Faced first with the truth that they were destroying whole civilizations that had preceded them on the continent, and later with the fact that the Union itself "is founded in unrighteousness and cemented with blood," Americans were forced to recognize the web—we call it culture now—in which the self was caught. They were discovering the "characteristically modern style of evil: indirect, impersonal, mediated by complex organizations and institutional roles."[61] They were beginning to live in the world that Goethe had prophesied in *Faust*, in which Mephisto understands that the messy human details (the misery of the poor, the brutal derangement of petty lives) have to be taken care of out of the master's sight, lest he be discomfited.

One case in point is a memorable chapter in Melville's novel *Redburn* (1849), in which a callow young American comes upon the sight of a starving woman squatting in a Liverpool gutter. He rushes about—to a local crone, to a group of sailors, to the proprietress and cook at his boardinghouse, to three policemen—looking for help for her. No one responds. "She deserves it," says one old hag, "—was she ever married? tell me that?" "It's none of my business, Jack," says a constable, "I don't belong to that street."

Although Melville displaced this Dickensian vision to England, it was being realized in America as Melville wrote. Today it is, of course, a commonplace for most city people—as one walks past a beggar and closes the mind to the encounter, sometimes with hands in one's pockets, sometimes with the offer of a hush-money quarter. In the antebellum years such anonymous supplicants were still a novelty, but the intellectual energy of American culture was shifting away from the conservators of tradition toward those who were repelled by their own way of life.

In the midst of this moral crisis, Americans' sacred founding documents, the Bible and the Constitution, seemed useless as guides through the slavery maze. Slave owners invoked Paul's admonitions that servants must obey their masters, while abolitionists burned the Constitution as a compact with the devil—"a compact formed at the sacrifice of the bodies and souls of millions of our race, for the sake of achieving a political object—an unblushing and monstrous coalition to do evil that good might come."[62] And so, for the first time in our literature, the modern affliction that was later to be called angst was acknowledged, as in this 1841 passage from Emerson that hints at cosmic dread:

> The sturdy capitalist, no matter how deep and square on blocks of Quincy granite he lays the foundations of his banking-house or Exchange, must set it, at last, not on a cube corresponding to the angles

of his structure, but on a mass of unknown materials and solidity, red-hot or white-hot perhaps at the core, which rounds off to an almost perfect sphericity, and lies floating in soft air, and goes spinning away, dragging bank and banker with it at a rate of thousands of miles the hour, he knows not whither,—a bit of bullet, now glimmering, now darkling through a small cubic space on the edge of an unimaginable pit of emptiness.[63]

This anxiety for the future of one's ambition is something we can readily understand. It is the sort of prose one expects from a modern writer—Dostoevsky or Kafka—and one is surprised to receive it from the sagacious Emerson. But the concomitant anxiety for the safety of one's soul is harder to recapture, since in recent decades we have pretty much buried the myth of westering pioneers and replaced them at the center of our history with their previously invisible victims.

In this new version of our past, the Marshalls and Jacksons, and even, in some quarters, Lincoln himself, can only be understood as hypocrites—and so they have lately been described. We do not imagine them in the grip of self-doubt. To read recent histories of the United States is like returning to familiar photographs of grinning relatives in some tourist paradise, only to discover that a flock of attendants whom we never heard about—valets and coolies and beggars—had been airbrushed out of the pictures. Grandpa, once revered, looks shameless now, and we fix our attention on his degraded servants instead. What we have not yet fully understood, partly because of this shift to the most conspicuous victims, is that the apparently insouciant winners were losers too. A moral panic was building beneath the rhetoric of Manifest Destiny, as Americans realized that living in the modern world imposed new obligations in keeping the costs of self-enlargement invisible. It was to this fear, above all, that Lincoln spoke; and by naming it, he transformed its overthrow into a saving moral obligation.

The truth about the collective American self which Lincoln finally had the courage to name ("[God] gives to both North and South, this terrible war, as the woe due to those by whom the offence [of slavery] came") had been intimated in literature for a long time. Some of the books that Americans read in the antebellum years were crude self-acquittals; in the mid-1830s, for example, the genre of the anti-Catholic exposé was booming—books like *Female Convents* (1836), *Six Months in a Convent*

(1836), and the enormously popular (300,000 copies sold before the Civil War) *Awful Disclosures of . . . the Hotel Dieu Nunnery at Montreal* (1836), all of which "pictured alcoholism, flagellation, prostitution, and infanticide within convent walls."[64] Such books had the great advantage of segregating evil outside the normal precincts of American life (the people they slandered were chiefly foreigners); they operated quite outside respectability, and thus provided the frisson of threatened infiltration. They were rather like the spate of Russian-invasion novels that appeared during the Reagan years—imaginative efforts to keep evil at a distance, at a time when its foreign features were beginning to blur and the rot of the domestic culture was beginning to show.

These books were emollients. But the real writers—Melville, Hawthorne, Thoreau—made it known that Americans were in a state of deepening moral embarrassment. Their books were not comfortable reading—such as Melville's haunting story "Bartleby, the Scrivener" (1853), about a proper Wall Street lawyer saddled with a defiant employee who forces him to ask himself hard questions about his responsibility toward his fellow man when corporate relations were replacing personal ones. Such stories taunted more than pleased; and they did not sell, because they exacerbated the moral nervousness of those who read them.

It was a nervousness that helps to explain why this first great period of capitalist expansion was also a time of explosive religious growth. The number of Lutheran and Presbyterian congregations increased tenfold between 1780 and 1860, Methodists by a factor of forty.[65] Something like fifty thousand ecclesiastical buildings were constructed in the same interval—structures that were, as Dr. Johnson remarked of the pyramids, "monuments to the insufficiency of human enjoyments." Religion continued to animate most social initiatives—temperance, women's rights, foreign missions, abolition; and not just the specialized vocabularies of reform but also the common talk of the people remained saturated with religious longing. Primary meanings of words like "enjoy" and "society," which have descended to us with their religious tinge leached out of them, were still then spiritual rather than civic: "to join society" meant to find religion or to become a member of a church; to "enjoy oneself" (we speak, today, more commonly of enjoying something external to the self) meant to awaken the mind, to bathe it in holy thoughts.[66]

John Greenleaf Whittier, in 1843, drew this portrait of antebellum Boston, which might be fairly generalized into a picture of the whole United States in the years before the Civil War:

> Consider well that Temple of the Second Advent—its thronging thousands, with wild, awe-stricken faces turned towards the East, like Mussulmen to their Kebla, in hourly expectation of the down-rushing of the fiery mystery of the Apocalypse; waiting with trembling eagerness and "not unpleasing horror" to behold with the eye of flesh the tremendous pageant before which the elements shall melt and the heavens flee away—the Baptism of a World in fire![67]

This craving for apocalypse was hardly confined to Boston. There was a sense throughout antebellum America that the self was becoming ineffaceably dirty; that it needed to pass through some cleansing flame. Even as the culture now permitted "optically edible" showgirls to strip naked and display themselves to gaping men in the city theaters,[68] new communities sprang up throughout the country as efforts to realize, by acts of collective will, the old Scripture promise of the reign of the saints on earth—a vision that drew on the millennial Protestantism that was rooted deep in American life. Americans were again trying to purge themselves of themselves. Shaker communities arose as far west as Kentucky; Mormons marched out of their New York Babylon all the way to the Utah Territory, drawing strength along the way from tauntings and persecutions that served to confirm their sense of being the new chosen people. Industrial reformers like Robert Owen (who came to America in 1825) proclaimed their mission "to introduce an entire new system of society; to change it from an ignorant, selfish system to an enlightened social system which shall gradually unite all interests into one, and remove all causes for contest between individuals."[69]

These experiments usually failed at a pace proportionate to their grandiosity. Owen's community at New Harmony, Indiana, collapsed in part because the middle-class technicians and propagandists who came with him from Britain, as well as American believers who joined later, had less taste for manual labor than they thought, and were more devoted to class hierarchy than they claimed. Yet however tracelessly they died, all the social and religious experiments—and the literary outcry—of the antebellum years expressed a fervent reaction against the moral deformations of the risen business culture. Americans were in headlong flight from the world they had made. One of the most poignant images left to us from this period of promiscuous dissent—an image now curated in a few Shaker museums, and marketed to the rest of us through shops full of blond "country" furniture—is the look of a Shaker room. On the wall, at a height just reachable if a woman strains, one finds a row of pegs placed for hanging the ladder-backed chairs when the floor is broomed. The dream was of a world made clean, no spot to be left unswept.

Jon Lovitz as the devil on Saturday Night Live
(NBC)

PART TWO

Modern Times

Drawing of Lottery Tickets.

"*Drawing of Lottery Tickets*" *from J. H. Green*, Gambling Unmasked! or, The
Personal Experiences of the Reformed Gambler *(1847)*

FOUR

The Loss of Providence

Niebuhr

"All human life," it has been said, "is involved in the sin of seeking security at the expense of other life."[1] The size of this expense—the moral cost of ambition—was what Americans had discovered as they became both beneficiaries and victims of the commercial culture of the nineteenth century. Slavery may have been the most obvious expression of this sin, but as they experienced for the first time the genius of capitalism in its full creative power and its concomitant brutality, Americans found that living in this new world required not only a new alertness to opportunity but a willingness to seal oneself off from awareness of the human casualties one leaves behind. To be successful, or even to survive, one *had* to be a sinner.

High among the requisite new talents was the ability to create a demand—for one's products, one's friendship, one's skills—in the minds of people who had not known they wanted them before they were advertised as being available. Thoreau makes this point with a little parable in *Walden*. A "strolling Indian," he tells us, studies the ways of the usurping whites who have dispossessed him, and concludes that in order to survive, he must go into their business of making and selling. So he weaves a basket, and offers it to a local lawyer, only to be refused with a curt "No, we do not want any." The guileless Indian has not yet learned that the white man's economy runs on desire as much as on necessity; he has not yet "discovered that it was necessary for him to make it worth the other's while to buy them, or at least make him think it was so."[2]

By 1850, America was rampant with people who had learned this lesson. It was becoming a place we recognize as our own, where desire for advancement is mixed with the dread of becoming someone else's prey.

Such a man may be outwardly cheerful even if the inner weather of his soul is, as Ishmael says in *Moby-Dick*, a "drizzly November." He tends to feel used, as if he were a rubbing post for a cat; yet he is condemned to search for opportunities to use someone else in the same way. He bumps up continually against disdain or jaded amusement from some functionary of an enterprise in which he seeks a position, some calculator who sizes him up the way a shopper in a fish market sniffs out the freshness of the fish.

He is a modern man, in other words, always on notice that his utility is being assessed. If "despondency [comes] readily to heart," in Emerson's words, it is because the structures of modern life (factories, firms, flat houses, chain stores, and most of all the cities that contain them) are profoundly isolating, and make him feel more like a function than a person. "The state of society," as Emerson had the prescience to see already in the late 1830s, was "one in which the members have suffered amputation from the trunk, and strut about so many walking monsters,—a good finger, a neck, a stomach, an elbow, but never a man."[3]

It is, therefore, one of the ironies of our history that the first signs that this dismembered self might be reconvened—that a society might be restored in which there could be again a " 'we' that is an 'I,' and an 'I' that is a 'we,' "[4] to use the Hegelian formula—came just as the nation itself was about to break apart. Even the usually phlegmatic Nathaniel Hawthorne remarked, after the shelling of Fort Sumter, that "it was delightful to share in the heroic sentiment of the time, and to feel that I had a country—a consciousness which seemed to make me young again." This "wholesome calamity," this chance "to redeem America for all its sinful years since the century began,"[5] turned out to be the last chance.

[1]

Attacks from the North against the slaveholding Satan had been building since the adoption by Congress in 1850 of a law requiring the return of escaped slaves (a slave who fled his master, the law said, had stolen himself) to their owners. With local authorities compelled to turn over escaped slaves to badged bounty hunters who were little more than hired thugs, many previously indifferent citizens in the North now discovered a violent distaste for the whole business of slavery, which had once seemed a faraway abstraction.

Harriet Beecher Stowe wrote her apocalyptic novel *Uncle Tom's Cabin* (1852) in just such a fever of outrage at the passage of the Fugitive Slave Law, stocking it with a gallery of devils whom she arranged along a spectrum of sin ranging from indifference to brutality. Her most famous malefactor is the odious Simon Legree, who works male slaves to death while using females as pleasure machines. Stowe's novel, which still has the power to grip readers today, sold 20,000 copies within three weeks of publication, 300,000 within the first year. It spawned sequels, stage adaptations, condensations for children, and moved huge audiences to weep over the slave drivers' cruelties. Southerners received it as a purely polemical—and outrageously distorted—attack on the very core of their civilization, and they countercharged that their putatively humane slave system, along with everyone, white and black, who lived under it, had been slandered. So America's regional division widened and became unbridgeable, and evil, to each side, became the exclusive property of the other region. The North saw itself as the country of free labor. The South saw itself as the last sanctuary for the right to property, for which the Revolution itself had been fought.

When tariffs and the prices of imports went up, Southerners, who depended on a relatively unrestricted export trade, and had to import most machinery and finished goods, felt that Northerners had conspired against them. When tariffs and import prices went down, they claimed victory over Northern "money-power." In either circumstance, they saw themselves in the Jeffersonian tradition as a virtuous people living close to the earth, holding out against city-vitiated, venal Yankees whom they called "scum," and "impious," and "infernal fanatics." They spoke of Northern women "abjuring the delicate offices of their sex, and deserting their nurseries, stroll[ing] over the country as politico-moral reformers, delivering lewd lectures upon the beauties of free-love and spiritualism." And they regarded Lincoln as a tool of antislavery interests who were calculating how best to reduce them to their own form of vassalage.[6]

Northerners looked with reciprocal contempt upon the South, but they no longer regarded slavery as a "peculiar institution" confined to a strange country of hogs and mosquitoes and sunbaked verandas. With the passage of the Kansas-Nebraska Act of 1854, slavery became a contagion that threatened everyone. The new law declared that "squatters," as the settlers in the territories were called, could vote on the legality of slavery when their territory was ready to seek admission to the Union. This plan raised the specter of each side summoning in sympathizers to swing the vote their way, as had happened in Kansas in 1850; and it raised legal and political questions involving representation in the territorial legislatures, which had the power to initiate petitions for statehood. Free-Soilers suspected that the whole business was a device to ensure the extension of slavery beyond the limits established by the Missouri Compromise— suspicions that were confirmed when, three years later, the Supreme Court ruled in the Dred Scott case that a slave, even if he were living in free territory, could not sue for his freedom because he was not a citizen of the Republic.

This deadly combination of congressional and judicial action seemed to Lincoln, among others, a bald plot to make slave property portable and secure. If the slave interests succeeded, *all* American territory could, in effect, become slave territory, and by the imperial logic of the slave system, *all* people could become slaves. Lincoln made this point to himself in a private jotting around the time of the Kansas-Nebraska crisis:

> If A. can prove, however conclusively, that he may, of right, enslave B.—why may not B. snatch the same argument, and prove equally, that he may enslave A.?—
>
> You say A. is white, and B. is black. It is *color*, then; the lighter, having the right to enslave the darker? Take care. By this rule, you are to be slave to the first man you meet, with a fairer skin than your own.
>
> You do not mean *color* exactly? — You mean the whites are *intellectually* the superiors of the blacks, and, therefore have the right to enslave them? Take care again. By this rule, you are to be slave to the first man you meet, with an intellect superior to your own.
>
> But, say you, it is a question of *interest*; and, if you can make it your *interest*, you have the right to enslave another. Very well. And if he can make it his interest, he has the right to enslave you.[7]

Kansas-Nebraska and Dred Scott were portents of things to come. But the plainest omen of war did not arrive until October 1859, when after years of rumors of emancipation plots and slave insurrections, news raced through North and South that an abolitionist named John Brown had crossed the Potomac River from the North with a band of followers (including three of his five sons) and seized a federal arsenal at Harper's Ferry—with the intention to distribute the weapons and incite rebellion among the slaves of Virginia. The rancorous decade was concluding with a military action by a man who all but proclaimed himself (using an unconscious pun that revealed his obsession with the glory of the crucifixion) to be Christ's second coming: "Remember," Brown wrote to his wife while preparing himself for execution, "that Jesus of Nazareth suffered a most *excruciating* death on the cross as a felon."[8] The prospects for reconciliation between North and South had vanished; Americans on each side were embarked on an effort to redeem themselves by fighting evil in their counterparts on the other side.

Harper's Ferry was the Bay of Pigs of its time. The enslaved people whom Brown intended to liberate did not rise up to join him, and when it became clear that he could not do the job alone, the governments of the free states did not come to his aid. Yet despite the debacle (and here the analogy breaks down), a single man had changed the world in a day. Something new was in the air: "this is sowing the wind to reap the whirlwind," wrote Longfellow, while Melville, invoking the old idea of heavenly portents, called Brown "the meteor of the war." The border between the slave world and the free had now for the first time been crossed with violent intent, and the day had been brought closer when Americans would no longer have to cope with "the fissure that separates them zigzagging itself half across the continent like an isothermal line."[9] For the first time in the history of the Republic, soldiers from one America had invaded the other.

If, in consequence, there was a rising new fear, it was for many an invigorating fear because however puny and easily repulsed Brown was (he was quickly captured by militia under the command of a Virginia colonel, Robert E. Lee), his incursion into the South broke a long slumber and furnished new reason to be alive. Thoreau knew that civil war had begun in all but name, and he delivered a speech even after the selectmen of Concord had refused to ring the town bell to announce it:

> These men, in teaching us how to die, have at the same time taught us how to live. If this man's acts and words do not create a revival, it will be the severest possible satire on the acts and words that do. It is the best news that America has ever heard. It has already quickened the feeble pulse of the North, and infused more and more generous blood into her veins and heart than any number of years of what is called commercial and political prosperity could. How many a man who was lately contemplating suicide has now something to live for![10]

In his excitement, Thoreau proclaimed the awakening of a generation that Emerson had written off not long before as having "lost all spring

& vivacity," and he sensed that Brown's campaign promised a thrilling resumption of holy war. The two Americas now set out, with no possibility of pulling back, on a work for which they had long been preparing: they demonized each other without mercy.

Paradise Lost was again the favored gloss on public events, and the language of righteous crusade reached its highest pitch since the Revolution. All pretense of mutual civility between North and South was dropped. Southerners, said one blunt New York businessman, are a "race of lazy, ignorant, coarse, sensual, swaggering, sordid beggarly barbarians," while others, steeped in Scripture, made the point more grandly. Oliver Wendell Holmes spoke of the coming struggle as a "Holy War" against "that great General who will bring to it all the powers with which he fought against the Almighty before he was cast down from heaven."[11]

When the anticipated war finally broke out in the spring of 1861, supporters of the Union seemed almost jaunty in their eagerness. "This is not a war of men," wrote one popular versifier, "but of Angels Good and Ill." Walt Whitman, looking back on these events, remembered exulting at "the prompt and splendid wrestling with secession slavery, the arch-enemy personified." And even Emerson, according to his Concord neighbor Hawthorne, was "breathing slaughter, like the rest of us."[12]

But the haughtiness dissipated in the Union's shocking defeat at Bull Run. After the disastrous battle, another newly engaged New England reformer, Julia Ward Howe, who had capacities for outrage comparable to Mrs. Stowe's, was en route back to Boston from the capital when she heard a group of beaten soldiers gamely singing the popular ballad "John Brown's Body" on the train. Attracted by the melody, she decided to compose for it some more elevating words; and the result was the "Battle Hymn of the Republic"—a pastiche of prophecies out of Isaiah and Revelation ("Let the hero, born of woman, crush the serpent with his heel . . ." "Mine eyes have seen the glory of the coming of the Lord . . .")—which became only the best-known instance in a flood of apocalyptic writing. The first Union campaign was a defeat; but the world had been invested with purpose again.

All across North and South men now rushed "to the front [of recruitment lines] like seekers at a backwoods revival, each vying with the other to be first on the list." Volunteers in the North were proclaimed "armed myriads of . . . angels" whom "the Supreme Majesty sent forth" against an enemy that had committed "an imitation on earth of that first foul revolt of the 'Infernal Serpent.' " "Confederate Lucifer" and "Lord of

Misrule" were among the terms applied to Mississippi senator Jefferson Davis, whom the Confederates chose as their President, and who was judged (by James Russell Lowell) to be an imitation of Satan, "the first great secessionist."[13]

In reply, one semi-literate Louisiana sugar planter employed equally fervid religious language and prayed

> that every black Republican in the Hole combined whorl either man woman o chile that is opposed to negro slavery . . . shal be trubled with pestilents and calamitys of all Kinds and Drag out the Balance of there existance in Misray and Degradation with scarsely food and rayment enughf to keep sole and Body to gather and o God I pray the to Direct a bullet or a bayonet to pirce the Hart of every northern soldier that invades southern soile and after the Body has rendered up its traterish sole gave it a trators reward a Birth In the Lake of Fires and Brimstone.[14]

Proclaiming themselves spotless, Americans had shunted off all evil to an infernal—but strangely welcome—enemy. They were ready for holy war.

[2]

For both sides, the symbol of the impasse was Abraham Lincoln. It was Lincoln, through what may be properly called his political ministry, who did most to retrieve and renew the dormant power of the symbols of good and evil that had been slipping out of public life. Yet the reason that Lincoln remains the most morally consequential figure in American history, the reason that it was he to whom the eulogists would attribute the *imitatio Christi* which Brown and others had claimed, is that he stood *against* the resurgent Manicheanism that produced the war. He accepted the war, and even participated in the conspiracy-mongering, but his Satan was ultimately no foreigner or alien or infernal other. Lincoln's Satan was the old symbol of limitation, the idea that the equality principle upon which the Republic had been founded was somehow to be hemmed in, hampered, and restricted to one race. For this idea Lincoln had nothing but contempt, and he spoke with sarcasm about the notion that slavery was a condition natural for, or desired by, blacks: "While I have often said that all men ought to be free, yet I would allow those colored persons to be slaves who want to be; and next to them those white persons who argue in favor of making other people slaves."[15]

Long before the war, Lincoln had seen that some sort of transformative event—the political equivalent of mass conversion—was needed if Americans were to feel that their destiny as individuals remained connected to the fate of the Republic. For him, this event had been the passage of the Kansas-Nebraska Act, which threatened to spread the scourge of slavery everywhere. Before Southerners had offered any open talk of secession, he had recognized that with the deaths of the founders (Jefferson and Adams were the last to go—dying, like predestined saints whose fates were bound together, on the Fourth of July in 1826), the Republic had been consigned to caretakers who had not bled for it. Lincoln is explicit on this theme in his eulogy upon the great Kentuckian, Henry Clay, who died in 1852. Cut off by time from the founders, the nation, he knew, had to resort to an untested symbolic system that tried—through flag, music, ennobling myths and fictions, regular political rituals, sacralization of the landscape through public monuments—to deliver some inkling of what it had meant to be alive in the Revolutionary years. Lincoln knew that the idea of the Republic (as Emerson had said of Christianity) had "fallen into the error that corrupts all attempts to communicate religion," and that all around him "men have come to speak of the revelation as somewhat long ago given and done."[16]

In doing his part to foster a quasi-religious revival of democratic ideals, Lincoln, like any zealot, had an incredulity that oscillated between pity and rage toward those who did not share his faith. He spoke in a voice trained on the models of Jeremiah and St. John: "Our republican robe," he said after the passage of the Kansas-Nebraska Act, "has been trailed in the dust. Let us repurify it . . . in the spirit, if not the blood of the revolution." For a man whose scripture was the Declaration of Independence, and the Union his church, the war with the secessionist Southern states was the logical outcome of his *religious* commitments. Lincoln confessed indifference to institutional religion ("I am not a member of any Christian church," he admitted when prodded—and the most he could muster when an opponent accused him of infidelity was that "I have never spoken with intentional disrespect of . . . any denomination of Christians in particular"), but his piety toward the Republic rose, as Alexander Stephens, Vice President of the Confederacy, was among the first to notice, "to the sublimity of religious mysticism." He defined the purpose of the war as the realization of the vision of the founders, who, he insisted, had intended the extinction of slavery within the borders of an inviolable union. As late as 1863, he remained ingenuously amazed at "the theory of the general government being only an agency, whose principals are the States"—an idea that "was new to me," he wrote, as if someone had dared propose to a believer that the soul was mortal or that Christ was merely one prophet among many.[17] No matter how often he encountered this idea, it remained for him a shocking novelty—in the way that vulgarity never ceases to offend a person devoted to tact. The idea that the United States had been signed into being as if by an abrogable treaty always struck him with the immitigable surprise of blasphemy.

Death-obsessed, gaunt, Lincoln had the unappeasable drive of an "ungodly godlike" man—two adjectives that Melville had used in *Moby-Dick* to describe the mad Captain Ahab, and which, in a telling coincidence, turn up in descriptions of the President by persons close to him (his friend Billy Herndon, and his wife's black seamstress, Elizabeth Keckley—unlikely readers, both, of Melville's epic), as well as in the tirades of political enemies who decried the "ungodly howling of Mr. Lincoln's Nigar Equality." These complementary words—godlike and ungodly—were as spontaneous as they were apt; and Lincoln became a beloved (and, by others, proportionately reviled) figure precisely because, like Ahab, he set out with a "bigotry of purpose" to achieve his end. He shared with Ahab a magnificent implacability: "I'd strike the sun if it insulted me," says Melville's mad captain. "I would rather be assassinated on this spot," said Lincoln in Philadelphia's Independence Hall on the way to the White House, "rather than surrender" the principles of the Declaration.[18]

Lincoln was a manic nationalist in the nineteenth-century mold of Mazzini and Bismarck. But first and last he was a democrat. At the outset of the war (he had been elected with only a bare plurality of the votes in a four-way election), his inclusion of blacks in his vision of universal rights was received as a buffoon's blather. But not long after his death, it began to be said that, as *Christ redivivus*, he had disseminated "his philosophy in parables," and had gone "through life bearing the load of a people's sorrows upon his shoulders,"[19] as if his flock had been culpably slow to understand him. Lincoln made people feel that he was returning them to contact with a vision of good—"our divine equality," as Melville called it—which they had once possessed. Refusing to portray the devil as a huntable enemy, he conceived of evil as the absence of this good, a *national* moral failure. When he said that Clay in 1850 had "exorcised the demon which possessed the body politic,"[20] he meant that the infernal idea of slavery had gotten loose from the cage in which the founders had left it to die—and that Clay had put it back in. But Lincoln always kept this demon from being personified. It was for him an atmosphere, an attitude for which he held *all* people responsible.

Lincoln's idea of evil was extremely demanding—as it had been since Paul and Augustine first refined it into a theological formulation. It required every prospective believer to come to terms with himself, because, as Lincoln knew and said, *no* American was uncontaminated by the racist history of the Republic. This was an extraordinary way to talk—this self-affiliation with the enemy—in the midst of a war. He always spoke without rancor about Southerners, whom he saw as having inherited a tragic history, and with candor about the complicity of his fellow citizens in the North, whom he deemed willing beneficiaries of the sweat and blood of slaves. Yet somehow Lincoln managed to sustain both his moral criticism and his war. Unlike his own generals, unlike his critics and enemies, he had a fundamental humility, but at the same time he was more certain than all of them that he knew the necessary course. His personal secretaries, John Hay and John Nicolay, called him—advisedly—"the tycoon."

The New York businessman George Templeton Strong, who kept a detailed diary during the war years, relates a story that helps to convey the peculiar coexistence in Lincoln of magnanimity and rage. Sometime in the early months of the war, the President received the visit of a simpler-minded Unionist, a senator who wanted to interest him in some parallels between the devil and Jeff Davis. The eager senator expected his President to have thought a good deal about the satanic nature of his foe:

> Story of Senator Dixon calling on the President and suggesting a parallel between secession and the first rebellion of which Milton sang. Very funny interview. Abe Lincoln didn't know much about *Paradise Lost* and sent out for a copy, looked through its first books under the Senator's guidance, and was struck by the coincidences between the utterances of Satan and those of Jefferson Davis, whom by-the-by he generally designates as "that t'other fellow." Dixon mentioned the old joke about the Scotch professor who was asked what his views were about the fall of the Angels and replied, "Aweel, there's much to be said on both

sides." "Yes," said Uncle Abraham, "I always thought the Devil was
some to blame!"[21]

Lincoln's visitor wanted righteous indignation, but he got something
more like a concurring nod and a smile—signs of the peculiar jocular
serenity that made the President mysterious, and even led some to suspect his sanity. The senator discovered that if Lincoln was a torment to
his enemies, his calculated callowness could be an even finer torture for
those who wanted him to breathe vengeance. He never did. In October
1863, on the costliest battlefield in human history, he addressed a crowd
that doubtless harbored hate in the midst of an unfinished war; but he
never mentioned the enemy. He drove his great speech at Gettysburg
with intransitive verbs—"dedicate," "endure," "perish"—that took no
resistant object and fostered no enmity. He held up a vision of a world
drenched in sin, but free of targetable devils. The only evil that Lincoln
understood, with a singleness of purpose that is both appalling and sub-
lime, was the evil of incompleteness. He was the greatest Augustinian in
our history.

[3]

"**M**r. Lincoln's war," as his enemies called it, began, like all wars,
with expectations of brevity and glory. "And the young men were
all elation / Hearing Sumter's cannon roar, / And they thought how tame
the Nation / In the Age that went before."[22] But it went quickly and
terribly wrong. It became a killing contest on a scale previously unknown.
It consumed not only white men but also black, who by late 1862 were
being admitted into segregated units of the Union army, and who num-
bered 200,000 by the war's end. "Never, since Cromwell's time," said
the white commander of a volunteer regiment of ex-slaves, "had there
been soldiers in whom the religious element held such a place."[23] But
soon the soldiers, white and black, became cannon fodder, and they knew
it. The conduct of the war settled more and more on the principle, as
the historian William McFeely has put it, that "total victory against other
committed Americans could be achieved only if there were more men
available for dying on one side than on the other," and it became a
grinding war of attrition. No matter what the politicians and generals said

in their (mostly florid) speeches, it seemed more a curse than a military contest, and it became harder and harder to see "God's hand through this darkness"[24] as if the old language could still be made to accommodate the new scale of mechanical mass killing. Faith was tested on all fronts —by the ironclads, the repeating rifles, the walls of withering fire into which men were forced to walk, as the flesh of their comrades in the rank before them was shredded and splattered in their faces.

The will to believe had to slacken in this hell. And so it did. Too many found the old gestures of religious affirmation archaic even as new hymns and sermons poured forth and calls to conscription were accompanied by prayers and drumbeat. First to feel the impropriety of the old slogans were Southerners, many of whom foresaw defeat early on, and whose civilians endured horrors of their own at places of siege like Petersburg and Vicksburg. The Southern commitment to the war had had more stoic dutifulness than eschatological fervor to begin with; the fight against the Yankees, some believed, was the obligatory resumption of the Cavaliers' unfinished campaign against the fanatic Puritans, who had never been entirely stamped out. At the same time, secular intellectuals in the North also sensed the new futility of the old idea of crusade and were hesitant to join the stampede. "Poor Fellows!" wrote the young William Dean Howells about the enlisted men, "I pitied them but being at work on a patriotic paper, I tried to see some sense in the business they had undertaken, but couldn't."[25]

In the South, which fielded its own praying army, skeptical gentry "counted [too many] generals in church and suggested that less piety and more drilling of commands would suit the times better," while in the North, as the dying went on, Lincoln's closest advisers confessed that "the immense slaughter . . . chills and sickens us all."[26] Too old to be confronted with the conscientious question of personal service, Melville climbed in his imagination to a New York City rooftop in order to view the fire and smoke that accompanied the "atheist roar" of antidraft riots in the streets below. It was the summer of 1863, six months after the Emancipation Proclamation had settled the question of war aims, but when the prospects for survival of the Union still seemed dim:

> *The Town is taken by its rats—ship-rats*
> *And rats of the wharves. All civil charms*
> *And priestly spells which late held hearts in awe—*
> *Fear-bound, subjected to a better sway*

> *Than sway of self; these like a dream dissolve,*
> *And man rebounds whole aeons back in nature.*[27]

The rats' "red arson" was a poor man's protest against the "nigger war" (the rioters were mainly Irish immigrants), but it signified an unease that pervaded American society even as it continued to mobilize. Before the demand for manpower overcame fear of racial mixing, local authorities throughout the North had instructed Union recruiters to tell "the d——d niggers to keep out of this . . . white man's war";[28] and beneath the high-flown rhetoric there was a murmur of outrage that whites were being sent to die for blacks. One of the reasons that Lincoln resisted emancipation for as long as he did was that he knew it would trigger a furious racist reaction.

He was right. The high purpose of the war became lost in a contagion of hate. Incensed mobs now stalked the streets beating blacks—children as well as adults—to death. "Shops were cleared out," reported one New Yorker, "and a black man hanged in Carmine Street, for no offence but that of Nigritude."[29]

When today we witness the will to persevere through this terrible war—through books or films or visits to the battle sites—we stand amazed. One recent reminder of this astonishment was the remarkable public television series that attracted an audience of nearly 20 million viewers in the fall of 1990. With its monotone narrator and plaintive music, it had the calculated hush of a documentary about Druids at Stonehenge or some such ruin of an irretrievable faith. It proceeded by accumulating images of the dead: piles of amputated limbs, skeletons at Andersonville, skulls washed by the rain out of the soil at Fredericksburg. The visual evidence of the war still available in our landscapes has become a great *memento mori*, forcing upon us the question of why these men went willingly to die. Faced with this question, and with the many evidences of dissent, we wonder: how willingly? Could Walt Whitman have been right when he wrote that "the brunt of its labor of death was to all essential purposes, volunteered," that "down in the abysms of New World humanity there had form'd and harden'd a primal hard-pan of national Union will . . . capable at any time of . . . breaking out like an earthquake . . . [into] the general, voluntary, arm'd upheaval"?[30]

Skeptical, we study the desertion rates and antidraft riots, the rich men cheating death by buying substitutes. We consider the young men's prewar illusions, the pernicious myths of chivalry and equestrian glory. We portray the soldiers as duped primitives who were cynically persuaded to give up their lives in exchange for the trinket of duty. But after the battles of Shiloh and Antietam and Chancellorsville, these explanations seem tinged with pettiness, and the questions persist. How could the generals, proclaiming their devotion to their brave boys, order them into such slaughter? Why did they go? The very fact that these questions are thinkable confirms something we know about ourselves—that in the realm of belief we have become frantically impoverished. Americans have not seen, and can barely imagine, any comparable surge of militance since Thoreau rang the Concord bell.

The Civil War was the great divide between a culture of faith and a culture of doubt. It began on both sides as a resurgence of mass belief, and ended as the last rally of a dying patient. At Gettysburg, more than 50,000 men were killed and wounded in three days; at Antietam, 25,000 in a single day; in one terrible frenzy at Cold Harbor, 12,000 men fell in eight minutes. Death, gorging itself, mocked belief. If the imperative to believe kept pace for a while with the horror, it was, as the historian Charles Royster has written, because "a people who had made war their salvation could not limit war by judging the implications of one battle or a series of battles. They were the nation; they were the war; they could not stop."[31] The Civil War may have been America's greatest religious revival, but it was also our spiritual suicide. Even as the hundreds of thousands went to their deaths, they must have wondered if out of the ashes would rise an infidel nation.

Before the war, Americans spoke of providence. After it, they spoke of luck. This spiritual collapse helps to explain why "the life of Lincoln's soul," as Richard Hofstadter wrote with bitter wisdom nearly fifty years ago, "was almost entirely without consummation." Hofstadter's assessment, offered in the aftermath of World War II, may have been driven by his own awareness of "the defeat inherent in any modern victory in war," but his choice of a quasi-sexual metaphor to describe Lincoln's spirit was exquisitely deft. Lincoln's mood of foreboding not only afflicted the man himself but soon gripped the whole nation with a kind of postcoital flatness and exhaustion, even a flustered wondering over what the exertions and excitement had been all about.[32]

[4]

As it turned out, the figure who embodied the future was not Lincoln, but a man who had been an indifferent student of tactics at West Point (where he had been sent because his father despaired of any career for him other than soldiering), a failed farmer "who could not bring in a crop of potatoes,"[33] and a small-town leather-goods merchant who could not muster the conviviality necessary to make a sale. Ulysses S. Grant gratefully discovered his talent and his purpose in the killing work of war. As such, he has recently been proposed as the representative modern American man who emerged—ready to rule—from the carnage:

There are many men in America who are articulate only to the extent of hinting in clichés at what is locked within them. They talk disparagingly of the weather and of people different from themselves; they joke about sex and theorize solemnly about ways to make money; and as they do so, they work monotonously at something they have no interest in talking about. Their predictable, ritual conversations with one another enable them to endure. Sometimes the talk stops . . . then such a man cannot keep going. The chatter that has been his barrier against nothingness is gone. The void that remains is terrifying. Grant had known that silence as he sought another kind. He wanted a silence born of confidence and command, a time when he could listen to other men's chatter but have no need to add to it himself. This is the silence not of a man deadened to the world, but rather of one come alive to engage it. It is the silence of Ulysses Grant as he appears in the Brady photograph, sitting on a bench hauled out of a church into the sun during the Wilderness campaign. There, as others busily talked, he sat silent and in control.[34]

This is persuasive writing. Credited by historians with inventing the modern war of "annihilation," decried by Mary Todd Lincoln as a "butcher," Grant was a preview of the dead-eyed murderers one meets in fictional and factual twentieth-century texts. He is like a figure who walks out of *In Cold Blood* or *The Executioner's Song*, or one of Jim Thompson's hard-boiled murder mysteries, in which men kill with mundane efficiency and detachment. A man who had no ground for faith in himself or in anything beyond himself, he was entirely at home in the modern, mechanized world of war where he found a comforting anonymity. He was very good at thinking about men as bodies capable of obedient motion. But he did not exactly think (there is a winning lack of self-consciousness in his *Memoirs*) about the vexations of modern life; he simply surrendered his spirit to them, and was grateful to have found a function. He is the first pure example on the American public scene of a personality that would later be the subject of much sociological commentary—the "organization man." Imbued with "majestical phlegm, an alienation in the midst of action, a capacity for watching in silence, and commanding without excitement,"[35] he seemed dead to the human consequences of his actions. If he had been in gestation for a long time, it took the Civil War to deliver him.

It was this modern monster who accepted Lee's surrender with laconic decency at Appomattox. But it was not long before a feeling spread that somehow there had been no proper victory, that both sides had been beaten, and that a new kind of American with Grant's peculiar combination of timidity and ruthlessness was emerging from the carnage. "The subsidence of that great convulsion," as Henry James put it, "introduced into the national consciousness . . . a sense of the world being a more complicated place than it had hitherto seemed, the future more treacherous, success more difficult." The Civil War was a last surge of unrequited ardor that left the country spent and unwilling to take further risks; it had created, as James said, a new American personality for the "days to come"—not the swaggering showman of the antebellum years, nor "a man of commitments," but "an observer"—in whom a certain callousness was required.[36] It was not clear that the war, after all, had had anything to do with good and evil, or that those concepts made any sense in the postwar world.

James recognized that this retreat into voyeurism (which became a leading theme in postwar fiction) was an expression of helplessness before the autonomy of systems. Postwar life continued to honor the military model. Transportation now ran by the clock, as local time differences, once determined by the variable behavior of the sun, gave way to standardized time zones because of the scheduling requirements of the railroads. It was in the 1870s that the phrase "on time" first came into use.[37] Working-class employees now knew their bosses in the way that infantry had known their generals. "Relations between investors and directors became increasingly impersonal, indirect, governed by technicalities of law"; and in the female world of the household, "domestic labor came to consist chiefly of budgeting and shopping rather than making."[38] One received, or was denied, the bounty of the industrial system as if it were rations distributed from some invisible HQ—a "machine process," as Thorstein Veblen would later call it, that "gives no insight into questions of good and evil"[39] because no responsible being can be detected in it. It seems somehow to run on its own.

Under these new conditions, daily experience was likely to include standing on line to pay for some product whose human origin (who made it? who brought it to the place of exchange?) was utterly removed from the scene of purchase. In the new "department stores . . . the seller fixes the price, and comes in contact with the buyer only through the intervention of a salesman who has no discretion as to the terms of sale."[40] The streets by which one traveled to and from these stores were illuminated by electric lights ignited without the torch of any lampman.

As writers tried to come to terms with this impersonal world, the impotence of the individual—especially that of young men—became a keynote. In Kate Chopin's well-known novel *The Awakening* (1899), young men of "high voice" and "serio-comic" charm do nothing but sit at the feet of unavailable ladies, giggling at their pleasantries; and in the regional stories of Sarah Orne Jewett (*The Country of the Pointed Firs* [1896]), old men drift into senility or are frozen in boyhood, keeping about them "a remote and juvenile sort of silence." Henry James populated his novels with commentators on these declensions: "young men," says the elder Mr. Touchett in *The Portrait of a Lady* (1881), "are very different from what I was. . . . when I cared for a girl—when I was young—I wanted to do more than look at her." Journalists agreed, one of them observing that even young men "of parts" walked in a "bent over fashion that was the style . . . of the day."[41]

Stimulated by new domestic and foreign supplies of cheap labor, by the quickening of westward expansion as the last pockets of Indian resistance were cleared away, and by the invention of new technologies brought on by the war itself, the United States lurched through a series of major recessions (1873, 1884, 1893) that changed everyone's fortune overnight. No one was immune. There was no controlling the convulsions; one simply had to ride them out. The economic expansion, driven by a will that seemed quite independent of human agency, looks retrospectively impressive in our textbook charts and graphs, but it was *experienced* by many people as a kind of dying. "The ash heap," as Henry Adams succinctly put it, is "constantly increasing in size."[42]

Under these circumstances, the idea that any individual could prosper through discipline and drive—an idea exemplified in a few conspicuously public lives, like those of Carnegie and, later, Edison and Hearst—seemed a lie sold to the poor by the faceless rich. To more and more Americans, trying to get ahead through the old virtues of self-reliance and individual exertion seemed like throwing snowballs at the sun. Workingmen huddled in defensive groups as if they were still at war, as the industrial landscape became a graveyard of American ideals. An entirely new vocabulary came into service for designating a new kind of treason: class disloyalty. The term "scab," for instance—once a synonym for prostitute because of its reference to venereal skin lesions—now came to mean a shameless man who takes a striking worker's job; an ironworker who consented to toil extra hours in the heat of the blast furnace was called a "hog" or "chaser" or "blackleg" or "boss's pet" or "Jim Grabs" in honor of his indifference to the safety and bargaining power of his comrades.[43] Such words were attempts to keep the idea of right and wrong alive in a world where virtue and fortune seem utterly disconnected from one another.

This was the world of the employed. But America had also changed in the sense that employment itself had become highly insecure, and millions now spent their lives seeking it, trying to hold on to it, treasuring it despite its deprivations. Already by 1877, when federal troops were withdrawn from the South and Reconstruction was effectively repealed, a massive depression had shrunk the national economy by a third and pushed unemployment rates in some cities over 30 percent. Murderous violence between troops and workers spread across the country. The nation seemed to be sinking into a godless sequel to the Civil War—fought out of sight of the "gentle" classes, in the mines and factories and ironworks and along the wharves and railroad beds; between workers and owners; but also among workers themselves.

In a striking passage from a Civil War novel published in 1867, religious exhortation and moral fervor are literally consigned to an irrelevant sermon printed in a dead man's newspaper:

I had just finished breakfast, and was lying on my back smoking. A bullet whistled so unusually low as to attract my attention and struck with a loud smash in a tree about twenty feet from me. Between me and the tree a soldier with his greatcoat rolled under his head for a pillow lay on his back reading a newspaper which he held in both hands. I remember smiling to myself to see this man start as the bullet passed. Some of his comrades left off playing cards and looked for it. The man who was reading remained perfectly still, his eyes fixed on the paper with a steadiness which I thought curious, considering the bustle around him. Presently I noticed that there were a few drops of blood on his neck, and that his face was paling. Calling to the card players, who had resumed their game, I said, "See to that man with the paper." They went to him, spoke to him, touched him, and found him perfectly dead. The ball had struck him under the chin, traversed the neck, and cut the spinal column where it joins the brain, making a fearful hole through which the blood had already soaked his greatcoat. It was this man's head and not the tree which had been struck with such a report. There he lay, still holding the New York *Independent*, with his eyes fixed on a sermon by Henry Ward Beecher. It was really quite a remarkable circumstance.[44]

Writers of all stripes have always managed unintentionally to slip into pedestrian monotony, but no one until now had actually *tried* to produce such a string of impassive sentences. This passage is a classic instance of what Edmund Wilson called "the chastening of American prose style." It is a prose purged of all rises and falls of affect; it has lost the ambition to build stanzalike paragraphs in the manner of Emerson or Thoreau, held together in emulation of nature by a web of linked images. Yet much more than a literary manner had died with the war. Gone for good was Emerson's idea that "every natural process is a version of a moral sentence," that "the whole circle of persons and things, of actions and events [is] one vast picture which God paints on the instant eternity."[45]

What, then, was left? In what could a man believe after the crusade turned out to be a pointless slaughter, and piety a form of nostalgia?

[5]

What was left was a stark sense that the world was run by chance. The emergence of chance and luck as the chief explanations and desiderata of life is perhaps the central story of modern American history, a story that runs its course in every Western nation, but that accelerated in the United States with notable suddenness after the clearing away of the Civil War dead.

The basic conviction on which Christian morals had been based—that the world is justly governed by an all-seeing God—now collapsed, and chance took the place of God as both mystery and explanation. In colonial and early republican America this concept had been virtually unknown and to speak of it had been a kind of blasphemy. One can see this in many popular texts, for example in a life of George Washington first published in 1800, but reprinted throughout the nineteenth century: George's father tests his son's piety by arranging for the gardener to plant some seeds in a pattern that, when the flowers come out, will spell out the boy's name. When they sprout, and young George runs to his father to show him the marvel, the father-tempter attributes it all to chance. "O Pa, you must not say *Chance*," is the boy's reply, and the satisfied father turns the colloquy into a religious lesson about God the designer.[46]

Over the course of the nineteenth century this lesson was radically revised, and "the irreducible presence of chance," as one scholar has called it, became the mark of the age. The line between fortune and providence was breaking down in public discourse as early as the 1820s, when the idea of chance first crept into the language of the clergy. "Many happy things are found or done by good fortune," we find Emerson saying in 1830 while he was still an ordained minister. But he quickly corrects himself: "I should rather say by the kindness of God." There is a clue in this little self-correction that helps to explain why he soon left the church. As the impious idea of fortune slipped into his diction, he found himself commenting on it instead of excising it—a sign, he knew, of slippage in his faith. By the time of the cholera epidemic that struck New York City two years later, full-scale public debate was under way over the meaning of the catastrophe, and there is a plaintive tone in the words of the believers: "Atheists may deny," wrote one New Yorker, "but the intelligence and piety, the real wisdom among us, will acknowledge the providence of God; and this acknowledgment will be made by the great majority of our population. They *feel* that God is chastising us."[47]

The Civil War hastened immeasurably this process of losing faith in providence. Even before the fighting, the old religious narratives were disintegrating. After the war it seemed clear that an entirely new kind of story would be needed for the narration of human lives and that the new stories would not be about God's supervision. They would be about blind luck. Chance was the name of the indifferent force that refuses to explain why one soldier comes home with shattered legs and another walks home whole. It was a cruel tease to maintain to the maimed boy or to the widow that the bullets had flown purposefully; and it was not much better to preach supine piety to victims of unregulated industrialization. The war turned the world into a theater of chance in which the living were randomly sorted from the dead.

Soldiers under fire became expert astrologers, reading the stars for hints to the future, decorating themselves with charms and amulets, betting on anything and everything—not just on cards and dice and wrestling matches, but on the day and time the regiment would move out, on the likely hour of the coming battle's first shot, on louse races run between bugs plucked from their hair and set loose in pairs on mess plates turned into racetracks. One Union boy was saved when a bullet struck the deck of cards he had stashed in his breast pocket, while his comrade, carrying a Bible, was killed.[48] Confederate soldiers gambled with cards imprinted with the likeness of Jefferson Davis, shuffling and dealing them till they were dog-eared from incessant games of poker, twenty-one, euchre, keno, and faro. A gambling den near Fredericksburg known as Devil's Half-Acre was as busy as any hospital or command post.

Gambling was a comfort, a need, a cabalistic rite. It seemed to many the best response to a situation where at one moment a man might fold his greatcoat for a pillow and an instant later, after a random shot, the coat was a sponge for his unstanchable blood. The tumble of the dice and shuffle of the cards replicated in miniature what seemed the overwhelming randomness of life. Memoirs of the war were filled with a sense of bafflement at the prospect of making sense of who lived and who died; one Indiana sergeant reported to his wife in 1862 that four of his comrades were hit while he was only grazed by a spent shell and his canteen torn away. After such evidence of divine protection, he reached back for the old language and dared to hope that "God will bring me safe home." But his supplicant piety did not last. Two years later, he was struck again, this time by one of the millions of bullets in the "leaden hail" at the battle of the Wilderness (directed by Grant); and on this occasion he wrote that "one half inch Difference" would have meant death. Saved by his belt buckle, he recounted his fate in a completely different voice: "I have been very *lucky*," he said, "I hope I will be as *lucky* as I have been all along and come out safe."[49]

This little shift in the habitual words of a common soldier, a minor detail in the grand, consuming story of the Civil War, affords a glimpse of one of those "soft, ambiguous moments [that are] moments of true origination"[50] in the history of a culture. More than a few soldiers survived like this Indiana boy, with their poise but without their pious habits. The process by which providence gave way to chance as the normative explanation of events was quiet yet incremental. One cannot poll the dead, but it is possible to follow these changes through inflections in the usage of commonplace words—words like "coincidence," which once simply implied simultaneity but was coming to mean an odd concurrence that mocked the observer with its symmetry; or "accident," which once had several related meanings (an irregular feature of a landscape, an inessential attribute of an artifact) but came to mean a disruptive event, a caprice without intelligible meaning.

The word "art," whose root meaning is "skill," had always implied mastery of the minutiae of a craft. Now the new "art" of photography, for example, involved so many uncontrollable contingencies—the fluctuating mix of natural and artificial light, the potency of the chemical bath, the unexpected juxtapositions of moving subjects within the compositional frame—that the finished work represented "a series of lucky (or unlucky) mechanical accidents."[51] Similarly, the word "sport": appropriating Kent's famous exclamation in *King Lear* that "as flies to wanton boys are we to the gods / they kill us for their sport," Paul Laurence Dunbar called his 1902 novel about black migration from country to city (one of many contemporaneous expressions of disillusionment with the legacy of emancipation) *The Sport of the Gods*. A few years later, the German social philosopher Max Weber wrote of the United States that "the pursuit of wealth, stripped of its religious and ethical meaning," had taken on "the character of sport." Mark Twain, who lost his beloved daughter to meningitis in 1896, wrote to his friend William Dean Howells (whose own daughter had just succumbed to an illness the doctors could not identify), "It is my quarrel that traps like that are set. Suzy and Winnie given us in miserable sport, & then taken away."[52] In the accelerating metamorphosis of such words, one sees the idea of providence receding by stages until it lingered only faintly, like sensation in a phantom limb.

Here is a sentence written, by the psychiatrist Robert Jay Lifton, not about a Civil War battle, but about Hiroshima—where dazed survivors, alive because they had brewed a second cup of tea, or turned their back to the blast to prepare a bath, wandered without comprehension among the dead: "Whatever his sense of good or bad fortune, whatever his claimed virtue or inner sense of the opposite, the survivor's concern about accidents of survival reflect his profound feeling that he was saved by an unknowable destiny or fate which he must both constantly propitiate and view with uneasiness—since these same larger forces willed the death of so many others."[53] The boys at Antietam and Fredericksburg and the Wilderness had seen the future.

The idea that conscious purpose might be driving history and nature seems vaguely insane to most Americans today; but in the late nineteenth century the idea had not yet quite been relinquished—or at least its aftereffects could still be felt. It was still news that nature, according to Darwin, "harbored no . . . purpose." It was still quite recent that in science the "assumption that the world and its parts were designed" was being purged, and teleological language rejected as what one modern philosopher of science has called a "vestigial . . . way of speaking."[54] This sort of linguistic sanitizing was a way to expunge the last traces of divine will from a world from which God had absconded. The residual prophetic elements of even scientific language were being rooted out, and the language pulled back into the confined function of description.

Poets (in this case, Edward Arlington Robinson) could find "no star"

In all the shrouded heavens anywhere
And . . . not a whisper in the air
Of any living voice but one so far
That I can hear it only as a bar
Of lost, imperial music.[55]

Well into the new century, prose writers conveyed the same sensation of groping about without points of reference in a land they once thought they knew. In works that bore titles like "The Open Boat" (1898), *Waste* (1924), *Barren Ground* (1925), *Obscure Destinies* (1932),[56] young writers turned the vertiginous emptiness of sea and plains and scrubland into a universal symbol. But it was an urbane old Easterner, Henry Adams, who best described

how the human mind . . . appearing suddenly and inexplicably out of some unknown and unimaginable void; passing half its known life in the mental chaos of sleep; victim even when awake, to its own ill-adjustment, to disease, to age, to external suggestion, to nature's compulsion; doubting its sensations, and, in the last resort, trusting only to instruments and averages—after sixty or seventy years of growing astonishment . . . wakes to find itself looking blankly into the void of death.[57]

The telltale repetition here is "void," which may seem a commonplace to us—the sort of thing we expect from some gabby neurotic in a Woody Allen movie—but which still had, in Adams's day, something scandalous about it.

For us today, this is old hat. If we preserve the idea of providence at all, we bury it in such expressions as "goodbye" (a contraction of the old valediction "God be with you"), used without consciousness of their origins. But the loss of providence was a fresh trauma for Americans a hundred years ago. Before the Civil War, the language of providence had been the ultimate explanation for one's fate. As late as 1857, the death of South Carolina congressman Preston Brooks, who had attacked Charles Sumner with a cane on the Senate floor a few months before, was judged "a providential visitation."[58] Lincoln's predecessor, James Buchanan, had spoken glibly of "superintending providence"[59] in the 1850s, and a belief in providence was the essence of Lincoln's credo. But after burying 600,000 dead in battlefield pits or, mangled beyond recognition, in anonymous graves, Americans faltered before this sort of language, and reference to providence became "morally unacceptable."[60] This is a key transition into modernity—the moment when the attribution of social pain to an inscrutable God became not only tenuous but offensive. "Science by its [very] definition," moreover, as Henry Adams pointed out, "must exclude the idea of a personal and active providence,"[61] even as death on its new modern scale made less and less intelligible sense—until providence as the explanation for one's survival became an affront to those who had died.

Sport, chance, luck, fortune—these were the bywords of the time. In some contexts they were terrible words, virtual obscenities. Millions of readers in the 1860s and 1870s learned from the fictional world of Horatio Alger that a ragged boy could lift himself by grabbing "the main chance," but readers knew that in the real world chance was a flirt and a tease, that it could tantalize a boy with an opportunity and just as quickly vanish. They knew as well that it was a great leveler, and that one of its effects was to mock their fathers' faith in the causal relation between merit and reward. For the first time, American cities had a significant population of single women, who were susceptible to what was commonly called "the sex game": a woman meeting a man "at a cafe table . . . by chance perhaps, and then by tacit consent or appointment" would have the course of her life determined by the "accident" of pregnancy or the luck of sex without conception.[62]

For the more stable and ever-growing middle class, insurance companies—whose profitability then as now depended on predictions derived from actuarial charts but whose sales appeal was based on people's fear of the mystery and unpredictability of chance—now became major financial institutions. Liability law proliferated. Chance made the difference between work and idleness for the unemployed who hung about the docks and warehouses and factories, hoping that some paid task would fall their way. Chance drove the lives of news reporters whose jobs depended on their "happening" to be in the right place at the right time —at the scene of a fire, or a brawl, or in a hotel lobby when a political deal was struck within earshot.

Among intellectuals, Darwinism had long before "opened . . . minds to the power of chance-happenings to bring forth 'fit' results if only they have time to add themselves together,"[63] but this process was not to be confused with the idea that nature embodied some discernible purpose. When Theodore Dreiser wrote *Sister Carrie*, his readers (including his own publisher, who issued the book reluctantly in 1900) were shocked not only by its sexual candor but by its unrelenting assault on the notion that a person's rise or fall has anything to do with a general economy of virtue and reward or of vice and punishment. Dreiser, whose fascination with coincidence rivaled that of his older English contemporary Thomas Hardy, described a world that ran on sex and accident; his feckless clerk snatches a last chance for pleasure by running off with a pretty girl and some of his employer's cash when the safe door accidentally fails to close. He does not exactly deserve his disgrace. Hounded by his bosses, he becomes a hanger-on in hotels, a scab in a streetcar strike, a beggar, and finally a suicide, while his disloyal mistress turns her minor acting talent into a big career. Their fortunes have no moral meaning; they simply happen.

A distinction between meaning and fact ("a fact," Emerson had said in 1838—in words that seemed to belong to some ancient language—"is an Epiphany of God") was moving beyond dispute. "Behind the bare phenomenal facts," the Harvard professor Chauncey Wright declared in 1877, "there is nothing." Emerson believed that "we lie in the lap of immense intelligence"; Wright believed that the world was an accident.[64] This distinction lay at the heart of all the writing that now poured forth from a new generation of American authors who recorded what they considered to be the central problem of modern life: the search for meaning in randomness. Yet even these gritty realists—from Frank Norris to John

Steinbeck—remained attached to the old world of immanent meaning; their work was rooted in the narrative tradition of the *exemplum*, the cautionary tale, and the parable. They called themselves *naturalists*, as a way of making clear their disbelief in anything *super*natural, but they were great readers of medieval romance. Their fictions begin as tales of temptation, but typically become stories about the miserable consequences of little accidents. A Union picket shoots blindly in the night at a rustle in the woods, and finds next morning the body of his brother (Ambrose Bierce, "The Mocking-Bird" [1891]). An intentional crash on a sled that is meant to kill the riders leaves them, by chance, maimed (Edith Wharton, *Ethan Frome* [1911]). Such cosmically trivial events would once have been called "casualties," but now they disfigure and destroy and, in the process, *teach no evident lesson*.

Chance was saturating modern experience. As social transactions became more and more glancing and impersonal (a shoeshine, a chain-store sale, a delivery), and city people heard frequent news of "mishaps" in the street or the factory, or of tenement and sweatshop fires from which only those who happened to be close to the doors escaped, chance seemed not just a persistent element in life, but ubiquitous and blisteringly alive. Americans were learning to ask themselves a modern question: "Why care for life-projects," as one philosopher has put it, "if there is no way of knowing what life will be there (if any) after the next drawing of lots?"[65]

Here, from Howells's aptly titled novel *A Hazard of New Fortunes* (1890), is his famous account of the city, which captures both the terror and the excitement of this new world of chance ("the inevitable ill fortune of life,"[66] as the reformer Henry Demarest Lloyd called it) as they are experienced by a man who has moved from Boston to the "planless" city of the future, New York:

There were certain signs, certain façades, certain audacities of the prevailing hideousness that always amused him in that uproar to the eye which the strident forms and colors made. He was interested in the insolence with which the railway had drawn its erasing line across the Corinthian front of an old theater, almost grazing its fluted pillars and flouting its dishonored pediment. The colossal effigies of the fat women and the tuft-headed Circassian girls of cheap museums; the vistas of shabby cross streets; the survival of an old hip-roofed house here and there at their angles; the Swiss-chalet, histrionic decorativeness of the stations in prospect or retrospect; the vagaries of the lines that narrowed together or stretched apart according to the width of the avenue, but always in wanton disregard of the life that dwelt, and bought and sold, and rejoiced or sorrowed, and clattered or crawled, around, below, above—were features of the frantic panorama that perpetually touched his sense of humor and moved his sympathy. Accident and then exigency seemed the forces at work to this extraordinary effect; the play of energies as free and planless as those that force the forest from the soil to the sky . . . The whole at moments seemed to him lawless, Godless; the absence of intelligent, comprehensive purpose in the huge disorder and the violent struggle to subordinate the result to the greater good penetrated with its dumb appeal the consciousness of a man who had always been too self-enwrapt to perceive the chaos to which the individual selfishness must always lead.[67]

Americans were being forced as never before to acknowledge unblinkable discrepancies between character and social status—with ruthless robber barons at the top and pitiable waifs at the bottom. Fortune seemed to have no respect for merit; only the stubbornly pious could ignore the claims of chance and continue to blame some persons for their misfortune while praising others for their luck. The terms "winners" and "losers" —as if life itself were a game—had become names for one's station in life.

This spreading prestige of chance raised many new problems for what Lincoln had called the American "political religion," the idea that every man—black and white—had the right to profit from his own labor and to turn that profit into capital. Such a religion could only flourish in a world in which prudence and diligence paid off, a world based on notions of rationality and justice. Now, to praise the businessman's virtue while condemning the gambler's vice became a sort of mental gymnastic, if not a contortion. Furtive questions made themselves heard: What was the difference between gambling and speculation? What was "the ethical distinction between putting one's money on a wheel of fortune" and "underwriting a policy of insurance" or "buying shares in a corporation"?[68] There was, of course, a conventional answer to such questions: that the spin of the wheel is random and therefore its winnings sinful; that the "fortunes" of business are earned and therefore just.

But such a glib answer requires a tractable audience, which, to the alarm of wealthy beneficiaries of the old complacency, was manifestly shrinking. Conservatives worried with good reason that Americans were coming to regard their experience with good and bad "breaks" as morally meaningless. Searching for some place to lay the blame, some people even blamed language itself: "We have no words in popular use," wrote one moralist in the 1890s (he particularly objected to the word "happen"), with which "to express the occurrence of events that exclude the idea of their being fortuitous."[69] And though textbook statistics show that Americans enjoyed substantial growth in per capita income, reduction in the length of the workweek, and a decline in death and birth rates, there was little solace in these numbers for those who actually lived through the new age of casino capitalism. By 1900, regulation of working conditions was just beginning to be accepted as a legitimate function of government, and the union movement, partly because its collectivist ethic was so deeply opposed to the tradition of American individualism, was still struggling for respectability. If the dogma of self-advancement through diligence had once been resisted in America because of its moral costs, it was now falling into doubt for entirely different reasons. To the millions upon whom fortune failed to smile, the theory of "opportunity" simply no longer worked, and exhortations to diligence from leaders of business, education, and religion sounded more and more hollow, even outrageous.

For the first time in American history, at least since the years immediately following the Revolution, it seemed a real possibility that full-scale social chaos was at hand. Before the Civil War, Horace Greeley had remarked that "as things now are, a man possessing the talent of a Fulton, the strength of Samson, the uprightness of Job, may perish of want in the streets . . . because no one knows his abilities or chooses to employ him."[70] By the end of the century, Greeley's man of inefficacious virtue had become the norm. The nation was failing to maintain the minimum condition required for protecting the social compact: *some* sense of causal relation between behavior and status within the shrinking circle circumscribed by chance. This was to happen again at the start of the Great Depression. For some people, the world remained a great coded utterance of God, but for most Americans the idea of an overseeing deity was by now a quaint legend, and "the gambling complex—seeing life in terms of the 'lucky break,' " was everywhere taking its place.[71] A Harvard economist, writing in a theological journal in 1908, put it this way:

> It is an evil to be cold and hungry, to have a tree fall upon one, to be
> devoured by a wild beast or wasted by microbes. But to evils of this

kind, unless they are in some way the fault of other men, we never ascribe any moral significance whatever.[72]

The United States had long been a country where every man lived for himself, but now it was a nation where every man hoped that it would be he—rather than his equally importunate neighbor—to whom chance dealt the better hand. In such a country, to pray for grace instead of to wish for luck was faintly embarrassing, like murmuring a rosary in a Protestant crowd. The concept of sin was thus weakened to the point of irrelevancy. "We live in an age," wrote one commentator in the 1880s, "which is rapidly losing the consciousness of sin."[73] How could it have been otherwise? Sin, after all, means transgression against God. But God had been replaced by fortune, and fortune makes no moral judgments. American culture had arrived at a place very close to our own, where virtually no one disputed the view that "the storm and the earthquake have no mind."[74] In what amounted to a new kind of paganism, the concept of evil devolved into bad luck, and "good luck" became the American benediction.

"Rankings in Murder," from Ernest A. Hooton, Crime and the Man
(HARVARD UNIVERSITY PRESS, 1938) (COLUMBIA UNIVERSITY LIBRARY)

FIVE

The Age of Blame

Ever since the idea of sin was first introduced into the Western mind in a story of flight and pursuit, it has made itself felt in the moment of capture:

> And the Lord God called unto Adam, and said unto him, Where *art* thou?
>
> And he said, I heard thy voice in the garden, and I was afraid, because I *was* naked, and I hid myself.
>
> And he said, Who told thee that thou *wast* naked? Hast thou eaten of the tree, whereof I commanded thee that thou shouldest not eat?
>
> And the man said, The woman whom thou gavest *to be* with me, she gave me of the tree, and I did eat.
>
> And the Lord God said unto the woman, What *is* this *that* thou hast done? And the woman said, The serpent beguiled me, and I did eat.[1]

Like all siblings and spouses, these first sinners have a reflex to accuse one another; apprehended, they immediately give in to this impulse to blame. When Milton rewrote the story of Adam and Eve in the seventeenth century, he spun it out to the same nonconclusion, with a man and woman caught in a vicious circle of mutual reproach:

> *Thus they in mutual accusation spent*
> *The fruitless hours, but neither self-condemning,*
> *And of their vain contest appear'd no end.*

In both the scriptural and Miltonic versions of this story, our primal parents run from God with all the dignity of roaches fleeing the kitchen when the light switch is thrown. They scramble to disown responsibility—"she did it," "he did it," "the snake did it"—and behave like flustered children caught in a forbidden act. (In the Jewish literary tradition there is a direct line from these quarreling children in Genesis to Portnoy sinning in the bathroom while his mother pounds on the door.) But if this story is to have any force, whether in its version as gospel or as farce, there *must* be at the center of it a discoverer who cannot be eluded.

By the late nineteenth century, this discoverer was gone. And so, with what Nietzsche called "the irreversible decrease in faith in the Christian God," there came a "considerable decrease in human consciousness of sin."[2] Nietzsche's account of the moral history of man anticipates the one developed by Freud, who believed that the "renunciation of instinct owing to fear of aggression by the *external* authority" (God or parent or lawgiver) is a primitive stage in the development of the moral sense, and that it is only with the "erection of an *internal* authority" that one can speak intelligibly of the consciousness of sin. But Freud himself acknowledged in 1930 that "present-day society has to reckon in general" with "people [who] habitually allow themselves to do any bad thing which promises them enjoyment, so long as they are sure that the authority will not know anything about it or cannot blame them for it." Such people, he thought, "are afraid only of being found out."[3] Even Freud, skeptical as he was of the value of religion, and committed as he was to the idea that the human mind regulates itself from within, realized that with the disappearance of God the idea of sin had become unsustainable.

In a world without God, the story of the fall becomes a fable—the last full-scale retelling in American literature had been Hawthorne's *The Marble Faun* (1860)—and "sin" becomes a word disconnected from its original meaning, which was transgression, violation, trespass. By 1900 it was impossible to reattach the word "sin" to its original sense, because the target of the violation—God—was gone. Though it was still heard in the churches, it had become the sort of word Emerson had in mind when he spoke of "a paper currency [being] employed, when there is no bullion in the vaults."[4]

[1]

There is a scene in Stephen Crane's novel *The Red Badge of Courage* (1895) that conveys with precision this evacuation of meaning from the old religious vocabulary. A terrified Civil War soldier who has just deserted his unit runs through the woods in flight from the blood and guns of a raging battle, until he reaches a place "where the high, arching boughs made a chapel" suffused with "a religious half light." This place has the look of a sanctuary promising succor and relief, a place where Emerson might take us to be refreshed by "the currents of universal being," and to experience ourselves as "part or parcel of God." According to literary convention, in such a place a guilty fugitive can learn the cost of his inconstancy. We expect him to be judged. For most of Western literary history, this sort of expectation would have been fulfilled in one way or another.

But Crane's soldier finds no such thing. He finds, instead, that he is "being stared at" by

a dead man, who was seated with his back against a columnlike tree. The corpse was dressed in a uniform that once had been blue, but was now faded to a melancholy shade of green. The eyes . . . had changed to the dull hue to be seen on the side of a dead fish. The mouth was open. Its red had changed to an appalling yellow. Over the gray skin of the face ran little ants. One was trundling some sort of a bundle along the upper lip.[5]

The face of this dead man is not the holy remnant of a being recently vacated by an immortal soul. It is an alpine challenge to the ants.

Crane's putrefying corpse is a sign of the driving fear of modern life: the fear that the world is not invested with meaning but is a place of speechless, pointless death. By the time Crane was writing, death was no longer conceived by many people as a journey toward a "sacred encounter"—because there was no ground left for believing there was anything on the other side. There was nothing merited or glorious or commanding about death, which had once been understood as a punishment proportionate to the sin that had brought it into the world in the first place. It had become a meaningless terminus to a meaningless life.

The endemic fear of death may be felt in the physical arrangements of the Victorian household, in its clutter of memorial knickknacks, ornamented furniture, opaque drapes, gaggles of family photographs, etched replicas of religious paintings—all of which bespeak a dread of blankness. This pack-rat style gave pride of place to mantelpiece images of death in gilt-edged frames, as if the real thing could be warded off by placing totemic images in its path. These images were like a hex that worked together with embossed leather Bibles and etiquette books, in which chapters on deportment at funerals and on the rules of proper mourning had become standard. They showed a fear of open spaces, and reassured their owners that someone, when the dread time comes, would place *their* picture on the bureau.

And so there arose an imperative to collect and to hoard. This impulse took hold of the middle classes as well as of the idle rich (this was the first great age of the American collector—Frick, Morgan, Barnes), whose urge to gather and curate had the quality, as Walter Benjamin put it in a well-known essay about the collector's impulse, of "a dam against the spring tide of memories." It was a drive to command the past, to place it on "the pedestal, [in] the frame, [on] the base, [behind] the lock of [one's] property" as a way of stopping it from being sucked into the vacuum of death. In most artistic and literary renderings, death had formerly been heroic; history paintings had typically featured a swooning hero surrounded by adoring followers, his face set in the traditional "expression of beatific ecstasy." In the sentimental fictions that Crane called "pink valentines," death would customarily appear as a gentle attendant at the patient's bedside, where it arrives as a fluttering last breath drawn amidst the loving family circle.[6]

But both these traditions were winding down. Death moved to squalid quarters, where it killed without an audience. Hurstwood in *Sister Carrie* dies alone in a "wooden, dusty" flophouse room, which he turns into a gas chamber by sealing the door with his overcoat before opening the gas jet. Lily Bart, in Edith Wharton's *The House of Mirth* (1905), drugs herself in a boardinghouse, savoring the narcotic as a "bath of oblivion."[7] Death was inglorious, tawdry; it did its work behind closed doors along with the other indecent bodily functions.

This concealing of the work of death was new. In the antebellum years when religion still had a certain vitality, the American cemetery had been a suburban salon for the dead, a "dormitory"[8] (literally "sleeping place") in which body and soul could sleep cozily until their resurrection into a new gracious home called heaven. Now the cemetery became a depository to which corpses were removed from view. Relatively recent bestsellers like Elizabeth Stuart Phelps's *The Gates Ajar* (1868) (who was hailed as "America's foremost authority on the home life of heaven") had represented the great beyond as a mansion with a well-stocked pantry, where the supply of gingersnaps in the cookie jar is perpetually replenished.[9] But death, once conceived as an extended visit to a rest home, now became an abyss. No victuals needed here. A minister could no

longer stand before a fresh grave and dish out his conventional line—
"What is the grave to us, but a thin barrier dividing time from eternity
and earth from heaven?"[10]—and expect pious nods.

Naturally enough, people looked for ways to fend off the fear that the
grave was nothing more than a pit of dirt and worms. The ancient metaphors with which human beings had always decorated death ("shuffling
off the mortal coil," "crossing the great divide") were periphrastic. Here
is a little condolence letter, written in the last year of the Civil War by
a soldier to his widowed brother. Strikingly free of the old pieties, it
sounds the new note:

> I feel very sorry for the great loss you have had which can sertainly
> never be replaced in this world. But I hop[e] its tri[a]ls will be of good
> service not only to you but to us all.[11]

This is the kind of condolence letter we write today. Its highest achievement is tact, and the fewer the metaphoric evasions—"passed on,"
"passed away"—the better. It has a modern brevity and frankness, as if
the comforter knows that anything grand or pious will sound impossibly
fake, and so it subsides into a meager gesture of concern.

The news from the battlefield that men were nothing but disposable
sacks of bone and blood had been a presentiment of what science now
confirmed for everyone: that, as Phelps put it in the 1880s, "we are not
men, but protoplasm . . . not spirits, but chemical combinations."[12]
Cursed with this knowledge, the living could no longer respectably say
that the dead will enjoy heavenly rest; all one could offer was a hollow
commendation of death as part of the survivor's education. "The language of service," as one historian puts it, "was shouldering aside the
language of sanctification."[13]

Yet in a country where some degree of "belief in the spirits [remained]
. . . nearly universal," the old pretty metaphors were not easily relinquished. Americans continued to be "superstitious with regard to
ghosts,"[14] and for such a people, the large-minded Kantian abstraction
(here reformulated by the philosopher Josiah Royce in 1899) that it is
"my *moral* existence . . . [that] extends . . . without limit, through the
whole range of the future temporal order," was pretty pallid stuff. It had
the ring of a preacher's platitude. One's moral choices may confirm one's
freedom and reverberate throughout all time, but believing it does little
to quell the fear of personal extinction. William James, Royce's colleague

at Harvard, expressed respect for his friend's efforts to expound the consoling notion of a "Soul of the world" through which each individual participates in a kind of immortality; but James saw that this did not much prepare us for the dread moment when the "buzz of life ceases . . . as a piano-string stops sounding when the damper falls upon it."[15]

The first hints of a new way of dealing with death can be noticed already during the Civil War, when, as was perfectly customary, the First Lady sought the services of a medium after the death of her firstborn child, and President Lincoln himself read at his son's memorial service from Shakespeare's *King John*—"I shall see my boy again."[16] The doctrine that held that the souls of the dead can communicate through a "medium" with the living came to be known as spiritualism, a successor to the "science" of mesmerism, which had flourished earlier in the century—a movement named for an Austrian physician, Anton Mesmer, who believed that stars emanate a vital fluid that can be channeled into concentrations with therapeutic value. The mesmerist would strap his patient to a tub filled with water and iron filings—a kind of magnet that was supposed to draw the life force down from the heavens and transmit it to the impaired body of the sufferer. It was not too far from these procedures to the hope that the mesmerist could actually bring the dead back to life. Spiritualism, like this precursor, was also an expression of belief that the gulf between earth and heaven could be crossed.

As a therapy for dealing with existential dread, spiritualism had a certain plausibility even for people who prided themselves on their up-to-dateness and rationality. It claimed the status of science, and peaked in the late years of the century when a great many people were infatuated with electricity. For the first time in history, the images and voices of the dead could now be preserved and reproduced on film and phonographic cylinders. New forms of invisible energy (X rays; isotopes) were continually being reported, and every year some new invention stretched the boundaries of the possible. Since it was now known that at certain measurable frequencies sound ceases to be audible to the human ear and light visible to the eye, it seemed possible even to some scientists that there might be a "vast Zone" (one writer confidently assigned it to the frequency between "38,000 and 396 trillion waves per second") that was truly the "sphere of souls, in which darkness, silence and death are unknown."[17] Man seemed on the verge of discovering a *scientific* basis for believing that the invisible world of the theological imagination might, after all, exist—if only he could find the right instruments for detecting it.

Spiritualists were sure they had found them. Their "central belief . . . [was] an existence beyond the grave," and, advertising their skills through street-corner barkers and pulp magazines, they spoke to a people cut off from "dreams [and] revery"—a people collectively experiencing something like what happens to the individual who is denied what we would now call REM sleep. Some spiritualist mediums attained immense prestige; usually women, they were regarded as persons whose "sense organs have been developed or quickened to that degree of vibratory activity that he or she is able under proper conditions to receive and give out communications from the so-called dead."[18]

Such claims that "the real is invisible" may sound mad or fraudulent to us, but spiritualists in turn-of-the-century America were not just schemers and hawkers of a worthless nostrum. They were deliverers of dreams. They were shouters in the canyon who were somehow able to convince others that the voice heard in reply was more than an echo. And their faith had enormous appeal: a few strange rappings could bring a whole town out into the night, as word spread that the spirits of the local "dead" were trying to cross the divide between the "realms of life visible and invisible."[19]

This craving for contact between the living and the dead was more encouraged than embarrassed by the rising prestige of science and, as such, was by no means a uniquely American phenomenon. Its devotees in Britain included luminaries like Arthur Conan Doyle and Alfred Lord Tennyson. By the 1890s a full-scale renaissance of ghost stories was under way on both sides of the Atlantic; most famous among the American examples was James's *The Turn of the Screw* (1898), but Howells, in such books as *Questionable Shapes* (1903) and *Between the Dark and the Daylight* (1907), made his own contributions, as did, later, Edith Wharton, in *Men and Ghosts* (1914). Even such an authority as William James, while conceding that "it would be . . . strange" if " 'Spiritualism' . . . [is] to be the chosen instrument for an era of faith," nevertheless concluded, "I see no other agency that can do the work."[20]

Many who embraced spiritualism did so because the alternative—that the world was a gigantic tomb from which no one emerged—was literally unspeakable. Its fundamental appeal was that it offered support to anyone still trying to preserve some belief in "the immortality of the soul;

the certainty of a future state corresponding to our deserts and conduct in this life; [and] God's government of the world through the instrumentality of good and evil spirits." Howells, for instance, looked back to his childhood and recalled that he could never bear to walk past a yard where tombstones were cut and polished, or listen to ghost stories with his friends at night, or look, without terror, at a painting of Death.[21] Newspapers were filled with reports of gentlemen losing their practiced reserve when they encounter a dead family member—a son, or wife, or parent —restored to all apparent vividness of life. One Brooklyn businessman in 1881 is thrilled, a New York newspaper reported, to see his dead son sitting in his parlor in the middle of the day—and remembers how, during the boy's final illness, he frequently "exclaimed 'Beautiful' and said that he had had a vision," now confirmed, of eternal life as "an open sea containing many beautiful objects indescribably bright."[22] A few months later, the same paper gave space to a letter from a reader distressed by the doubts of both skeptics and Christians:

> Why . . . throw ridicule on all so-called spirit manifestations? Why try to rob fathers and mothers of the comforting belief that they have once more seen the dear one! After death the spirit goes somewhere, does it not![23]

If this kind of howl had remained the private wail of individuals who only occasionally let it out into public expression, its significance for the history of our culture would be difficult, and possibly pointless, to measure. But, in fact, it became much more. It became a public pathology, a fear generalized into an expectation of doom not only for the self but for all

> mankind . . . [which was] in a position similar to that of a set of people living on a frozen lake, surrounded by cliffs over which there is no escape, yet knowing that little by little the ice is melting, and the inevitable day drawing near when the last film of it will disappear, and to be drowned ignominiously will be the human creature's portion.[24]

This sort of apocalyptic vision—common at the ends of centuries—had a long history, of course. But in its scriptural form, chiefly in the Book of Revelation, it had always carried with it the promise that the dead at judgment day would be gathered to God's bosom.

Now, however, God had become a bodiless abstraction: "I spell my God with two *o*'s," said one respectable "believer" as early as the 1870s, and, for emphasis, he added that he spelled his "devil without a *d*."[25] Despite the rash of claims from people who said they were in contact with the "dead," for most educated Americans the spirit world was an object less of knowledge than of desire. At the same time, the knowable world of material reality disclosed ever more compelling evidence that it was undergoing continuous breakdown and dissolution.

This anxiety amounted to the most pervasive pathology of modern life: the fear of annihilation. Once again, William James cut to the heart of the matter:

> The purely naturalistic look at life, however enthusiastically it may begin, is sure to end in sadness . . . the lustre of the present hour is always borrowed from the background of possibilities it goes with. Let our common experiences be enveloped in an eternal moral order; let our suffering have an immortal significance; let Heaven smile upon the earth, and deities pay their visits; let faith and hope be the atmosphere which man breathes in;—and his days pass by with zest; they stir with prospects, they thrill with remoter values. Place round them on the contrary the curdling cold and gloom and absence of all permanent meaning which for pure naturalism and the popular-science evolutionism of our time are all that is visible ultimately, and the thrill stops short, or turns rather to an anxious trembling.[26]

With this announcement of a "curdling cold" world, we have truly arrived at the twentieth century.

[2]

American culture, by 1900, was a culture in panic. Panic is an emotional state in which what has once been background noise becomes unbearably invasive. We close our eyes and try to shut out the ruckus, and when these measures fail, the panic, unstinted, grows. When, as happens from time to time, this sensation spreads throughout an entire culture, the quacks come out with their potions and nostrums. They promise that if only the people will buy them, there will be relief. And the best-selling remedies are always those that identify the source of the affliction as being *external*. This is what happened now in the United States. It was as if the whole culture paused to take a breath in the midst of reciting its belief in its own permanence, and noticed a figure strolling toward it on a course that will leave it crushed under his boot:

> I tremble with horror when I think of what is crawling toward us, with noiseless steps: couchant, silent, treacherous, pardlike; scarce rustling the dry leaves as it moves, and yet with bloodshot, glaring eyes and tense-drawn limbs of steel, ready for the fatal spring. When comes it? To-night? To-morrow? A week hence? Who can say?[27]

Part of the horror is the invader's obscurity. No one could be certain what it was, or when it would come; its mystery and elusiveness made the waiting victim feel cornered and stalked. And so, on a scale never before approached in American history, though there had been surges of xenophobia in the 1790s and 1850s and it had always been present in chronic form, people now tried to blunt the panic by identifying the danger, by giving it a face and a name. America had entered upon its great age of scapegoating.

To put the matter into a psychoanalytic vocabulary, Americans converted "the death fear of the ego" into aggression. The times were marked by judicial rulings and new laws that restricted the rights of blacks and immigrants; by legal travesties like the Haymarket case, in which several immigrant German anarchists were executed for a bombing to which they had no provable relation; by police actions like the Palmer raids, in which government violated civil liberties in order to move against what Attorney General A. Mitchell Palmer called "aliens of . . . misshapen cast of mind and indecencies of character." One historian has summed up the legacy of the Civil War this way: "After the great bloodletting, which established the illegality of chattel slavery, [white Americans] engaged in a general rejection of the aliens who had caused the disastrous struggle." Americans were making a full-scale commitment to the project of finding a " 'representative' or 'vessel' of certain unwanted evils, the sacrificial animal upon whose back the burden of these evils [could be] ritualistically loaded."[28]

The most convenient sacrificial beast was the Negro. Lynchings increased in the South, as vigilantes struck back at those who, according to Thomas Dixon's 1905 novel *The Clansman* (upon which D. W. Griffith's famous film *Birth of a Nation* was based), had forced "delicate and cul-

tured [white] women [to live] on cowpeas, corn bread and molasses—
and of such quality they would not have fed it to a slave . . . [while]
droves of brutal negroes roam at large, stealing, murdering, and threatening blacker crimes." Once "chattel to be bought and sold," the Negro
was now widely regarded as a "beast to be feared and guarded." Mark
Twain, in a 1901 essay entitled "The United States of Lyncherdom,"
published a blistering protest against the new mood. But the hatred not
only persisted; it spread North. In 1917 the worst race riot in American
history broke out in a small Illinois town to which thousands of black
workers had been lured by the industrial company that ran it in an effort
to break the power of the union that was trying to improve the workers' lot. A few years earlier, the leading black intellectual of his time,
W. E. B. Du Bois, while preparing a defense of a Georgia black man
accused of raping a white woman, discovered that the man had already
been lynched and his knuckles put on display in a grocery store just down
the street.[29]

This kind of compensatory hatred went beyond race retribution. The
idea of evil had become generally synonymous with one sort of alien or
another. It was the worst of times to be deemed "un-American"—and
not just for blacks. In the West, as loans were called in and foreclosures
mounted during the periodic economic contractions, there arose a rhetoric
of resentment against Eastern urbanites for whom Westerners furnished
food and on whom they depended for credit. "Scum of creation" became
a standard populist epithet for city dwellers who ate up the nation's store
and gave nothing in return. The hives in which such people lived (New
York, it was said by the populist writer William Harvey, was an "un-
American city") were "monstrous, malignant growths on the body politic." Cities were seen as basins of sin filled with a new race of "Goths
and Vandals" attracted to America by manufacturing interests (decried
from the heartland as Jews) who, in turn, "didn't care a curse how much
harm to our future" was entailed in their greed for cheap labor.[30]

Why the ferocity? And why at this time? The shadow of racism tends
to deepen in times of social stress, and American life had of course always
been darkened by bigotry and race hatred. Some of the most shocking
pages in our literature are to be found long before this age of retrenchment. The diaries of certain eighteenth-century gentlemen report, at the
height of the Enlightenment, that whipping the favorite slave of one's
wife can be a splendid way of reproaching her during a domestic quarrel:
"My wife caused Prue to be whipped violently notwithstanding I desired

not, which provoked me to have Anaka whipped likewise who had deserved it much more." The most frightening sentence in a long horror tale of shipwreck and cannibalism written by Poe in the 1830s, when fear of slave rebellion ran high, comes when the narrator realizes that he and his companion are "the only living *white* men upon the island." And in the 1840s, when Melville remarked that "if our evil passions must find vent, it is far better to expend them on strangers and aliens, than in the bosom of the community in which we dwell," he knew full well that one of the functions of black people had always been to be this accusable stranger whose very existence protected whites from acknowledging the savagery in themselves.[31]

These literary moments were and are windows through which we may catch a glimpse of the lives of those deemed strangers in our putatively democratic culture—people who wait for their violent end, like Jews huddled in the shtetl for the next pogrom. Now it came. It had always been bad in America to be conspicuously different, especially to be black. But since emancipation and reconstruction, it had gotten much worse. The relatively new doctrine of racism *as an ideology*, as a developed theory of racial hierarchy, had all the appeal of a hot new fashion. Even the slaveholding founders of the Republic had been agnostic on the question of whether blacks were actually mentally inferior to whites; it was their doubt on this question that had made slavery a moral embarrassment.[32] Now the doctrine became dogma.

The fad of race hatred caught on in the salons as well as in the streets. Infecting all classes, it was, for the unlettered, a blood-fury; for the bookish, it furnished a universally explanatory category for organizing man's knowledge about himself. To be black, or Asian, or any new arrival in the United States of the last quarter of the nineteenth century, was to be, first and foremost, an exploitable and expendable resource. To be white, especially if you were a "steak-and-potato-eating American worker," meant to "be in 'deadly competition with those who live on a bowl of rice and a rat a day,' " as one Midwestern senator put it in the 1890s.[33] Among dockworkers in Eastern port cities, the word "Slav" (used as a generic term for an array of European immigrants) became a term of contempt for men willing to work long hours for small pay. In the iron industry, blacks were excluded from such relatively well-paid tasks as "puddling" and "rolling," and relegated to shoveling, stacking, and other sorts of gang labor. Railroad workers in the South were almost exclusively black; in the West, where menial workers tended often to be Japanese or Scandinavian, they were commonly supervised by armed bosses who "locked up their belongings" at night "and patrolled the sites, in order to assure that transportation and store debts were repaid."[34]

While laboring men reviled the shiftless niggers and foreign scabs who threatened their jobs, their scholarly counterparts were proposing a concept that a Columbia professor, George Edward Woodberry, writing in 1903, called "Race Power"—in order to explain why some peoples seemed to produce artistic works of lasting value while others did not. This was an academic version (*The Bell Curve* of its day) of the "Darwinism" that had already become a conventional justification for the nation's expansion beyond its continental boundaries to Cuba, Hawaii, and the Philippines, places inhabited by people whom President William Howard Taft called our "little brown brothers." Rudyard Kipling's dictum, by which he had defended England's reign over India, that "Asia will never attend Sunday school, or learn to vote, save with swords for tickets," was now commonly echoed by American voices. "It is inherently as admissible to subjugate the Philippines with the sword," wrote one contributor to the *International Journal of Ethics* in 1900, "as it is to subjugate France by industrial superiority."[35]

To certain indignant historians in our own day, this outburst of national arrogance is best understood as an organized event directed by businessmen whose interests were served by foreign conquests, or as a plot by capitalists who feared the specter of a multiracial union movement. These interpretations have much force. But the turn toward race as an ultimately satisfying category cannot be sufficiently explained as a superstructure of belief built atop a foundation of material interests. It was deeper than that. It was a lunge for something graspable, for some clear scheme of value, in a world that had become spiritually incomprehensible.

One reason that Americans took comfort in enumerating and naming enemies is that they were learning that hatred can be a way of striking back at the "King of Terrors,"[36] death. Losing their place in the cosmos, they were at the same time losing their country, as Thomas Bailey Aldrich wrote in 1895, to

Men from the Volga and the Tartar steppes,
Featureless figures of the Hoang-Ho,
Malayan, Scythian, Teuton, Kelt, and Slav,

> *Flying the Old World's poverty and scorn;*
> *These bringing with them unknown gods and rites,*
> *Those, tiger passions, here to stretch their claws.*[37]

Unlike death, these enemies could be resisted, perhaps even defeated. They set off an answerable alarm about the impending doom of the American "race"—a term that had previously been used interchangeably with the word "nation" ("God has predestinated . . . great things from our race," one spokesman for Manifest Destiny had proclaimed in 1850, and "the rest of the nations must soon be in our rear"[38]). But now "race" implied blood kinship more than shared membership in a favored community. Race became a matter of color and blood, not of citizenship; and the white race had to be defended at all costs.

In 1891, a sociologist named Edward Ross coined the term "race suicide" to describe the plight of the besieged Anglo-Saxons, whose birth rate was falling (because of late marriages, a culture of sexual self-control, and the beginnings of modern contraception) below those of the sweaty Negroes and aliens who engaged, it seemed, in incessant copulation. For some, the color of the peril was chiefly yellow. Infamous for their fecundity, Asians were, according to the Democratic Party platform of 1884, "unfitted by habits, training, [or] religion . . . for the citizenship which our laws confer." (Forty years later, the conventional image of the Chinese male was the sinister Fu Manchu, who first appeared as a popular stereotype in 1917.) Others were alarmed by the concupiscence of the Jews: "there is no swarming," wrote Henry James in 1903, "like that of Israel." A year later, Theodore Roosevelt summed up the varieties of xenophobic resentment with an article entitled "True Americanism," in which he borrowed Ross's phrase about the coming suicide, and declared it the duty of everyone of "native American descent" to bring forth at least four children in order to forestall the extinction of the race. All who failed in this duty, he said flatly, were "criminals."[39] The terms had been set for a procreation contest—and the stakes were thought to be immense.

[3]

This explosion of racial fear introduced a new way of thinking about evil. Thrown out along with other superannuated ideas like providence and destiny and God himself, the old morally comprehensible devil, who had once embodied the concepts of sin and pride and the fall (ideas now "popularly ignored," Melville wrote in *Billy Budd* just before his death in 1891), was now truly a relic. He had been discarded because he no longer correlated with experience. Yet now, as the Old World spewed forth its human detritus into America's cities, the question of whence evil—though no longer susceptible to a theological answer—took on new life as a public problem.

An immediately satisfying answer was that the face of evil was *foreign*, for the foreign devil was everywhere. Foreigners were lazy, greedy, shiftless, sneaky; they were poisoning the country. Some sections of New York, according to one advocate of urban reform who personified sin as if he were writing medieval allegory, contained houses "where Murder has stained every floor . . . and Vice skulks or riots from one year's end to the other."[40] "Satan's Circus" was the popular name for the increasingly Italian area of lower Sixth Avenue;[41] and the very idea of the criminal became interchangeable with the image of the "bewhiskered, ranting, howling, mentally warped, law-defying"[42] immigrants—whose males tended to be represented as priapic and whose females were thought to be in continual heat.

This civic culture was a preview of our own—filled with foreboding that its once vernal world was being despoiled by alien invaders. "What has become of the American?" asked a supporter of the Ku Klux Klan in 1928. "Is he vanishing from the earth? America today is not the America of twenty-five years ago, but stands mongrelized, alienized, and demoralized in the eyes of her own citizens."[43] Then as now, Americans seemed to have no genuine moral language for describing what was happening to them. And then as now, they resorted to the formula of blame. The links between this time and our own are manifold and direct: there also arose, on the principle that death itself could be somehow sweated out of the body, the first national fitness craze, a kind of spiritual calisthenics that focused on the bullish figure of Teddy Roosevelt. A theme was inaugurated that has persisted in American life through Vic Tanny and the cult of "vigor" in the Kennedy years, to Jack LaLanne and the Nautilus gym culture of our own day. Such popular how-to books as *Bodybuilding; or Man in the Making* (1905) and *The Construction and Reconstruction of the Human Body* (1907) were part of a flood of publications that purported to explain how one could restore spiritual health and confidence through enhancement of the body. In 1899, the first widely celebrated bodybuilder in American history, an entrepreneurial crackpot named Bernarr Macfadden, founded a magazine called *Physical Culture*, which within twenty years reached a circulation of more than 150,000, and was emblazoned with a motto that touched the national nerve: "WEAKNESS IS A CRIME. DON'T BE A CRIMINAL."[44]

The logic was dubious but the imperative was clear. In order to protect the strong, the criminally weak had to be kept at a distance. Accordingly, the leading institutions of "civilized" life set about establishing various kinds of quarantines. In 1896 the Supreme Court ruled in *Plessy* v. *Ferguson* that racial segregation was not only constitutional but necessary to keep inferior peoples from pressing against the privileges of their superiors. Encouraged by such rulings, white Southerners ensured that "the opening years of the twentieth century saw the nearly total disfranchisement of black voters";[45] while in the North, Ivy Leaguers sang a bar song that alarmed the authorities of one university sufficiently to rouse them, by the 1920s, to create a Jewish quota:

> *Oh, Harvard's run by millionaires,*
> *And Yale is run by booze,*
> *Cornell is run by farmers' sons,*
> *Columbia's run by Jews.*[46]

Also in these years, there arose, among "true Americans" of college age, the ritual of football as a male solidarity rite, a kind of weekly olympiad in which the brawn of the racially pure would prevail.[47] In the same year as *Plessy* v. *Ferguson*, when the newspapers covered a game between Harvard and the Carlisle Indian school, what came through the headlines was a miniature race war. After the Crimson's last-quarter rush, the sore Indian losers were reported to have grumbled that "they have stolen a continent from us, a wide, wide continent, which was ours, and lately they have stolen various touchdowns that were also ours."[48]

As the white man mocked his opponents for their weakness and their whining, he himself—in war as in sport—affected a certain swagger. But he was whistling in the dark. In this age of the Rough Rider and the Boy Scout, all his claims to racial superiority were half-baked theories and semi-truths, and somewhere people knew it. The ideology of race was riddled with contradictions. In comparison with hale Americans, immigrants and Negroes and Indians were supposed to be puny and contemptible—yet they were also virile and fecund. They constituted an immense threat—yet they were underdeveloped. They were sexual supermen—yet they were bent-backed simperers. They talked in grunts—"ugh" and "how" and "heap"—yet they constituted a threat. They were slothful and cowardly—yet the nation to which they swarmed, and in which they now propagated like rodents, was the greatest nation on earth precisely because it had been built up by "energetic, restless, and courageous men from all parts of Europe [who] have emigrated during the last ten or twelve generations." Yesterday's immigrants were pioneers—yet today's immigrants were lower-order organisms, leeches, suckers, germs.

Such contradictions could be explained "scientifically," of course. If Negroes and Indians performed better than whites on the new sensory perception tests, it was because whites were "more deliberate and reflective." And if Negro children scored higher than whites on memory tests, it was because they had less on their minds that would interfere with the ability to recall the past.[49] Here is one expert on the vexed issue of rehabilitation, explaining why most criminals are beyond redemption:

Take the boy begotten and reared in the slums of the city . . . of ignorant, vicious parentage . . . tell him how a law is made and what for, and read it to him, and . . . he would be like the Indian who was being taught to read in the New Testament in his own language and translate it into English, and was given the parable of the prodigal son and it was explained to him in its allegorical sense. This was his translation: "Old man—heap money—two boys. One boy no wait. Take heap money—go away. Have big drunk—money all gone—go home. Old man glad—make music—eat heap."

"Not the slightest perception," the author concludes, "of the lesson sought to be conveyed by the parable."[50]

In other words, the lesser races were congenital idiots—both intellectually and morally. And suddenly the country was full of authorities on how to deal with them. Here is one such expert—this time a dentistry professor holding forth on the analogies between primitive biological entities and these new, outlandish Americans:

The parasitic "guest" dependent on its "host" for lodging alone, or it may be for both board and lodging, is in a fair way to become degraded in structure, and, as a rule, exhibits marked degradation, where the association has persisted sufficiently long. Parasitism and servile dependence act very much in structural lower life as analogous instances of mental dependence on others act on man.[51]

This writer, perhaps thinking of the bacterial sludge he scraped every day from his patients' teeth, regarded certain human beings as fungi hiding in the damp crannies of the body politic. In its time, this sort of reasoning was conventional and unsurprising. And it led to a plain conclusion: such vermin must be gotten rid of—exterminated, if necessary —until the infested body has been returned to purity and health. It would not be long before a word in another language came into use as a description of what would be left after the requisite cleaning. It was a German word, *rein*—meaning purified—as in, for example, *Judenrein*.

[4]

And so, out of the endemic fear of death (individual, racial, universal), a new *biological* theory of evil had emerged. It associated moral evil with feebleness of body and mind and, implicitly, with foreigners. It suggested that evil revealed itself physiognomically—in "prominent ears . . . projecting cheek-bones . . . large lower jaws . . . deeply placed eyes, [a] shifty, animal-like gaze."[52] Picking up where the old "science" of phrenology (the art of reading character in the bumps and contours of the skull) had left off, it defined a new class of inferior human beings who could be classified according to head shape and brow size and facial expression. And it generated a new vocabulary—words like "moron" (invented in the early 1900s to designate adults who scored at the level of children in intelligence tests) and "eugenics" (coined in England in the 1880s from the Greek for "wellborn" to designate the idea that mankind could be improved through artificially selected breeding).

The most important premise of this new "science" of eugenics was that deficiencies of character and mind were inherited. Still innocent of the biochemical basis of genetic transmission, "geneticists" of the time were really statisticians eager to demonstrate that patterns of inferiority are passed down through the generations in certain families and races. From this premise it was a short step to the conclusion that one could save the healthy from contamination by the sick by preventing the sick from reproducing—or, as certain inventive men in another country eventually decided, by doing away with them altogether. In 1887 the superintendent of a Cincinnati sanitarium made the first public suggestion in the United States that some criminals should be sterilized. Soon eugenics bills were being introduced in state legislatures; in 1907 a statute authorizing sterilization of "confirmed criminals, idiots, imbeciles, and rapists" was enacted in Indiana; by 1915 thirteen states had similar laws on the books; by 1930 the number had risen to thirty.[53]

In 1927, just after immigration had peaked and begun to fall off under new exclusion laws and quotas that limited the influx of Asians and Jews, the biological theory of evil received its most prestigious endorsement. Writing the majority opinion for the Supreme Court, Justice Oliver Wendell Holmes, Jr., upheld the constitutionality of a Virginia law that permitted involuntary sterilization of "feebleminded" persons held in state institutions. "Experience," Holmes wrote, "has shown that heredity plays an important part in the transmission of insanity, imbecility, etc."; and so "it is better for all the world, if instead of waiting to execute degenerate offspring for crime, or let[ting] them starve for their imbecility, society can prevent those who are manifestly unfit from continuing their kind."[54]

Quite apart from the question of how anyone can know, as Holmes blithely assumed, that sterilization is "not felt to be [a sacrifice] by those concerned," the intellectual bankruptcy of the eugenics movement makes it seem grotesque in retrospect. The whole grisly business seems but one step removed from the systematic genocide that, we now know, was about to break out in Europe. Yet in Holmes's time—not, after all, so long ago—the idea of an inheritable "linkage between weak minds and weak morals"[55] was not only credible but respectable, even self-evident, not just in America but throughout the developed West.

Many eugenicists, moreover, thought of themselves as progressives. Adherents to the cause included such well-known liberals as Charles W. Eliot, president of Harvard, as well as the English socialists Beatrice and Sidney Webb and, later, Harold Laski. The marriage of liberalism and eugenics had been encouraged by the collapse of the Lamarckian theory of "acquired character," which had explained the evolution of species as a result of the efforts of individuals to cope with their environment. As long as Lamarckian theory ruled (the best-known illustration of this theory had been the giraffe's neck—which became long and flexible, according to Lamarck, because of the animal's repeated efforts to reach higher and higher vegetation), it had been possible to construe social progress as analogous to evolution. If one generation of slum children acquired good habits, they would be passed on to the next.

By the early twentieth century, however, the theory of "acquired character" had been discredited. The classic refutation was an experiment in which the tails of mice were severed over many generations; when no change could be detected in the tails of the offspring, scientists were forced to conclude that "so long as the hereditary material was unaffected, no bodily or behavioral alterations, no matter how enduring, would be inherited."[56] It was now an irresistible inference that species evolve not through learned skills or imposed effects upon individuals, but through random changes in their genetic structure, coupled with the process of "natural selection" that Darwin had described.

The Darwinian idea of "natural selection" was the decisive idea of the nineteenth century, and as it reverberated into the twentieth it seemed to confirm what experience more and more suggested: that the universe was ungoverned. In the natural world, certain individuals reproduce more successfully than others because they survive in larger numbers to maturity, and because they possess characteristics attractive to prospective mates (this is the related principle of "sexual selection"). Life is a partnership of accident and procreation through which advantageous characteristics are passed on from parents to progeny. Learning, as a Berkeley biologist wrote in 1891, has nothing to do with it:

> If natural selection be indeed the only factor used by nature in organic evolution and therefore available for use by Reason in human evolution, then, alas, for all our . . . schemes of *education*, intellectual and moral.[57]

The only hope left to the reformer who wants "permanent improvement of the human stock" is to find some way to "exercis[e] . . . influence upon the selective process."[58] To do this, one must treat human beings in the same way that farmers improve their livestock or botanists grow hardier crops—i.e., breed them selectively. And one way to introduce this principle of "artificial selection" into human society is to forbid some human beings from breeding at all.

The Darwinian idea behind this movement for purifying the human race was an immensely powerful explanation for the evolving nature of all living things in a world from which God had departed; and it compelled belief with the force of a religion. If it found an especially hospitable reception in the United States, this was partly because the ideas of eugenics and its various counterparts had been present in dormant form since the outset of the culture and needed only to be resuscitated.

The idea of the biological transmission of character, for instance, could be construed as an updated version of the idea of original sin. Augustine himself, despite his commitment to a privative conception of evil, had argued that sin is transmitted from generation to generation through human semen. And when populists of the 1890s railed about degraded people overrunning America's cities, they were unwittingly echoing Thomas Jefferson, who, falling into a quasi-biological vocabulary, had decried the dependence of city dwellers on the "casualties and caprice of customers," and who worried that dependence "begets subservience and venality, [and] suffocates the germ of virtue." The idea of evil as eradicable disease had been active in American culture for a long time, evil as what one Puritan minister called an "impostumed . . . body," a "corrupt matter" that must be cut out from the healthy tissue before "gangrene" sets in.[59]

These themes—rural purity versus urban corruption, the idea of sin as transmittable "uncleanness"—were old in American life. They amounted to a perennial way of apprehending evil as a positive, malignant entity— an attitude that was powerfully active in the American imagination, and still is. But there are times when these metaphors for evil seem to take on a particular virulence. The end of the nineteenth century was such a time. What was new—a novelty of great advantage to those who believed evil to be something alien and diseased—was the "obsession," as the historian Carroll Smith-Rosenberg has called it, "with describing the abnormal, and with defining the legitimate."[60]

[5]

There were, of course, dissenters—Randolph Bourne, for instance, who wrote in 1916, "Let us speak, not of inferior races, but of inferior civilizations," among which he counted any that conform to the "tight and jealous nationalism of the European pattern"; and John Dewey, who applied the word "savage" not to aliens but to all peoples who "have identified their experience with rigid adherence to their past customs." For Dewey, evil was the failure of the imagination to reach beyond itself, the human failure to open oneself to a spirit that both chastises one for confidence in one's own righteousness and promises the enduring comfort of reciprocal love. There is a sense in which all of Dewey's thought was an extended commentary on Emerson's remark that "the only sin is limitation."[61] This understanding of evil as incompleteness found expression in the progressive movement—in its confidence in the insatiable human drive, as Dewey put it, "to arouse energy, to stimulate the means necessary to accomplish the realization of ends" through such means as education and social reform. Such a view of the human imagination as restless within established forms had no room for the idea of a fixed standard by which deviance from the truth could be measured and denounced.

But despite his prestige, Dewey was finally a dissident. American society had taken a decisive turn toward conformity and a spirit of exclusion; it was set on a path that allowed less and less "margin for the deviant." It was becoming a culture in which men and women devoted themselves to the ideal of what one historian, writing about the 1890s, has called "undemonstrative sobriety" and "impeccable inexpressivity." To become a member of this lockstep tribe one had to be native-born and white, to dress in conventional middle-class clothes, and to learn that the first rule of public deportment is that "singularity is to be avoided." Americans were demonstrating the sociological rule that deviance is "an integral part of all healthy societies" inasmuch as it "brings together upright consciences and concentrates them" into a regulating force that may be called "the public temper."[62]

In response to this formidable new force called the "public," serious American writers now undertook to measure the cost to dissidents of living within its range. Whether it was Howells writing about the loneliness of a divorcée in the twilight Puritanism of Boston, or Wharton writing about an adulterous woman shunned in New York society, or Sherwood Anderson writing about the misery of being homosexual in a Midwestern town, all the major American writers turned to the experience of deviants living in a society more and more committed to a conception of evil as departure from a merciless norm. Of course, some transcendent norm operates in any culture at any time; yet the impulse to parade the insolence of the self is also indispensable if the culture is to remain vital. Locked in mutual dependence, the dissenter needs the conformist in order to achieve a bracing sense of independence, and the conformist needs the deviant in order to feel the delicious relief of being *normal*. As a consequence, one measure of any culture's resiliency is the extent to which the rights of the insolent self are protected against the indignation of conformers.

Like a bellows or a lung, every culture has its rhythm of expansion and contraction. When it inhales, it makes room within itself for a variety of human identities; when it exhales, some of what it once contained is expelled. Turn-of-the-century America was a culture in a state of extreme contraction. This assessment may at first seem odd, because few societies have been so economically expansive as the United States in the late nineteenth and early twentieth centuries. But as the GNP soared, tolerance plummeted and normality became a national obsession. The litany of normality was rehearsed in private letters—as when Theodore Roosevelt (writing in 1896 as Police Commissioner of New York City) commended Stephen Crane for having written a terrific gunfighter story, but urged him to compose "another story of the frontiersman and the Mexican Greaser in which the frontiersman shall come out on top; it is more *normal* that way!"[63] And the vocabulary of normality infused public events, too: in 1920, a man was actually elected President of the United States by running on a platform of returning the country to *"normalcy."* From the Spanish-American War, when dissenters were labeled as sissies, through World War I, when one writer declared the German to be a "new gorilla [whose] mentality and . . . moral principles are even more warped and twisted than his physique—a combination of big body, small head, and reptilian heart"—to the McCarthy period, when Communists and fellow travelers were characterized as "secret, sweaty and furtive, like . . . homosexuals in a boys' school,"[64] treason in America was increasingly understood as a crime against nature.

In other words, to be un-American came to signify not merely disloyalty but *abnormality*. And of all the forms that abnormality could take, the most alarming concerned those that afflicted the people on whom the future of the "race" most directly depended—women. Just as racial characteristics had to be distributed in an elaborate hierarchy of "normalcy" —from the refined Anglo-Saxon at the top to the simian Negro at the bottom—characteristics proper to each gender had to be scrupulously discriminated. It was imperative that the character of the *normal* man and *normal* woman be clearly delineated as standards from which deviance could be measured.

One example of how this requirement was set out can be seen in the way even progressive advocates of women's rights resorted to an idea of treason against nature. In 1913, the pioneer feminist Charlotte Perkins Gilman declared, as part of her plea for a national commitment to support nurseries and other institutions devoted to the welfare of children, that "any mother who is capable of giving all that a child needs, and keeps such unusual power exclusively for her own, is a social traitor." Similarly, the new women's colleges (Vassar had been founded in 1865, Smith ten years later, Bryn Mawr a decade after that) were modeled not so much on the older male colleges as on the way that "medical superintendents . . . administered institutions to cure the insane."[65] At the center of their curricula were strict regimens of calisthenics, dietary supervision, and open-air exercise—all designed to train female students to live normally according to their natures, to compel them to obey their "natural" instincts and rhythms. Menstruation was regarded as a kind of biological sabbath, a periodic interruption of active life that must be observed with due reverence. To do otherwise—to exert oneself during this natural bloodletting—was to blaspheme against the body. What all this added up to was the idea that woman was basically "neurasthenic"—a creature of porcelain character who must be swaddled and kept quiet lest she be broken by too much stress.

There was, predictably, a "scientific" basis for the hygienic management of these delicate creatures. In the jargon of the day, women were classified as "anabolic" beings—a term borrowed from biology, where it designated organisms that produce more energy than they can use. According to this theory, females are properly understood as a species of ambulatory plant—not only in their physical differences from men (their comparatively greater accumulation of fat, retention of urine, ability to function on little sleep) but also in their character (their tendency to contemplate rather than to act, to save rather than to spend).[66] This sort of biologism encouraged one to believe that women were suited to a placid habitat, a slower-paced world than the contentious world of men, and that it was unnatural for them to mingle with men for purposes other than procreation and domestic service.

In the end, all these warnings and decrees amounted to an effort to find in nature itself some stable source of truth—something trustworthy and dependable. A woman's body was supposed to be the repository of this principle; she was, as Henry Adams put it, a "goddess" worthy of worship "because of her force; [because] she was reproduction—the greatest and most mysterious of all energies." Yet experience seemed less and less conformable to the standards of nature even as they were being invoked as axioms. For instance, women were portrayed as naturally delicate, passive and inert, but this was also the time when pioneers of the birth-control movement acknowledged that female sexuality had something more than a reproductive function, that it was demanding and even voracious, that although abstinence and withdrawal might be effective means of preventing pregnancy, they were deficient precisely because they frustrated a woman aroused. By the early 1920s, some male writers had become candid enough to write of a woman's voiced pleasure as a "ghastly, reiterated female sound."[67] The sound of her passion was disturbing because it was the sound of implacable desire. It could not be dampened, tuned down, turned into the grateful whimper with which women were supposed to praise the prowess of their masters.

This fear of sexually voracious women has an extensive history. It had long been at work in the common racist fantasy that blacks and Jews are the hugely endowed monsters for whom America's belles had been restlessly waiting. But the fear now took subtler form—in, for instance, the new vogue of vampire fiction. Beginning with stories by writers as diverse as Ambrose Bierce and Mary Wilkins Freeman, it has continued up to the present-day gothic fictions of Anne Rice. The most successful of the fin de siècle vampire stories was, of course, an English one—Bram Stoker's *Dracula*, published in England in 1897, but also a big American seller that spawned American imitations. Stoker's novel—the story of a virginal young woman whose "purity [turns] into voluptuous wantonness" as she is transformed by the nocturnal Count into a sexual carnivore—set the standard.[68]

These disturbing images of the sexually deviant woman were only some among many versions of the larger concept of deviance itself. (Krafft-Ebing's *Psychopathia Sexualis* was translated into English in 1892.) As public discussion of what made a criminal or pervert was now more and more conducted under what one contemporary writer called "the head of defective development," the source of these weaknesses was in some vague sense increasingly understood to be organic. (As late as 1900, certain forms of insanity were still treated by oral administration of a "brain emulsion" made from the brains of calves or sheep and mixed with salt, whiskey, malt, and other "preservatives."[69]) More and more criminologists looked upon the frequent offender in the way that a surgeon looks upon a tumor: short of eradication, there is nothing to be done.

As late as 1938 (the year, in another country, of *Kristallnacht*), a Harvard anthropologist published a scholarly book devoted to the classification of deviants by hair color, skull shape, lip size, etc., and declared that it is "from the very dregs of its germ plasm" that each race produces its "regiments of criminals." Everything, in such an intellectual enterprise, is to be measured against an understood norm. Every adjective tends toward its comparative form: criminals have "deep*er* chests, long*er* faces, narrow*er* foreheads, long*er* ears absolutely and relatively to their breadth, and jaws which are narrow*er* in relation to forehead breadth." In the background of such sentences there is always an ideal type, a *normal* man—natural partner to the *normal* woman—who has the right-sized chest cavity, the proper thickness of hair, the appropriate nose (criminals, says the Harvard expert, tend to show "more compressed or narrower nasal wings"). Even moles on the bodies of evildoers are calculated to be more profuse than on normal skin.[70]

This sort of thing may sound bizarre, yet the ideas of this expert had been entirely conventional for years ("the shape of heads and their bumps mean something," insisted a widely reprinted article, "How to Read a Customer," from a salesman's trade journal in 1905, "and . . . the contour of the face is invariably indicative of character"[71]), and remained so for a long time. Two years after the Harvard anthropologist published his compendium of common "knowledge" about race, during the first, gingerly phase of American rearmament in the face of another prospective war, an irate West Virginia man, who had heard that a black officer had been promoted to the rank of brigadier general, wrote to President Franklin D. Roosevelt that "it is incomprehensible to normal Americans for you to appoint a member of the red, yellow, or black race to [such a] high rank."[72] The idea of the normal had staying power. It was the mark of a culture that had moved steadily toward the judgment that character was inherited and that criminals and certain races were not only morally but also genetically deficient, in ways that could be read on the surface of their bodies. The imperative was no longer to pray for them or to teach them or even to punish them—but to cut out their gonads so that they might be the last of their kind.

[6]

In reviewing these baroque variations on the themes of racism, misogyny, and bad science, it is easy to look back upon them in a spirit of mockery and condescension. We want to have outgrown them. The muscle flexing and contempt for sissiness, the posse mentality and the fear of racial contamination, the anxiety over what we nowadays would call "gender confusion"—all these are attitudes we like to think we have left behind. Yet if one keeps in mind the dread that underlay the hue and cry, one begins to suspect that the madness may not, after all, have been so much an aberration as one among a series of periodic convulsions that always signaled more to come. Less than a month before becoming Speaker-elect of the House of Representatives in 1994, Newt Gingrich of Georgia spoke on national television about Democrats as "the enemies of normal people."[73]

For anticipation and confirmation of this inveterate American need to divide the world between the clean and the polluted, we may turn, once again, to Melville, who in 1850 had written a prophetic book about a man so horribly wounded that he directs his mind in manic concentration toward the quest for revenge. Here, in one of the transcendent passages in all of American literature, is Melville's explanation of Captain Ahab's rage against the white whale—his insatiable need to find something on which to fix the blame:

> All that most maddens and torments; all that stirs up the lees of things; all truth with malice in it; all that cracks the sinews and cakes the brain; all the subtle demonisms of life and thought; all evil, to crazy Ahab, were visibly personified, and made practically assailable in Moby-Dick. He piled upon the whale's white hump the sum of all the general rage and hate felt by his whole race from Adam down; and then, as if his chest had been a mortar, he burst his hot heart's shell upon it.[74]

Anyone who has contended with this greatest of American novels knows that one of its mysteries is the transfixing appeal of this peg-legged captain. Ahab is a study in hatred. As he seethes, one wonders how he draws his unsuspecting men to his cause. How does his hatred spread? How does he turn the men from the enterprise for which they think they have shipped—the business of filling barrels with whale oil and collecting their share of the spoils—to a mad quest for a singular whale that will be worth nothing to them in coin? How does he put his vengeance in their minds?

He does it by compelling them to feel his suffering as their own. He touches their private heart-wounds. He makes them *feel* how "Ahab and anguish [had lain] stretched together in one hammock," how "his torn body and gashed soul [had] bled into one another,"[75] and in so doing he makes them feel that he is at one with them—victims all, wounded discards, sufferers *almost* beyond recompense. The celebration of this feeling is his genius; and by displaying it so eloquently, Melville wrote in advance the story of the twentieth century, which became—as we know all too well—the century of the demagogue.

The American demagogue developed a specialty in stirring up hatred across what W. E. B. Du Bois, in 1903, called "the color line." In his ensuing incarnations, he would sometimes wear the robes of the Ku Klux Klan (which held political control of several Southern and Southwestern states for decades), or bear names like Senators Theodore Bilbo ("the integrity of our white blood is at stake"), Huey Long, and Joseph Mc-Carthy. But in the end, whatever his style or region or tone, the demagogue invariably drew his strength from his ability to sweep away people's fear that their sufferings were meaningless, and to convince them instead that there exists a gloating consciousness that has arrayed the world against them. The demagogue replaces the sense of life as a series of random defeats with the possibility of righteous struggle against a huntable enemy. It was the "dream of the late Professor Franz Boas . . . a Jew," wrote Senator Bilbo, to bring upon us "a brown race—a mixed race—mongrels—products of sin itself."[76]

Here, after another economic spasm had again stirred up the resident demons of the American mind, is one exemplary American demagogue —the proto-fascist priest Charles Coughlin, who made common cause with victims in a weekly radio address during the 1930s:

> How tremendous, then, is the sufferer! With what dignity is the sufferer's soul surrounded! Those who are oppressed, those who are victims . . . those whose bodies feel the stripes of the lash . . . whose brows are circled with the thorns of worry, whose hands are pierced with the nails of poverty, whose hearts are opened with the spear of calumny—they are living crucifixes who stand clear of the wrangling world around them! . . .
>
> My dear shut-ins and sufferers . . . Remember us . . . as you suffer in the Gethsemane of your heartache, in the Pilate's Hall of your poverty, or on the Calvary of your bed of pain.[77]

These words masquerade as Christian compassion. But in fact they are the voice of despair. The demagogue's catalogue of demons—capitalists, industrialists, prohibitionists, usurers, tax-evading financiers, blacks, Jews, and other devils innumerable—may vary in its details, but it is always recited in Ahab's "high raised voice" until it drops into an "animal sob."[78] And it never includes the one true devil: pride.

The most insidious thing about the demagogue is that along the way he may express, as Richard Hofstadter has said in his great essay on "The Paranoid Style in American Politics," "certain defensible judgments."

There was truth, for instance, in Coughlin's charge that some supporters of prohibition were animated by the desire to see men working in their factories rather than dissipating in bars; and there was substance in his claim that corporate internationalism can be a form of tax evasion. (Even Hitler had a point when he claimed that injustice had been done at Versailles.) The moral inventory of the demagogue is never entirely fraudulent. But sooner or later the demagogue leaves truth behind and embarks on a crusade against an enemy who is "totally evil."[79] In America, mercifully, this voice of despair subsided before it overcame the whole society with a spirit of retributive fear. But by the time it had been quieted, its counterparts in other nations had released into the world more hate and blood than had been imagined in all the centuries that had gone before.

"I . . . want to be able to hate," wrote Joseph Goebbels in a confession of blood-freezing candor. "Oh, I can hate, and I don't want to forget how. Oh, how wonderful it is to be able to hate."[80] To listen to this voice is to realize again what Augustine knew and what Melville put into the form of a story: that the crusader who construes evil as a malignant, external thing—a thing alien to himself—is by far the worst kind of barbarian. The struggle of the twentieth century was to keep this proficient hater from seizing the world.

*"This, ladies and gentlemen, is Exhibit A, the sneakers
that urged my client to Just Do It."*

Cartoon from The New Yorker *(December 7, 1992)*

SIX

The Culture of Irony

Since the heyday of the racial purists, no word in our language has undergone a greater loss of prestige than their once cherished word "normal." Formerly a synonym for virtue, it has become a dirty word, a throwback to the vocabulary of light-skinned men who looked into the mirror and proclaimed their own image to be the perfect realization of normality. Not long thereafter, a crime without parallel in human history was justified in Europe by a similar ideology, and ever since, the word "normal" has not been allowed to regain anything like its lost dignity.

Its official repudiation was achieved in 1942, when the Supreme Court, in an opinion written by Justice William O. Douglas, reversed its earlier position on eugenic sterilization by striking down an Oklahoma law that permitted sterilization of a person convicted three or more times for "felonies involving moral turpitude." The power to sterilize, in "evil or reckless hands," Douglas wrote, could "cause races or types which are inimical to the dominant group to wither and disappear."[1] Ever since this overdue expression of revulsion, it has not been possible to hear the word "normal" without hearing at least a faint echo of the eugenicist's cant or the fascist's rallying cry. One asks, with proper outrage, who appointed these judges? What authorized them to determine what was natural and unnatural? How dared they say where the dividing line fell?

[1]

These questions, which have become commonplace in our time, were first widely articulated in America in the aftermath of World War I, a war to which high purposes were initially attributed, but whose motives and tactics seemed in retrospect to resemble those of prep-school rivalries—inexplicable except in terms of tribal pride and territorial competition. For many Americans, the war began a process that has continued apace ever since: the discrediting of what has been called "the versus habit"—a way of perceiving the world as a battleground of normality vs. abnormality in which "one of the poles embodies so wicked a deficiency or flaw or perversion that its total submission is called for."² This "habit of simple distinction, simplification, and opposition" was a way of thinking from which the generation formed by World War I turned away in disgust.

Although the turn "beyond good and evil" accelerated after World War I, it had been adumbrated before the war in the robust Progressivism of figures like Clarence Darrow, who, in a notorious speech to the prisoners in the Cook County Jail, declared in 1902 that "there is no such thing as a crime as the word is generally understood. . . . I do not believe that people are in jail because they deserve to be. They are in jail simply because they cannot avoid it on account of circumstances which are entirely beyond their control and for which they are in no way responsible." Darrow was animated by outrage at the casualness with which helpless people were condemned without any sense of compassion or complicity on the part of the insulated rich who judged them. For other secular intellectuals, however, the moral norms of the culture were less an expression of class prejudice than a noxious residue of religious superstition about sin and judgment and an answerable God—concepts that had been discredited by the racism and xenophobia that were often dignified by Christian platitudes. This kind of disgust, which made no distinction between the concept of sin and its application to certain designated sinners who were disproportionately foreign, dark-skinned, and poor, found expression in the vogue of Nietzsche, a writer introduced in the United States by such champions as H. L. Mencken, who celebrated him as one of the great "sham-smashers and free-thinkers" of all time.³ Nietzsche's appeal (which is deeply ironic, considering his later popularity with the ideologues of German racism) was his contempt not only for the superseded norms of Victorian moralism but for the life-crushing concept of sin itself. He treated the very basis of the moral system that we now call "Judeo-Christian" as a hoax, and declared that the idea of sin itself was nothing but a ruse invented by a wretched band of "ascetic priest[s]" (Jews, of course)—shamans who had achieved a magical hold over men by playing the "ravishing music" of guilt in their souls. Here is his account of how the idea of sin first took hold in the human mind:

> At odds with himself for one physiological reason or another, rather like a caged animal, unable to comprehend his plight, avid for reasons (reasons are always comforting) and for narcotics, man must finally have recourse to one who knows the hidden causes. Behold, he is given a hint by his magician, the very *first* hint as to the cause of his suffering: he is told to look at himself, to search his own soul for a guilt, a piece of his personal past; to view his suffering as a penance. . . . The sufferer takes the hint, he has *understood*, and from now on he is like a hen about whom a circle has been drawn. Now he will never escape from that confining circle; the patient has been transformed into a "sinner."[4]

Fed up with the pinched values of their predecessors, Americans who came of age in the early twentieth century adopted this style of iconoclastic irony. "Irony," as F. Scott Fitzgerald wrote in 1922, "was the final polish of the shoe, the ultimate dab of the clothes-brush, a sort of intellectual 'There!' " Irony was "the Holy Ghost of this later day," and those who believed in it gratefully discovered in Nietzsche (and, soon, in Freud) a writer who mocked the sense of sin and guilt that had once been at the heart of middle-class culture, and redefined it as a pathology. The ancient association of sex with sin was now exposed as life-killing prudery, and the restorative power of myth proclaimed. Some of the brightest young intellectuals (Ruth Benedict, Margaret Mead) gravitated toward the burgeoning discipline of anthropology, whose basic premise was that the old distinctions between "primitive" and "civilized" were specious. In some circles, a cult of the Negro as exotic primitive came into fashion as a belligerent way for white bohemians to dissociate themselves from the provincial past. The pale, old Puritan founders of American culture were regarded as "oligarchs," and the once celebrated worthies of American literature (Emerson, Longfellow, Whittier) were dismissed as unbearably respectable gentlemen from whose writings, in the words of Ernest Hemingway, one would never "gather that they had bodies. They had minds, yes. Nice, dry, clean minds."[5]

This "discourse of disbelief," in Ann Douglas's words, "became the only thoroughly accredited modern mode." But the new freedom and the repudiation of the old constraints had a cost, as Walter Lippmann pointed

out in 1929, in a book hopefully entitled *A Preface to Morals.* Despite his
gestures at rebellion, the "modern man," as Lippmann called his professional and intellectual peers, was increasingly subject to

> moments of blank misgiving in which he finds that the civilization of
> which he is a part leaves a dusty taste in his mouth. He may be very
> busy with many things, but he discovers one day that he is no longer
> sure they are worth doing. He has been much preoccupied; but he is
> no longer sure he knows why. He has become involved in an elaborate
> routine of pleasures; and they do not seem to amuse him very much.
> He finds it hard to believe that doing any one thing is better than doing
> any other thing, or, in fact, that it is better than doing nothing at all.[6]

Lippmann's generation found its poet in Hemingway, who caught the
peculiar ennui of the postwar years in staccato sentences that "choked
to death," as Clifton Fadiman once put it, all the "Big Words . . . Love,
Imagination, Mind, Morality, the Will."[7]

Yet if Hemingway was a debunker of the old pieties, he was not san-
guine about what succeeded them. Recognizing, like Lippmann, that
their passing was not without cost, he regarded the postwar generation,
however brazen and iconoclastic it may have seemed, as finally nerveless
("shallow, cynical, impatient, turbulent, and empty," was Fitzgerald's
assessment).

Americans were slow to grasp that the discrediting of the old moral
geography would leave them in a world without any moral map at all.
They did not apprehend, as the cultural historian George Steiner put it
later, that

> the mutation of Hell into metaphor left a formidable gap in the co-
> ordinates of location, of psychological recognition in the Western mind.
> The absence of the familiar damned opened a vortex which the modern
> totalitarian state filled. To have neither Heaven nor Hell is to be intol-
> erably deprived and alone in a world gone flat. Of the two, Hell proved
> the easier to re-create. (The pictures had always been more detailed.)[9]

Among those who did recognize that the "world [had] gone flat," and
that (in Douglas's words) "the defacements of significance will one day
be all that is left of significance," was a group of theological writers who
have come to be known as "neo-orthodox." Beginning in the 1920s, they
argued—against Nietzsche and the party of irony—that the catastrophe

of modern man was precisely the *loss* of the concept of sin. Led by Paul Tillich, a refugee theologian who had fled the Nazis, and Reinhold Niebuhr, who spent most of his career as a pastor and teacher at Union Theological Seminary in New York City, they insisted on speaking the discredited language of sin to an audience that had given it up. "The demonic," Tillich wrote, "is the elevation of something conditional to unconditional significance."[10] This was as much a response to the brutalities of Marxian totalitarianism as to the rise of fascism—which writers like Tillich and Niebuhr regarded as twin expressions of the self-deceiving arrogance by which human beings imagine that history has elevated their values, structures, and society above all others. In this sense, such writers were ironists too; they kept steadily in view the ridiculous spectacle of people celebrating local practices and beliefs as if they were universal principles. But in restoring the language of sin to currency, they were responding to a tendency of human nature that menaced civilization even as it escaped the range of secular thought, and against which mere debunking irony had no force. They offered a way to acknowledge the human capacity for radical evil that was, for a moment, belatedly evident to even the most resolutely secular sensibility.

One poignant instance of this belatedness may be seen in the career of the German-Jewish refugee Ernst Cassirer, an idealist philosopher who had always described "human culture" as "man's progressive self-liberation." Cassirer did his major work, *The Philosophy of Symbolic Forms* (1923–31), in Germany, became the first Jewish rector of the University of Hamburg, then resigned and left his native country in 1933. When he looked back in 1945 from his sanctuary in New Haven upon the ruins of Europe, he reflected ruefully that "when we first heard of the political myths"—the fables that proclaimed the superiority of the master race— "we found them so absurd and incongruous, so fantastic and ludicrous that we could hardly be prevailed upon to take them seriously." By the end of the war, however, it had "become clear to all of us that this was a great mistake. . . . The mythical monsters were not entirely destroyed. They were used for the creation of a new universe, and they still survive in this universe."[11]

Cassirer, speaking implicitly for an entire generation of émigré intellectuals who added immeasurably to American life in the 1930s and beyond, was among those who pioneered the modern view of man as a symbol-making animal (today it is our conventional view), a creature definable "only in terms of his consciousness," who "is always inclined to regard the small circle" of reality described by his symbols as "the standard of the universe."[12] This definition was supple enough to accommodate the fact of man's provincialism; it agreed with the ironists' contempt for the local, and with the anthropologists whose purpose was to break out of the small circle into which one happens to be born; it agreed with the modernists who exploded the formal and moral boundaries of literature and art; it even agreed with Niebuhr's denunciation of the self that "imagine[s] himself the whole." But it did not begin to explain how, at certain critical historical moments—such as the one at which he was living—the collective mind of an entire culture may abruptly close the circle and drive itself into a frenzy of hate against outsiders. It did not explain (and it was the poignancy of Cassirer's later work that he recognized the inexplicability) how his own native country could suddenly devote itself to turning millions of people—simply because they fell outside the circle of the normal—into smoke and ash.

Religious intellectuals responded to this crisis of explanation by trying to make their secular contemporaries aware that this profound and explosive irrationality is always present, even when it seems muted and on the wane. Americans for whom the threat seemed faraway and abstract were chided for their complacence by journalists like William Shirer, who reported throughout the 1930s on the transformation of Germany into an armed fascist state, and by novelists like Sinclair Lewis, whose *It Can't Happen Here* (1935) imagined a fascist putsch in the United States itself. Writing in *The New Republic* in the spring of 1940 (not long after the Nazi invasion of Denmark and Norway), Lewis Mumford excoriated his fellow secular liberals for being "unaware of the dark forces of the unconscious," and declared, by comparison, that "though the theologian's view of the external world might be scientifically weak, his view of the internal world, the world of value and personality, included an understanding of constant human phenomena—sin, corruption, evil—on which the liberal closed his eyes." Yet despite this and other calls to awareness (Mumford and his colleague Waldo Frank, who wrote a piece after the Nazi invasion of France called "Our Guilt in Fascism," both resigned from the *New Republic* editorial board when it refused to endorse their call for intervention), for most Americans the reality of brownshirts and goose-steppers continued to seem a distant charade.[13]

There is a remarkable passage in the memoir of Frances Perkins, Franklin Roosevelt's Secretary of Labor, that reveals a moment at which this feeling of theatrical distance was obliterated by a shock of recognition. Perkins registers an encounter between an urbane, secular American mind for whom the fascists remained mysteriously distant and a fundamentally religious account of man's capacity for evil that made them immediately comprehensible. She recalls that, early in 1944, a young minister at Roosevelt's church in Hyde Park commended to the President the mystery writer Dorothy Sayers and remarked that Sayers had been much influenced by the writings of Kierkegaard. " 'Who is Kierkegaard?' the President asked." When he learned, as Perkins put it, that "the inner core of Kierkegaardian teaching . . . was a fresh emphasis on the doctrine of original sin and its implications for man," he asked a number of "questions, jotted down names of books by Kierkegaard . . . and listened more than he talked." Perkins goes on:

> Some weeks later I happened to be reporting to Roosevelt on problems concerning the War Labor Board. He was looking at me, nodding his head, and, I thought, following my report, but suddenly he interrupted me.
> "Frances, have you ever read Kierkegaard?"
> "Very little—mostly reviews of his writings."
> "Well, you ought to read him," he said with enthusiasm. "It will teach you something."
> I thought perhaps he meant it would teach me something about the War Labor Board.
> "It will teach you about the Nazis," he said. "Kierkegaard explains the Nazis to me as nothing else ever has. I have never been able to make out why people who are obviously human beings could behave like that. They are human, yet they behave like demons. Kierkegaard gives you an understanding of what it is in man that makes it possible for these Germans to be so evil."[14]

There is a certain ingenuous sense of discovery in this reaction, as if Roosevelt were surprised to find that the moral abstractions of a remote philosopher turn out to be not only applicable but essential for grasping the motives and actions of human beings in his own time. What the Nazis did for Roosevelt's generation was to restore to life a moral idea—the idea of radical evil—that, in the age of irony, was quickly losing its meaning.

[2]

Since the Nazis' reinvention of hell took place while the world was not watching, one of the central disclosures of the twentieth century has been that even the most brazen sins can be committed in safety. Despite his musings on the evil of Nazism, Roosevelt, as the historian David S. Wyman has documented in *The Abandonment of the Jews: America and the Holocaust, 1941–1945*, "gave no priority to the rescue" of their victims. Most people wished not to see and not to know. When American troops reached the town of Gotha in central Germany in the spring of 1945, they found on the outskirts a "work camp" complete with facilities for torturing and executing inmates unwilling or too weak to work. When the citizens of Gotha denied having known what was going on in the camp, General Eisenhower issued his now famous order that "all men, women and children be turned out at bayonet point to parade through the camp and form work parties to bury the dead." At the same time, he arranged for his own troops to visit the site so that they could see first-hand what the retreating enemy had left behind. According to witnesses, as he himself was leaving the camp, he "suddenly turned to an unidentified GI sentry," and asked, "Still having trouble hating them?"[15]

The concentration camps shamed the ironists. Auschwitz and Bergen-Belsen and Treblinka remained for twenty years or so at the center of moral awareness for American intellectuals, because they were the purest expression of the characteristic form of evil in the modern world: the ability to erase the humanity of other beings and turn them into usable and dispensable things. Those who turned to the Marxist tradition for an understanding of this process (they were numerous in the 1930s, especially before the signing of the Hitler-Stalin pact, and reemerged in the 1960s as the "New Left") attributed it to a capitalist market system that assigns persons their worth strictly according to the exchange value of the things they make or the services they provide. But the Marxist tradition has always been of limited use in coming to terms with evil because, as Niebuhr put it,

> it fails to recognize that there is an ideological element in all human rational processes which reveals itself not only in the spirituality of the dominant bourgeois class, and not only in the rationalization of economic interest; but which expresses itself in all classes and uses every circumstance, geographic, economic and political, as an occasion for man's as-

sertion of universal significance for his particular values. This defect in human life is too constitutional to be eliminated by a reorganization of society; a fact which constitutes the basic refutation of the utopian dreams of Marxism.[16]

The moral obscenity of the camps may have been the immediate occasion for Niebuhr's remarks, but within the specific experience of American civilization, the purest social expression of this "constitutional defect" had been chattel slavery, which was a perpetual war against the human dignity of black people—a war of which most white people had kept themselves blithely unaware. It also made itself known, with incremental horror, in our military "progress"—in the repeating rifles of the Civil War; then, during America's first great foreign engagement, in trench warfare where the enemy became an indistinct mass into which gas was dispensed as if into a swarm of hornets; then, in World War II, in the practice of carpet bombing, where the extinction of human lives was signified by distant thumps and puffs of smoke as the plane, having relieved itself, banked for home; and, finally, in atomic incineration. In our own time we have taken it a step further with "smart bombs" that with eerie silence report themselves to the sender as blips on a video screen. What all these technologies have in common is their ability to destroy a human target whose humanity is out of range.

Through his interpretations of the Old and New Testaments, of Augustine, Calvin, and Edwards (whom he elevated to first rank among American theologians), Niebuhr was trying to expose this human capacity for willed insouciance that seems to grow with every technological advance. He tried to expose it by reiterating the basic Christian idea that sin is the confusion of the self with the world. "Evil," he wrote on the eve of the Cold War, "is always the assertion of some self-interest without regard to the whole"—an idea flexible enough to accommodate the child's demand for incessant attention and the sadist's ability to value his pleasure more than the person whom he is torturing. But even as he believed in the continuing relevance of the old concept of sin to new events, Niebuhr was also aware that evil had taken on a distinctly modern characteristic. In this sense, he belonged to another lineage as well—to the literary tradition that runs from Goethe to Melville and Dostoevsky and Conrad, and expounds evil as the capacity to render invisible another human consciousness. Sin, in this view, is the failure to meet what Kant called the "categorical imperative," by which one is compelled to treat other persons as ends rather than means. "To accomplish his object," as Melville put it, writing about his mad captain's willingness to use his men as instruments of his personal revenge, "Ahab must use tools; and of all tools used in the shadow of the moon, men are most apt to get out of order."[17]

This conversion of human beings from obstructions into instruments is one of the obligatory themes of modern literature, for the good and sufficient reason that the economic and political organization of the modern West (capitalism and colonialism) has ensured its presence. Here, at the outset of the tradition, is Goethe's Faust—one of the first literary portraits of the grasping modern consciousness—explaining why he has ordered Mephisto to clear out an old couple whose cottage stands on a spot that he, Faust, covets as a building site:

> *That aged couple should have yielded,*
> *I want their lindens in my grip,*
> *Since these few trees that are denied me*
> *Undo my worldwide ownership*
>
> . . . .
>
> *Hence is our soul upon the rack,*
> *To feel, amid plenty, what we lack.*[18]

Faust is loudly indignant when he learns that Mephisto, having taken his wishes seriously, has killed the old couple and burned their house to the ground. But the offense, we suspect, is not the deed so much as the tactless fact of his being told about it. He wants not so much that the old man and woman should have been spared as not to know what was done with them.

In the middle decades of the twentieth century, American writers took up this theme as their own. Even before the war it had been Lillian Hellman's theme in *The Little Foxes* (1939) and Richard Wright's in *Native Son* (1940); after the war, it occupied the imagination especially of young Jewish writers like Saul Bellow (a Canadian immigrant) and, somewhat later, Bernard Malamud. Evil was a preoccupying subject in the movies —in Alfred Hitchcock's brilliant study of malice disguised as avuncular charm, *Shadow of a Doubt* (1943); in William Wyler's *Detective Story* (1951), about a cop who "can smell evil" in others but is oblivious to his own; in a rash of thrillers about sadistic murderers, including *Kiss of Death*

(1947), *The Night of the Hunter* (1955), and *Cape Fear* (1962); and in horror films like *The Bad Seed* (1956) and *Village of the Damned* (1960), about innocent-seeming children who are monsters within.

Evil became a compelling topic in the academy as well. In 1947, Niebuhr's professorial neighbor on Morningside Heights, Lionel Trilling, published a novel, *The Middle of the Journey*, about the onset of a postwar America whose physical configuration expressed the Faustian denial—a world of whitewashed houses in which the middle class huddled, shutting out even the sound of the crickets in which they feared to hear the "ceaseless noise of time rushing away." Designed in every respect to "refuse knowledge of the evil and hardness of the world," this suburban sanctuary is invaded by sin when the town drunk strikes his child, who dies when a blood vessel bursts in her brain. It happens in church, in full view of the congregation; but despite the invasion, sin and death remain unfit subjects for discussion. At the mere mention of death, Trilling's suburbanites withdraw "in a polite, intelligent, concerted way . . . as if they were the parents of a little boy and were following the line of giving no heed to the obscenities their son picked up on the street and insisted on bringing to the dinner table."[19]

To read the literature of the postwar years is to encounter everywhere the same collective stammer, which the young Arthur Miller (writing also in 1947, in *All My Sons*) described as an insult to the dead:

> I got an idea [says a young war survivor about his fallen comrades]—watching them go down. Everything was being destroyed, see, but it seemed to me that one new thing was made. A kind of . . . responsibility. Man for man. You understand me? — To show that, to bring that on to the earth again like some kind of a monument and everyone would feel it standing there, behind him, and it would make a difference to him. . . . And then I came home and it was incredible. . . . there was no meaning in it here; the whole thing to them was a kind of a—bus accident.[20]

All these writers—theologians, critics, novelists, dramatists—touched a nerve when they insisted that to endorse accident or circumstance as concepts adequate to recent events was to give up on the possibility of meaning in human experience. "Educated people," as Trilling said, "more and more accounted for human action by the influence of environment and the necessities and habits imposed by society"[21]—a circumstantial explanation never adequate to the reality of evil. With its penchant for attributing evil to pernicious habits and systems, the historicist explanation was shared by Marxist ideologues, who saw class conflict as the source of all evil, and anti-Marxist zealots, who saw the world threatened by a satanic conspiracy against property and liberty. For the neutral ironists, who began to reemerge after the war, evil was nothing more than a psychological illusion.

Trilling, who became the closest thing to America's official intellectual in the 1950s, tried to dissociate himself from all these parties. But in his postwar critique of liberalism as squeamish about evil, he had chiefly in mind the evil of Joseph Stalin, not of the Red-baiters who, in the name of anti-Communism, were turning the United States into a fear-drenched society in which internal espionage was an expected aspect of life. He had "at heart," he insisted, "the interests of liberalism," and aimed to make it "aware of the weak or wrong expressions of itself"[22] that laid it open to seduction by the sort of rationality by which Marxists—domestic and foreign—claimed to explain the tragedy of history.

If Trilling was writing from within the liberal tradition, a more ferocious attack on its principles and practitioners as soft on Marxism was being mounted at the same time from without. It came from opportunists like Senator Joseph McCarthy and fanatics like the Director of the Federal Bureau of Investigation, J. Edgar Hoover, who also understood the postwar world as a place in which evil went unrecognized and unresisted. Assessing fascism and Communism as comparable political systems, both men saw the latter as "the senior totalitarianism," and were relatively reticent about the former. One of the charges McCarthy made against the "supine and treacherous" George C. Marshall, architect of the postwar plan for European recovery and his favorite bête noire, was that he had failed to invite Generalissimo Franco to dispatch his troops, renowned for their "warlike quality," for the defense of Europe against the Russian beast.[23]

"How can we account for our present situation," the senator demanded in 1951, thinking of the "surrender" of China (due, in large part, to the treachery of a "pro-Red . . . clique of young Foreign Service officers"), "unless we believe that men high in this Government are concerting to deliver us to disaster?" And then came the famous phrase, "a conspiracy so immense," which McCarthy repeated in many public speeches with a kind of lingering vibrato:

This must be the product of a great conspiracy, a conspiracy on a scale so immense as to dwarf any previous such venture in the history of man. . . . What is the objective of the conspiracy? . . . to weaken us militarily, to confuse our spirit with talk of surrender in the Far East and to impair our will to resist evil.[24]

The result of this demagoguery, with its attendant technique of public innuendo about treasonable diplomats, policymakers, intellectuals, and a host of fellow travelers, was a society, as the columnist Joseph Alsop put it in 1954, where "the accuser speaks; the next morning's headlines announce the accusation; and the accused is marked thereafter as a traitor to his country."[25] Responsible writers like Arthur Miller reacted (as in *The Crucible* [1953], an allegorical play that likened McCarthy to the Salem witch-hunters) by denouncing his method as another confirmation of the irremediable human impulse to project evil outside the self.

It is difficult in our post-Communist world to recapture the pervasive sense of menace that gripped the United States in the 1950s. The symbolism of the Cold War infused not only politics but historiography (it was in these years that Lincoln was reinterpreted as the lonely hero who saved the country not just from the slave-conspirators, but from the appeasers), the movies (as in the showdown genre exemplified by *High Noon* [1952]), and popular fiction (the best-selling novelist Mickey Spillane had his private eye, Mike Hammer, rail against the Mafia as "an oversized mob of ignorant, lunk-headed jerks who ruled with fear,"[26] and who looked a lot like their thuggish counterparts in the Kremlin).

As the anxiety began to lift in the 1950s with the stabilization of Europe, the death of Stalin, and the rise of Khrushchev, a distinction was reasserted between realism and paranoia, and new writers (Norman Mailer, Thomas Pynchon, and the British novelist John le Carré, whose books flourished in the United States) introduced the notion that the struggle against totalitarianism had become a totalitarianism of its own. These were fresh voices expressing an old theme: that the essential modern evasion was the failure to acknowledge evil, name it, and accept its irreducibility *in the self*. Evil, in other words, was one's near neighbor as well as an alien force. Toward the end of Saul Bellow's masterpiece, *Herzog* (1964), Moses Herzog, a man of good instincts but flabby will, finds himself in court, listening to testimony in the trial of a young couple who have been charged with murdering their three-year-old son. The mother, he gathers from the testimony, came from Trenton, born lame. . . . She had a fourth-grade education, I.Q. 94. An older brother was the favorite; she was neglected. Unattractive, sullen, clumsy, wearing an orthopedic boot, she became delinquent at an early age. . . . Because she was a poor crippled creature, she had often been molested, later sexually abused by adolescent boys.

Her child, it is surmised by the medical examiner, had been "often beaten," with the heaviest bruises "in the region of the genitals, where the boy seemed to have been beaten with something capable of breaking the skin, perhaps a metal buckle or the heel of a woman's shoe." As the testimony proceeds, more "background" details are revealed: someone testifies that he once witnessed the boy, hungry, with his mother at a Howard Johnson's while she ate and failed to feed him.

> I fail to understand! thought Herzog, as this good man, jowls silently moving, got off the stand. I fail to . . . but this is the difficulty with people who spend their lives in humane studies and therefore imagine once cruelty has been described in books it is ended.

Now the circumstances of the boy's death are related from the witness stand:

> Mostly . . . the child cried a lot. Tenants complained, and when he [a neighbor] investigated he found the kid was kept shut in a closet. For discipline, was what the defendant told him. But toward the end the boy cried less. On the day of his death, however, there was a lot of noise. He heard something falling, and shrieks from the third floor. Both the mother and the boy were screaming. Someone was fooling with the elevator, so he ran upstairs. Knocked at the door, but she was screaming too loud to hear. So he opened it and stepped in. Would he tell the court what he saw? He saw the woman with the boy in her arms. He thought she was hugging him, but to his astonishment she threw him from her with both arms. He was hurled against the wall.

Herzog rushes for the corridor, gurgling " 'Oh my God!' and in trying to speak discovered an acrid fluid in his mouth that had to be swallowed." In his mind's eye he is in the elevator with mother and child:

> The child screamed, clung, but with both arms the girl hurled it against the wall. On her legs was ruddy hair. And her lover, too, with long jaws

and zooty sideburns, watching on the bed. Lying down to copulate, and standing up to kill. Some kill, then cry. Others, not even that.[27]

After the camps, the Bomb, and the witch-hunters, how could evil—with all its dreadful ordinariness and its evasions and disavowals—not have been the leading theme, even the only theme?

[3]

As the Holocaust faded into the commemorated past, and McCarthyism (a term coined by the cartoonist Herblock) was discredited as a national shame, Americans discovered, as if blinders had been lifted, that the deadly connection of evil and insouciance they had belatedly identified in foreign despots and their minions could be found throughout their own culture. They discovered that their government had forced thousands of its own citizens into prison camps because they were "racially" Japanese.[28] And within a decade of the end of the war, the Supreme Court ruled that the segregated system of public education—considered by many to be sanctioned by nature itself—was, in effect, a form of racial incarceration. J. Robert Oppenheimer, who led the development of the hydrogen bomb, put the discovery this way: "In some sort of crude sense, which no vulgarity, no humor, nor overstatement can quite extinguish, the physicists have known sin; and this is a knowledge which they cannot lose."[29]

Even some conservative writers loyal to the idea of Anglo-American world leadership were as shaken by the power the United States had twice released as by the power against which it was unleashed. After visiting the bomb site at Nagasaki, the usually serene and local-minded novelist Louis Auchincloss remarked that "the man who can contemplate the hospital, large as Bellevue . . . gutted from one end to the other, in a single moment, and say 'it's all for the best,' must have a giant faith in the victory formula of the Anglo-Saxon world."[30] If one's loyalties went beyond race and nationality and encompassed, say, the whole of what used to be called "Christendom," one had to conjure with the sight of a Pope (Pius XII) who had genuflected as usual before the image of a crucified Jew, then gone about his parochial business while Jews burned. And as for those who wanted to believe in the civilizing influence of art, how could they take solace in music after the Nazi murderers had listened, rapt, to Furtwängler and Karajan while the trains to the death camps unloaded their cargo of doomed children?

Among the earliest and most effective expressions of this discovery of complicity with evil was John Hersey's *Hiroshima*, published in 1946 as the first work to which an entire issue of *The New Yorker* was devoted—a series of sketches that had the effect of showing an album of family snapshots to someone who has previously heard of the subjects only from afar. Hersey gave the anonymous victims of the nuclear firestorm faces and names. He showed the citizens of Hiroshima in the kitchen, on the porch, putting their children in pajamas in the moments before the bomb fell. He showed them blown about like tossed debris amid window shards and the splinters of what had been roofs and walls. He made it difficult to represent them with a number (70,000 or 100,000, depending on whether one took account of post-blast radiation effects) and a dismissive name (Japs).

The attack on invisibility became the main business of serious American writing. In 1951, Ralph Ellison published the most accomplished novel yet composed by a black American, *Invisible Man*, in which he examined the myriad ways in which blacks are rendered into playthings or objects of disdain or experimental subjects—anything except fully sentient human beings. In 1962, Rachel Carson published her epochal *Silent Spring* (which had also run, serially, in *The New Yorker*), in which she quoted Albert Schweitzer's remark that "man can hardly even recognize the devils of his own creation," and spoke of pollution as "a chain of evil . . . [that] is for the most part irreversible." She applied, in effect, the Niebuhrian definition of sin to the whole culture, which she believed was saturating itself—unknowingly, but still culpably—with invisible poisons. The name of her primary devil was DDT, which "she hated," as one historian has put it, ". . . not only for the palpable harm it did but for the war-inflamed ideal it fostered, of total eradication of all enemies, boundless control and infinite mastery of the earth."[31] In 1963, Betty Friedan brought out *The Feminine Mystique*, in which she asserted that the subjugation of women was a "problem [that] lay buried, unspoken, for many years [even] in the minds of American women" and that was only now struggling into consciousness. And in the same year, Michael Harrington published *The Other America*, an effort to "pierce through the invisibility of 40,000,000 to 50,000,000 human beings" who lived in poverty as "internal alien[s]" in the richest nation in the world. Its first chapter was entitled "The Invisible Land."

The generation that grew up with these books wanted to believe that America was through with xenophobia and the fortress mentality, and was entering an age when some truly fundamental reimagining was about to take place—a revolution not only in political and social relations but in sexual relations as well. Herbert Marcuse, whose *Eros and Civilization* (1955) became virtually a cult classic in the 1960s, was most explicit on how even Freud had been locked into a provincial sense of what constituted normal human sexuality. The utopian future, according to Marcuse, would see an unprecedented "spread of the libido" beyond the pinched forms of sexual expression permitted by the rules of bourgeois society. This expansion of unrepressed desire would manifest itself

> in a reactivation of all erotogenic zones and, consequently, in a resurgence of pregenital polymorphous sexuality and in a decline of genital supremacy. The body in its entirety would become an object of cathexis, a thing to be enjoyed—an instrument of pleasure. This change in the value and scope of libidinal relations would lead to a disintegration of the institutions in which the private interpersonal relations have been organized, particularly the monogamic and patriarchal family.[32]

These apocalyptic books ("we must perceive passionately," Harrington wrote, "if this blindness is to be lifted from us") were an answer to the call that had been made in the terrible afterglow of Hiroshima by one of Trilling's Columbia colleagues, a young historian named Richard Hofstadter, who declared an end to the "spirit of sentimental appreciation" in which our own history had been traditionally received, and announced that a new age of "critical analysis" was at hand.[33]

Yet with all their critical passion, these works have not worn as well as their more ironic contemporaries like Joseph Heller's *Catch-22* (1961) or Stanley Kubrick's *Dr. Strangelove* (1963). Writers like Carson and Hersey attributed transcendence to values that only the stubbornly devout still think of as established by God or nature. Hersey was the son of missionaries. Carson had been aptly described as a "Transcendentalist" engaged in "ecstatic contemplation of a world without man." Even Martin Luther King, Jr. (who had read Niebuhr as a student at Boston University) sounds today like a voice from a distant age when in his *Letter from Birmingham Jail* (1963) he invokes natural-law theologians from St. Thomas Aquinas to Martin Buber, and declares that "segregation is not only politically, economically and sociologically unsound, it is sinful."[34]

[4]

What overtook these books, and makes them sound anachronistic when read today, was the corrosive spirit of irony that reasserted itself after its dormancy during World War II and the Cold War, and that has since grown into the dominant style of American culture. The transformation of outrage into irony was hastened in the 1960s by a series of stunning assassinations that drove an entire generation away from politics as an arena of hope. It announced itself most clearly in a famous cartoon that first appeared in 1970, after the literature of self-indictment had come to focus almost exclusively on the war in Vietnam. Paraphrasing the words of Oliver Hazard Perry after the battle of Lake Erie in 1813, "We have met the enemy, and they are ours," Pogo changes the report: "We have met the enemy, and he is us." By the time this cartoon appeared (it was used on the first Earth Day poster in 1971), what had begun as a few dissident voices in the Cold War years had become, in Trilling's phrase, a full-fledged "adversary culture."

"The salient feature of irony," as Kierkegaard had put it with astounding prescience more than a hundred years before,

> is the subjective freedom that at all times has in its power the possibility of a beginning and is not handicapped by earlier situations. There is something seductive about all beginnings, because the subject is still free, and this is the enjoyment the ironist craves.[35]

There had long been a domestic American strain of this kind of romantic irony, which Emerson expressed in its purest form when he proclaimed his intention to "write on the lintels of the doorpost, *Whim*," and which Walker Percy, more than a century later, called "the locus of pure possibility," the condition in which "what a man can be the next minute bears no relation to what he is or what he was the minute before." But only a very few people in any generation are willing to act on this principle of radical freedom, to "shun father and mother and wife and brother when my genius calls me."[36] For the rest, after a period of adolescent rebelliousness in which whim may rule, the craving for new beginnings remains just that—a craving, unslaked.

At first, it seemed that the generation of the 1960s might prove an exception to this pattern of spontaneity followed by reversion to conformity, that it might actually commit itself for the long run to what Irving

Howe called *"the psychology of unobstructed need."*[37] Something sorely needed had been injected into American culture—a sense of humor that did not spare the self. And for a time, the spirit of the 1960s remained irreverent rather than corrosive, playful rather than anarchic. This was a different spirit from the jaded weariness of Hemingway and Fitzgerald. Irony seemed ready to deliver now on the Emersonian promise: to liberate the culture from the oppressive sense that possibility was foreclosed. This has always been the indispensable work of irony, which is the recourse of the oppressed (it is no accident that Jewish and black humor are the strongest comic traditions in American life), and an antidote to the kind of poisonous cultural narcissism that allows demagogues to prosper.

But to Howe and his contemporaries, who had been children in the 1920s and had come of age during the horrors of the 1930s and 1940s, it was clear that the antinomian irony reignited in the culture of the 1960s would not burn hot for long. It would, they predicted, subside into a cool, performative routine. Writing in 1961, Trilling had already detected in his students what "we might call the socialization of the anti-social, or the acculturation of the anti-cultural, or the legitimization of the subversive."[38] With a precision that was as uncanny as it was unwitting, he echoed what Scott Fitzgerald had said about the generation of Americans who came of age between the two world wars—that "the young people in America are brilliant with second-hand sophistication inherited from their betters of the war generation who to some extent worked things out for themselves."[39]

The clearest manifestation of this secondhand irony was the emergence into the mainstream culture of a style called Camp. It began as a covertly homosexual style, an expression of a closeted subculture whose members knew what it meant to live perforce in disguise, and for whom caricaturing the strictly sex-differentiated straight world with exaggerated fey gestures or with the macho style of crew cuts and combat fatigues was a kind of solidarity ritual. Camp, as its chief exegete, Susan Sontag, explained, was "the love of the exaggerated, the 'off,' of things-being-what-they-are-not. . . . Camp sees everything in quotation marks. It's not a lamp, but a 'lamp'; not a woman, but a 'woman.' "[40]

The immediate antecedent of this new ironic style was what Norman Mailer had, in the 1950s, called Hip:

if our collective condition is to live with instant death by atomic war, relatively quick death by the State as *l'univers concentrationnaire*, or with a slow death by conformity with every creative and rebellious instinct stifled . . . why then the only life-giving answer is to accept the terms of death, to live with death as immediate danger, to divorce oneself from society, to exist without roots, to set out on that uncharted journey into the rebellious imperatives of the self. In short, whether the life is criminal or not, the decision is to encourage the psychopath in oneself, to explore that domain of experience where security is boredom and therefore sickness, and one exists in the present, in that enormous present which is without past or future, memory or planned intention, the life where a man must go until he is beat, where he must gamble with his energies through all those small or large crises of courage and unforeseen situations which beset his day, where he must be with it or doomed not to swing.

And the source of Hip was "the Negro [who] has been living on the margin between totalitarianism and democracy for two centuries."[41] Mailer, who discerned an encroaching totalitarianism throughout American life, wrote about it in an electric prose that cut to the bone. But when, in its subsequent expression as Camp, it became an accoutrement of the respectable middle class (like jazz and folk music, it was a style co-opted by the consumer culture), it lost its authenticity and became just another fashion.

It hit the world of interior decoration and clothing design, of television (in the *Batman* series that ran from 1966 to 1968, the Gotham battlers for good against evil came across as fey fools), and of the movies. Its quotation-mark style meant that every member of the culture who had not embraced it was still locked into a prescribed role in which the actor's improvisational talents were suppressed in favor of some scripted assignment. To this kind of dull-minded submissiveness, Sontag preferred the "haunting androgynous vacancy behind the perfect beauty of Greta Garbo," who refused to be conventionally soft and pliant and fulfilled by some male protector. "To perceive Camp in objects and persons is to understand Being-as-Playing-a-Role. It is the farthest extension, in sensibility, of the metaphor of life as theater." In any such theatrical performance, the devious Bad are more attractive than the predictable Good. After watching Emile De Antonio's film *Point of Order* (1963), about the Army-McCarthy hearings, Sontag found that "all the good guys come off badly—Army Secretary Stevens, Senator Symington, lawyer Welch, and the rest, looked like dopes, stuffed shirts, ninnies, prigs, or opportunists —while the film irresistibly encourages us to relish the villains aesthetically."[42] This, to use a later phrase whose abbreviated coyness comes straight out of the Camp sensibility, was irony "to the max."

One of the best examples of this Camp aesthetic was Truman Capote's best-seller *In Cold Blood* (1965), about the murder of a Kansas family by a couple of drifters, a book that launched the vastly successful "true crime" genre more recently pursued by Joe McGinniss and other journalists. Capote's most evocative writing is reserved for the murderers, especially for the misshapen Perry, who has a semi-dwarfed body for which he tries to compensate by building up his torso and oiling his hair until it is "lotion-soaked and scented." He was once encouraged by a prison mate who "thought he divined in the cripple-legged body builder with the misty gaze and the prim, smoky voice 'a poet, something rare and savable.' " His "eyes, with their moist, dreamy expression, [are] rather pretty—rather, in an actorish way, sensitive."[43]

In contrast to this poignant killer, his victims are an unbearably wholesome family, all of them strangers to hardship and pain. For the teenage girl who dies at Perry's hands, the biggest issue in her life has been the question of who would take her to the senior prom. She is "a straight-A student, the president of her class, a leader in the 4-H program and the Young Methodists League, a skilled rider, an excellent musician (piano, clarinet), an annual winner at the county fair (pastry, preserves, needlework, flower arrangement)."[44] With every item in this inventory of middle-American virtues, one imagines Capote wincing.

This kind of writing was the result of drinking deep from the cup of irony—deeper even than the writers of the 1920s had done, in whose works there is often a residual Midwestern earnestness. At first, the effect of giving oneself up to this kind of undilute irony may be a delightful giddiness, like that which Emerson had in mind when he remarked, "Turn the eyes upside down, by looking at the landscape through your legs, and how agreeable is the picture, though you have seen it any time these twenty years!" At first, irony is a release from the stultifying world in which the customary is confused with the just and conventions are regarded as commandments. It transports us, as Melville knew it could, to a world where "what we deem wrong, may there be deemed right; even as some substances, without undergoing any mutations in themselves, utterly change their color, according to the light thrown upon them."[45] In this world turned topsy-turvy, the good becomes bad and the bad becomes good. "This is a vision," as Howe put it at the end of the 1960s, of life beyond good and evil, not because these experiences or possibilities of experience have been confronted and transcended, but because the categories by which we try to designate them have been dismissed. There is no need to taste the apple: the apple brings health to those who know how to bite it: and look more closely, there is no apple at all, it exists only in your sickened imagination.[46]

One of the literary and artistic legacies of the 1960s was a dismissive style known as "minimalism"—the perfect style for a "world gone flat" —in which all differentiations (foreground, background; light, dark; surface, interior) have been obliterated. This style came into its own in the monochrome canvases of Barnett Newman and Ad Reinhardt and later in the fiction of some short-lived literary celebrities of the 1970s and 1980s like Jay McInerney and Bret Easton Ellis. Derived from a group of laconic French novelists who had earlier introduced a new kind of fiction in which events like the sole of a shoe were written about with the same clinical precision as one brought to an account of, say, the birth of a child, this kind of writing brought the leveling tendency of Hemingway's prose style to a new extremity. It was ironic art in the fullest sense: "stripped of all 'illusions,' it has lost belief in 'essences' themselves."[47]

These painters and writers imagined before the fact the undifferentiated world we live in now, in which anyone who makes assertions about "natural" differences between "male" and "female," say, sounds like a fundamentalist raver—since these terms, which once signified a division thought to be inherent in nature, now denote the ways in which certain behaviors are assigned by culture to the two biologically distinct entities that comprise the human race. Similarly, the once unassailable distinction between good and evil is suspect, since it is now conventional to believe that "the apparent assertion of [moral] principles functions as a mask for expressions of personal preference," and the question arises, as Walker Percy put it in *Lancelot* (1977),

What would happen if you could prove the existence of sin, pure and simple? Wouldn't that be a windfall . . . ? A new proof of God's existence! If there is such a thing as sin, evil, a living malignant force, there must be a God! . . . if you could show me a *sin* . . . a purely evil deed, an intolerable deed for which there is no explanation . . . People would sit up and take notice. I would be impressed. You could almost make a believer out of me.[48]

Percy, who was reared and lived most of his life in the South (and was therefore perhaps more sensitive than his Northern counterparts to the process by which old moral "truths" are revealed as ruses for power), recorded the ironic "explosion of all formulas, all myths" with unusual precision. He set his novels in a world without distinctions, where television advertisements for shaving cream coexist with news footage of war, and fewer and fewer people notice the difference. Here is a little stretch of dialogue from *The Last Gentleman* (1966) between the titular protagonist—a new version of Lippmann's "modern man"—who is trying to convince himself that there is durable truth in the fading bourgeois virtues, and another man, who has long ago given them up:

"It is better to do something than to do nothing—no reflection, sir."
"No reflection."
"It is good to have a family."
"You are quite right."
"Better to love than be loved."
"Absolutely."
"To cultivate whatever talents one has."
"Correct."
"To make a contribution, however small."
"However small."
"To do one's best to promote tolerance and understanding between the races, surely the most pressing need before the country."
"Beyond question the most pressing need. Tolerance and understanding. Yes."
The engineer flushed. "Well, isn't it better?"
"Yes."
"Violence is bad."
"Violence is not good."
"It is better to make love to one's wife than to monkey around with a lot of women."
"A lot better."
"I am sure I am right."
"You are right."[49]

Every one of these assertions is nerveless, robotic, and received with bland indulgence. They reveal themselves, in the saying, as dead platitudes. The dialogue has an odd obliqueness that makes it sound truncated, like a series of chords that does not return to the tonic. But at the same time it reads like a transcript of a conversation we are now continually having with ourselves—a conversation in which all talk about morals has come to sound moralistic.

Since Percy and Capote's day, we have literally enveloped ourselves in quotation marks; to be fashionably dressed today is to be either androgynous or satirical in pinched-waist dresses or square-shouldered suits that make mock allusions to some hyperfeminine or hypermasculine style in the past. Irony has become the normative style of contemporary life —a fact that is, of course, an irony of its own, since irony begins its career, as Augustine noted long ago in recalling his days among the "Subverters," as an expression of resistance to cultural prescriptions, until it is left with nothing to resist except itself.

The influential German social theorist Jürgen Habermas (writing, like all postwar German intellectuals, with a haunting awareness of how the ironic sensibility that flourished during the Weimar Republic turned out to be the prelude to Nazism) has described this situation as a "legitimation crisis," a moment in social development when "later generations no longer recognize themselves within the once-constitutive tradition" of the culture to which they putatively belong.[50] Not only to intellectuals but to millions of citizens who have some sense of history, our own past has become a scandal or, worse, an object of indifference. One quick way to grasp what this means in the United States is to visit the Lincoln Memorial in Washington, then take the long walk down its steps, and further downhill to the subterranean Vietnam War Memorial that stretches out like a fortified trench in its shadow. Chiseled in the marble walls around the figure of Lincoln are the texts of the Gettysburg and Second Inaugural addresses. In the granite of the Vietnam memorial (which is all wall, enclosing nothing) there are simply the names of the dead. This mute tombstone is the only kind of monument we now dare build.

[5]

Since every generation is inclined to believe that its own experience is without precedent, one of the rewards of looking into history is to discover that this is not so. In the aftermath of the Civil War, for instance, one finds Whitman complaining that "the men believe not in the women, nor the women in the men," and that "the aim of all the *littérateurs* is to find something to make fun of." These sentences—eerily apt for our own time—suggest that irony tends to surge in periods of retrenchment, after a culture has exerted itself on behalf of old pieties and paid the cost in blood and hope. (One of the first, and bitterest, effusions of post-Vietnam irony was Robert Altman's film *M*A*S*H** [1970], which became a long-running television show in which the one-liner rhythm of the sitcom is transposed to a jungle field hospital.) "Irony," as Hayden White puts it, "represents the passage of the age of heroes and of the capacity to believe in heroism."[51]

If one scrolls through the history of American culture, a few ironic voices do emerge before the twentieth century above the din of consensual piety. But they leap from the page because of their rarity, as when an intellectual gadfly named Abner Kneeland gave vent to irony in the 1830s (contemporaries compared him to "beer from a bottle, all foaming") and found himself hauled in for trial on the charge of blasphemy. "A Parisian," he wrote,

> will be surprised to hear that the Hottentots cut out one of the testicles of every little boy; and a Hottentot will be surprised to hear that the Parisians leave every little boy two. Neither the Parisian nor the Hottentot is astonished at the practice of the other because he finds it unreasonable, but because it differs from his own.[52]

This man believed precociously, as we now do conventionally, that history is nothing more than a chain of contingencies. He was a modern before his time. If in one country little boys are permitted to keep their genitals intact and in another they are subjected to testicular excision, this is because they have come accidentally into the world at different times and places—not because there is anything intrinsically better about having one testicle or two. In country A, tampering with the genitals is denounced as mutilation. In country B it is an affront to God for a child to keep his scrotum intact. To condemn or approve either view is to proclaim oneself a provincial—a person imprisoned in the prevalent stories of one's own time and place. When Kneeland expressed these opinions, he was being deliberately scandalous; but today he would be considered just another cultural relativist—one of the many who regard all past doctrines as a series of universal claims for local practices. Once this judgment is made, there is no longer any scripture to which the missionary may turn when he wants to bring light to the savages. Indeed, there are no more Christians and no more savages.

Yet if there are historical analogies for our situation ("genuine belief has left us," Whitman wrote in 1870), the triumph of irony has never been as complete as it is today. We have reached a point where it is not only specific objects of belief that have been discredited but the very capacity to believe. This is new. In the past, when old ways of seeing the world gave way, it was possible to discern at least the outlines of a new way that would take their place; and the succession, it was generally believed, would result in a better vision of truth. (This is what happened at the end of the seventeenth century, for instance, when the idea of possession by ghosts gave way to associationist psychology. It happened again in the nineteenth century, when the doctrine of divine creation was replaced by the idea of evolution.) But the process we are living through today is sufficiently different in degree that it has become different in kind. It is divestiture without reinvestment.

We are living in "a stillness between tides, neither going out nor coming in,"[53] in E. L. Doctorow's phrase, and as we wait to see what the tide will bring in, the rule of irony compels us to ask certain urgent questions. Can irony yield any sense of evil? Is the ironist capable of making discriminations of value? Or is he condemned to live in a contingent world of morally indistinguishable actions and events, in which all ideas are denigrated as ideologies? If, for example, we read today the words of John Foster Dulles in 1948, when he decried the expansion into Europe of Soviet Communism "by methods of penetration, propaganda, and terrorism . . . the like of which men have not seen since, one thousand years ago, the new and dynamic Moslem faith struck out against the established institutions of Christendom,"[54] we are quick, and right, to ask the ironist's questions. By what arrogance did Dulles dare exempt from his moral indignation the Inquisition or other crimes committed in the name of "Christendom"? And what about the brutal "Christian" conquest of the New World, or indeed the whole history of European class warfare, racism, and imperialism? Dulles's analogy between the Russians and the Muslim hordes sounds the unmistakable note of what we would now call "Orientalism"; and so we consign him to the dismissible category of Cold Warrior.

But after these points have been made, does the ironist ask whether Dulles was right about Stalin? Is it possible for such a question to arise in the ironist's mind? In the face of some new Stalin or Hitler, is it possible to shake off the lethargy induced by irony and rise to the fight? History does not encourage an affirmative answer to these questions. This is so because, as the philosopher Paul Ricoeur has said, "there is no taboo in which there does not dwell some reverence, some veneration of order."[55] Without reverence for *something*, there can be no proscriptions—and it should be clear enough to any observer of contemporary culture that we are short on both. Irony has proven to be a more potent solvent of our erstwhile beliefs than any contending belief. Yet for all its power to dissolve the presumptions of the past, it cannot produce future commitments. Its energy is negative. When it does the work of exposure, it can open up the view like any demolition work. But afterward, it is of no use in the work of rebuilding.

Take, for instance, the case of feminism, perhaps the most important social force of the last twenty-five years, and one that claims to have revealed a form of evil that had hitherto remained hidden behind the unexamined axioms of gender hierarchy. Writing in the early days of the women's movement, the critic Mary Ellmann addressed what she called (before the term had become a cliché) "phallic criticism." She had just read a review by a male critic of a new novel by Françoise Sagan, the French writer who, as a teenager, had made a sensation with her coming-of-age tale *Bonjour Tristesse* (1954). The reviewer did not like Sagan's new book, and said so in these terms:

> Poor old Françoise Sagan. Just one more old-fashioned old-timer, bypassed in the rush for the latest literary vogue and for youth. Superficially, her career in America resembles the lifespan of those medieval beauties who flowered at 14, were deflowered at 15, were old at 30, and crones at 40.

Ellmann's response was to offer "a review of a new novel by the popular French novelist François Sagan," cast in the same terms:

> Poor old François Sagan. . . . Superficially, his career in America resembles the lifespan of those medieval troubadours who masturbated at 14, copulated at 15, were impotent at 30, and prostate cases at 40.[56]

Finding herself for no discernible reason in a culture where "the literal fact of masculinity, unlike femininity, does not impose an erogenic form upon all aspects of the person's career," Ellmann availed herself of the vocabulary that was customarily used to force women's lives into a preposterous "erogenic form." She knew that it sounded normative when applied to women, and outrageous when applied to men. This is a fine particular instance of the ironist's general point—that if one shifts the context of any received idea, it will be revealed as a convention. The ironist's tactic is a version of the child's maddening game of asking "why" after every assertion or command. Even as the parents grow exasperated, they know that the child has a point—that there is no good answer to the "why" and that the game will end with a decree and a fiat: "Because I said so."

This discovery of what the deconstructionists call *absence* at the core of authority ("by vast pains we mine into the pyramid," as Melville put it long ago, "by horrible gropings we come to the central room; with joy we espy the sarcophagus; but we lift the lid—and no body is there!—"[57]) gives impetus to the reformer who would deny the metaphysical claims of those who hold power. In the ironist's eye every pretender to legitimate authority becomes a Wizard of Oz, and the point is to draw aside the curtain.

But when the exposure has been performed and the next point is reached—the point at which the world that was dismantled must be rebuilt—irony is of no use. If one reveals the foundations of the culture as floating on nothing, if one exposes its empirical approach to experience, its instrumentalist view of nature, its "possessive individualism" —the whole catalogue of inheritances from the Enlightenment—as historically evolved rather than naturally sanctioned, how, then, do we respond when the absence of these principles in other cultures seems to have something to do with the horrors they perpetrate? How does the radical feminist react, say, to the fact that female genital mutilation is a regular cultural practice in some non-Western societies? Adept as she is at exposing the contingent nature of all cultures and the arrogance of imputing superiority to one's own, how is she to justify her outrage? When she shudders at the idea that some adolescent girls have their labia sewn together or their clitoris amputated, is she not reacting from within a specific cultural context in which her own sensibility was formed? What basis does irony give her to intervene or even object?

The truth is, if she is to invoke the ideology of individual rights—the rights, in this case, to own one's own body and to experience sexual pleasure—she is reverting to a cultural vocabulary which has claimed universalism but which she has exposed as contingent. The historian David Hollinger has recently brought attention to this issue in what he calls "the case of the Masai women." He reviews it with some irony of his own:

> If these women are but breeding stock and, when barren of sons, are treated by their warrior masters as inferior to cattle, who are we to criticize? It is part of Masai culture, after all. And we probably should not even talk about it, as such talk might flatter Western prejudice and might lead us to forget how much violence and injustice are suffered by women in the United States and Western Europe.

He continues in this ironic vein; the only way that we could rescue the Masai and remain true to our principle of refraining from comparative cultural judgments would be

> if the Masai peoples eventually die off amid the economic, political, and ecological transformation of East Africa. [Then] we could, on ethnocentric principles, rescue the last surviving Masai woman as she crawls starving across the Ogaden. The price of her emancipation would then be the death of her culture, which we are restrained from countenancing by our principled anti-universalism and our healthy suspicion of Western imperialism.[58]

In other words, to make a judgment and save a life is to suspend one's irony about one's own culture. It is to repudiate someone else's belief on behalf of one's own. This has become an increasingly difficult act to imagine, much less perform, since as a society we seem to have virtually no beliefs left. When we use the old words—rights, responsibility, and, above all, evil—we are reverting to a world that the new ironist believes he has left behind.

One of the best descriptions of this kind of paralysis has been offered in a remarkable book by Richard Rorty called *Contingency, Irony, and Solidarity* (1989). It is, like *The Last Gentleman*, a reprise of Lippmann, and a reminder of how much contemporary America resembles the America between the wars about which Lippmann was writing. Rorty's own concession to irony is to substitute the feminine pronoun for what was, until recently, the unexamined universal *he:*

The ironist spends her time worrying about the possibility that she has been initiated into the wrong tribe, taught to play the wrong language game. She worries that the process of socialization which turned her into a human being by giving her a language may have given her the wrong language, and so turned her into the wrong kind of human being. But she cannot give a criterion of wrongness. So, the more she is driven to articulate her situation in philosophical terms, the more she reminds herself of her rootlessness.[59]

Most Americans today recognize the feeling of rootlessness that Rorty describes here and know all too well what it means to live without a "criterion of wrongness." We recognize it because it is a description of where, and who, we are.

[6]

It is now customary to think of "consciousness," in the words of the critic Fredric Jameson, as "a kind of construction rather than a stable substance . . . a locus of relationships rather than an ego in the older sense."[60] Within the covers of an academic book, this "postmodernist" view of consciousness is a harmless abstraction, a way of asserting that the self is authored by the world rather than the other way around, as certain literary critics like to say. The cardinal principle of this postmodernist irony is that it is unintelligible to talk about the self before the advent of language: that the self is merely the name given to the stream of instincts, reflexes, and attitudes that are funneled into a human organism by the history of its antecedents.

But when this theory or idea gets loose from the books, it becomes another matter altogether. For it is a way of thinking about the self that is incompatible with personal responsibility. In this sense, the most articulate ironists of the last few years have been not professors but killers like the Menendez brothers—persons who variously identify some compulsion originating outside themselves as the initiator of their actions. "The architecture of [their] self-defense," as Elizabeth Hardwick has put it, is always organized around some form of coercion, and the most common form of coercion is sexual abuse ("as pertinent to the therapist," Hardwick says, "as a kidney to the urologist")—a form of terror that, as the young Lyle Menendez expressed it on the witness stand, left him "no choice but to kill his parents." In the case of Lorena Bobbitt, who cut off her abusive husband's penis, it was "the weapon of her torture— that is, her husband's penis," which she identified as the source of her misery and which she attacked with the kitchen knife.[61]

Intended to exonerate, these are only two of the better-known in a rash of responsibility-evading claims that come spewing forth from criminal defendants in America today. The question of where responsibility lies for the perpetration of evil is, of course, an ancient one; but the brazenness of these disavowals is new, and it is one of the most striking features of contemporary culture—a mutant form of irony, but a form nevertheless. In an essay that argues for Richard Nixon as the single greatest influence on contemporary American literature, the novelist Charles Baxter has called this trend "the concept of *deniability*," or "the almost complete disavowal of intention in relation to bad consequences." Not long ago a book was published about Adolf Hitler's childhood in which the argument was advanced that "the life of [this] mass murderer reflects the countless murders to which the child was subjected."[62]

The line between explanation and excuse is always a thin one, and many scrupulous people have tried hard to locate it precisely in order not to cross it; but the question of where to draw this line has never been so resistant to an answer as it is now. One looks back wistfully to the singular historical moment when Niebuhr, in a book entitled *The Nature and Destiny of Man* (can one imagine any academic luminary today affiliating himself with such a title?), wrote of "responsibility despite inevitability":

> While all particular sins have both social sources and social consequences, the real essence of sin can be understood only in the vertical dimension of the soul's relation to God because the freedom of the self stands outside all relations, and therefore has no other judge but God. It is for this reason that a profound insight into the character of sin must lead to the confession, "Against thee, thee only, have I sinned, and done this evil in thy sight" (Psalms, 51).[63]

It was with this same structure of responsibility in mind that Telford Taylor insisted at the Nuremberg trials that "it is important that the trial *not* become an inquiry into the *causes* of the war," that there should be no "effort or time spent on apportioning out responsibility for causing the war among the many nations and individuals concerned. . . . Contributing causes may be pleaded by the defendants before the bar of history, but not before the tribunal." Justice Robert Jackson, the American prosecutor at Nuremberg, opened the case against the Nazi defendants with the statement that "the wrongs which we seek to condemn and punish have been so calculated, so malignant, and so devastating, that civilization cannot afford their being ignored, because it cannot survive their being repeated."[64]

The world of Niebuhr, Taylor, and Jackson is lost to us. Today, we live instead in the world that Edwards predicted, where it is no longer clear whether "anybody [is] to be either blamed or commended for anything." As Michael Wood has written, it is a world

> full of uncaused events, littered with things that are just one of those things. We are all wrongly accused. We live inside a curious, sentimental reversal of Kafka's *Trial*, where the *court* is always found to be stacked and guilty. We have been lynched by life.[65]

This is an unimprovable description of the ironic reversals and claims of victimization (the main fare of Oprah Winfrey, Phil Donahue, and other impresarios of the professional victim) that now characterize American culture, a parodic reiteration of Benjamin Franklin's claim that for a "creature . . . able to do only such things as God [or fate, or circumstance] would have him to do . . . there can be no Merit nor Demerit." Wood then turns to one of the most familiar citizens of the cinematic version of our world, and reminds us of how he responds to one of its self-proclaimed victims who speaks in this self-excusing way:

> "Wish me luck. I got a raw deal," a tough, embittered woman says in *The Big Sleep*. Bogart, as Philip Marlowe, wiser and stricter and meaner than a problem movie, replies, "Your kind always does."[66]

Here is the essential point. Bogart, whose crushed hat and trench coat now constitute the inventory of upscale chain stores, and whose stubble and tough talk we like to imitate, possessed all the superficial attributes of irony—worldliness, fatigue with the self-righteous and the prissy and the prudish. He had seen it all, had had it all, had betrayed and been betrayed. But in the end, in the archetypal American film *Casablanca* (in which, as Wood says, he hides his "passionate altruism behind a mask of selfishness and diffidence"), he reveals himself to be an incorruptible moralist. Having lost Bogart's substance, all we have left is his pose.

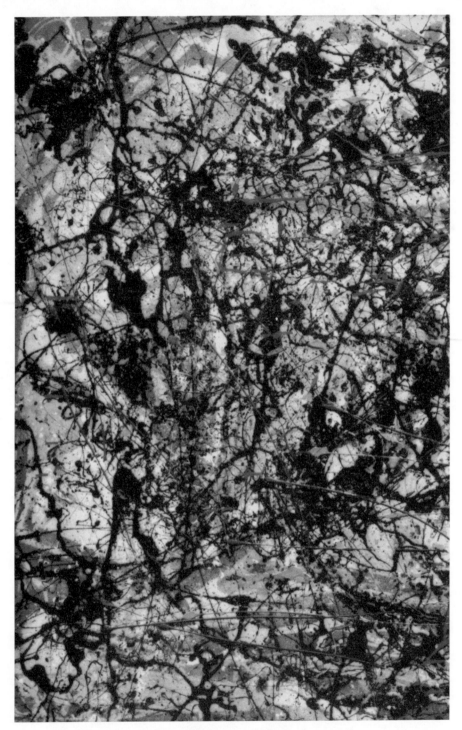

Jackson Pollock, Lucifer *(detail) (1947)*
(ARTISTS' RIGHTS SOCIETY)

SEVEN

Prospects

[1]

Some years ago, when my daughter was not quite three, I discovered one night while I was reading to her that she had never seen a star. Her storybook contained an illustration of a starry night, and it became clear that she did not know what the picture represented. I was startled, but realized that it was because she had lived most of her life in a city where the mercury lights that are supposed to make the streets safe also have the effect of obscuring the night sky.

So the next time we were in the country on a clear day, we went outside after dark and looked up. I was doing pretty well at faking an explanation of what stars are ("little suns," "lots of gas") when my daughter brought me up short by asking about *shooting* stars, a term she had heard and was confused about. It seemed shabby to answer her question as if it were easily disposable, so I stopped, and made some gestures of deferral.

Some time later I was reading a work by an early American writer who made some comments about the very fast- and slow-traveling stars (meteors and comets) which he had learned about and even seen with his own eyes. Such spectacular events were, he said, adornments of the "great and glorious volume of [God's] Works." The world was the Lord's published book, over which inattentive persons might nod if God, like a printer who highlights certain parts of a text with boldface type or arrows in the margins, had not placed

in the Margent . . . Red Letters, Asterisms, or pointing Hands, to awaken unto a more heedful attention and serious consideration, the dead-hearted sleeping and secure World of Mankind.[1]

In other words, comets and meteors were God's instruments for awakening people to his glory. They were his marginalia, his italics, his exclamation points.

Yet even in the seventeenth century, some impious persons doubted that this could be so. These persons were ahead of their time and halfway to ours. They were the ones who suspected that comets were a meaningless kind of fireworks—"periwigged Heraulds that have appeared on the aethereal stage" for no evident reason. After a flash in the night, when the pulpits rang with warnings that God was preparing a judgment—a flood, or an Indian attack—these were the people who snickered in the back pews. If no disaster came, they felt confirmed in their disbelief. They were the first American ironists.

Outraged by such people, the writer whom I was reading retorted that the signals in the sky might refer to some faraway event, that their "blasting influences might be direfully operative in remoter and less known parts of the Earth."[2] As I read this marvelously irrefutable rejoinder, I found myself thinking that it would be a comfort to live as he did—in a pre-CNN world where news of distant catastrophes never arrives and need never be denied. One could read the heavens without ever having their portents discredited.

Although there would be a certain satisfaction in living imaginatively in such a world, on balance it is probably a good thing that we have lost it forever. Whether we welcome or mourn this loss, it is the central and irreversible fact of modern history that we no longer inhabit a world of transcendence. The idea that man is a receptor of truth from God has been relinquished, and replaced with the idea that reality is an unstable zone between phenomena (unknowable in themselves) and innumerable fields of mental activity (which we call persons) by which they are apprehended. These apprehensions are expressed through language, which is always evolving, and which constitutes the only reality we recognize. Our world exists in this ceaseless movement of human consciousness, a process in which the reception of new impressions is indistinguishable from the production of new meanings: "mind's willful transference of nature, man, and society—and eventually of God, and finally of mind itself—into itself."[3]

Even though we may understand intellectually that we cannot reverse this process, as we watch our children grow up, at moments—such as the night in the unilluminated country when I went outside with my daughter to find the stars—the loss seems unbearable. Fortunately, we are usually aware more of the compensations than of the costs—for instance, that in the age of science our children (especially daughters) are likely to live longer and with less pain than did their stargazing predecessors at a time when nature was still largely unfathomable. Yet one fears for them. How will they live without some residue of the idea, diminishing as it may do with each generation, that (in the words of Poe) "the multitudinous myriads of stars . . . roll and glow in the majestic presence of their Creator"?[4]

Many Americans—and many millions throughout the world—have refused to give up their belief in this presence. These include people who hold fast to traditional religious beliefs, as well as those who come to the defense of "Mother Earth" against "the Faustian urge [of modern civilization] to dominate nature"[5] and attribute to nature a kind of pantheistic unity of consciousness that mankind has insulted and offended. They include millions of churchgoing Christians, devout Jews, Muslims, Buddhists, and members of such quasi-religious organizations as Alcoholics Anonymous who remain committed to the idea that responsibility and predestination are compatible terms for describing human experience under the watch of God.

By and large, I have left these people out of this book—because the story I have tried to tell is the story of the advance of secular rationality in the United States, which has been relentless in the face of all resistance. It is the story of a culture that has gradually withdrawn its support from the old conception of a universe seething with divine intelligence and has left its members with only one recourse: to acknowledge that no story about the intrinsic meaning of the world has universal validity. With this acknowledgment, all such stories—from the pre-Socratics to the Christians to the Romantics and beyond—become fairy tales. It is now considered a mark of maturity, as Richard Rorty has said, to put them away as childish things:

> The suggestion that truth, as well as the world, is out there is a legacy of an age in which the world was seen as the creation of a being who had a language of his own. . . . [But] the world does not speak. Only we do. The world can, once we have programmed ourselves with a language, cause us to hold beliefs. But it cannot propose a language for us to speak. Only other human beings can do that.

Over the short history of what we now call the United States, the American people have followed a course that Rorty, again, summarizes with precision:

> Once upon a time we felt a need to worship something which lay beyond the visible world. Beginning in the seventeenth century we tried to substitute a love of truth for a love of God, treating the world described by science as a quasi divinity. Beginning at the end of the eighteenth century we tried to substitute a love of ourselves for a love of scientific truth, a worship of our own deep spiritual or poetic nature, treated as one more quasi divinity. . . . [and now we have arrived at] the point where we no longer worship *anything*, where we treat *nothing* as a quasi divinity, where we treat *everything*—our language, our conscience, our community—as a product of time and chance.[6]

This remarkable paragraph is a miniature history of our culture. I have told this history mainly through our literature, at whose center Melville stands like a polar star, because American literature is the most sensitive record we have of American historical experience. It has been a literature concerned "more than anything else," as Lionel Trilling once put it about modern literature in general, "with salvation."[7]

In telling the story this way, I have tried to show how some of the metaphors we once used to describe the world have withered away. If a comet was once the harbinger of divine wrath, for instance, we now understand it to be "a nebulous body with a 'hairy' tail that makes a transient appearance in the sky . . . an irregularly shaped mass composed of ices . . . mixed with substantial amounts of soot-like matter—perhaps carbon in the form of fine dust."[8] And though the poets have always objected to this sort of deadly empiricism ("Science! . . . How should he love thee? or how deem thee wise? / Who wouldst not leave him in his wandering / To seek for treasure in the jewelled skies"[9]), most intellectuals urge us on toward what is sometimes called "demystification," in the hope that we may someday reach the point where the last vestiges of religious metaphor will have been expunged.

There are several reasons that I wanted to tell this story with more human detail than can be contained in a compressed summary like Rorty's. One reason is that I believe it is important to recognize that the process of secularization has always been resisted; during the Civil War many soldiers still regarded the sight of the aurora borealis as a harbinger of death. Large stretches of America's contentious history—including our current turmoil over issues like abortion and euthanasia—can only be understood as conflicts between those who accept the idea that "the world does not speak" and those who do not. At certain times—during the eighteenth century, for instance—the contest between these two views was particularly acute; and though it has sometimes subsided, it has never been fully resolved. In our own time, as the cultural historian Garry Wills has pointed out, when the evangelist Jimmy Swaggart admitted on television that he had committed sexual sins with a prostitute, millions of Americans thought they were witnessing the public humiliation of a faithless hypocrite, while millions more saw a penitent sinner humbling himself before his flock in the presence of God.[10]

In the 1950s, the English writer C. P. Snow coined the term "two cultures" to describe the cleavage between scientists and humanists that he believed pertained throughout the developed Western world. In the 1960s, the Kerner Commission appointed by President Lyndon Johnson used the term "two societies" to describe the widening division between blacks and whites in America. Now, at the end of the twentieth century, we are, I believe, dividing between two sensibilities that correspond to belief and irony.[11] The conflict between these two sensibilities has, I believe, more potential for rancor and ferocity than any of the preceding oppositions.

Thus in telling this American story—of how our language has been evacuated of religious metaphor—it is important to acknowledge that many people feel bereft. I am not sure that Niebuhr was right when he wrote that "the only ground of an effective ethic" is a paradoxical God who stands "as both the creator and the judge of historical existence," but I am quite sure that the author of a recent book entitled *The Postmodern Condition* is wrong (about America or any other culture) when he asserts that "most people have lost the nostalgia" for the old God-dominated world with "its great hero, its great dangers, its great voyages, its great goal." This kind of statement ignores the fact that "previous philosophy . . . has left stratified deposits in popular philosophy,"[12] and it seems to me that the party of rationality is prematurely convinced that people can endure life without the old metaphors.

This party of secular liberalism, of which I consider myself a member, has deluded itself into believing that human beings can manage without any metaphor at all. In Susan Sontag's book of about twenty years ago, *Illness as Metaphor*, for example, she described her own personal struggle, as a cancer patient, against certain prevalent ideas that associated her disease with moral meanings actually embedded *in* nature. She found that some people around her (friends and colleagues as well as strangers) implied that the disease from which she suffered somehow manifested a repressed personality in which sexual desire or artistic creation had been bottled up until it started eating the self from within. In the face of these insults to her dignity, Sontag called for the rejection of metaphor and for "the most truthful way of regarding illness—and the healthiest way of being ill," a way that is entirely "purified of . . . metaphoric thinking."[13]

Moving as Sontag's testamental book is, I find myself doubting that it is possible to live free of metaphor or to be cured, as Isaiah Berlin once put it, of our "deep metaphysical need."[14] If we fall back on scientific language for describing what happens to the cancer patient—that "normal" cells become "abnormal," that the body undergoes a process we think of as illness—are we not still asserting a vision of life that involves norms and violations of norms? Are we not still dividing the world between "healthy" entities and "sick" ones? Are we not still according greater value to the consciousness of the human sufferer than to the molecular processes within the body that lead to its death? What justifies this hierarchy of value except our own imagination?

Modernity, in other words, has doomed us to see the world through metaphors that cannot be ratified by any appeal to transcendence. And Sontag is, of course, quite right that the images associated with her cancer (and, as she argues in a later book, with AIDS) are pernicious and ought to be discarded as a noxious residue from the world where disfigurements of the body were judged to be marks of sin. No one should underestimate the destructive effects of the theological beliefs that have fallen away. No one should forget that for much of Western history, as Whittier put it more than a century and a half ago, "Satan [was] a sort of bandog of priestcraft, held in its leash and ready to be let loose upon the disputers of its authority" by ruthless churchmen who turned the world "into a great prison-house of suffering" for anyone who defied them. Yet, despite the monstrous uses to which Satan has been put, I believe that our culture is now in crisis because evil remains an inescapable experience for all of us, while we no longer have a symbolic language for describing it. Sontag herself expressed the crisis in the form of a question: "How," she asks, can we find our moral bearings "when we have a sense of evil but no longer the religious or philosophical language to talk intelligently about evil?"[15]

[2]

Around the time that Sontag was calling for the banishment of metaphor, Richard Selzer, a surgeon who writes uncommonly well about the effects on the mind of cutting and scooping and stitching people's bodies, acknowledged his own persistent hunger for spiritual significance, even though this need runs against the instincts that his scientific training is supposed to have developed in him. Here he describes an emergency operation which, in his imagination, he turned into a religious war:

The patient is a young man recently returned from Guatemala, from the excavation of Mayan ruins. His left arm wears a gauze dressing which, when removed, reveals a clean punched-out hole the size of a dime. The tissues about the opening are swollen and tense. A thin brownish fluid lips the edge, and now and then a lazy drop of the overflow spills down the arm. An abscess, inadequately drained. I will enlarge the opening to allow better egress of the pus. Nurse, will you get me a scalpel and some . . .

What happens next is enough to lay Francis Drake avomit in his cabin. No explorer ever stared in wilder surmise than I into that crater from which there now emerges a narrow gray head whose sole distinguishing feature is a pair of black pincers. The head sits atop a longish flexible neck arching now this way, now that, testing the air. Alternately it folds back upon itself, then advances in new boldness. And all the while, with dreadful rhythmicity, the unspeakable pincers open and close. Abscess? Pus? Never. Here is the lair of a beast whose malignant purpose I could but guess. A Mayan devil, I think, that would soon burst free to fly about the room, with horrid blanket-wings and iridescent scales, raking, pinching, injecting God knows what acid juice. . . .

With all the ritual deliberation of a high priest I advance a surgical clamp toward the hole. The surgeon's heart is become a bat hanging upside down from his rib cage. The rim achieved—now thrust—and the ratchets of the clamp close upon the empty air. The devil has retracted. Evil mocking laughter bangs back and forth in the brain. More stealth. Lying in wait. One must skulk. Minutes pass, perhaps an hour. . . . A faint disturbance in the lake, and once again the thing upraises, further and further, hovering. Acrouch, strung, the surgeon is one with his instrument; there is no longer any boundary between its metal and his flesh. They are joined in a single perfect tool of extirpation. It is just for this that he was born. Now—thrust—and clamp—and *yes*. Got him!

This account of the surgeon as exorcist, coiled into an almost sexual fervor of unity with his instrument, is a brilliant evocation of the deepest spiritual aspirations that our culture fails to satisfy. There is a sense of long-awaited discovery; the modern language of clinical description breaks down, and the old religious language of moral triumph is restored:

> Transmitted to the fingers comes the wild thrashing of the creature. Pinned and wriggling, he is mine. I hear the dry brittle scream of the dragon, and a hatred seizes me, but such a detestation as would make of Iago a drooling sucktit . . . Within the jaws of my hemostat is the whole of the evil of the world, the dark concentrate itself, and I shall kill it.[16]

The vocabulary of physical description, which one expects to be dispassionately empirical, is invaded by words from another sphere; the physical world has been imbued with moral qualities in the old way. This is Ahab against the whale.

The intercourse of vocabularies is a great pleasure for the writer, who exults in his restoration to the role of spiritual healer. But after the operation, when the deadpan pathologist, acting as ambassador of modernity, deflates him by identifying the creature as the larva of a warble fly —usually deposited in cows—the surgeon is incensed. And when he is told that "it was about to come out on its own," he curses silently: *"imposter, sorehead, servant of Satan,"* not yet ready to relinquish his moment of moral glory, but embarrassed to admit that it had swept him up.

In 1975, when Selzer was writing, the spectacle of a man of science invoking religious vocabulary was a striking one. In the twenty years since, it has become less so, because there is mounting evidence that the exhortations of religion and the disclosures of science may not, after all, be at odds. "The concept of 'evil,' " as Robert Wright has written in his recent book *The Moral Animal: Evolutionary Psychology and Everyday Life* (1994),

> doesn't fit easily into a modern scientific worldview. Still, people seem to find it useful, and the reason is that it is metaphorically apt. There is indeed a force devoted to enticing us into various pleasures that are (or once were) in our genetic interests but do not bring long-term happiness to us and may bring great suffering to others. You could call that force the ghost of natural selection. More concretely, you could call it our

genes (*some* of our genes, at least). If it will help to actually use the word *evil*, there's no reason not to.[17]

I would, and have, put it more emphatically: the idea of evil is not just a metaphor that "some people find . . . useful"; it is a metaphor upon which the health of society depends. Wright's larger point is that certain human behaviors that used to be understood under the rubric of original sin (aggression, sexual wantonness, greed) are being disclosed by post-Darwinian science to have an objective reality as constituents of human nature.

The story that Wright tells goes something like this: Certain essentially selfish impulses were written into our genes as instincts favorable to the species. Then, late in the natural history of the human creature, these behaviors were denounced by man himself. He called them evil. His religions cursed and proscribed them, offering instead the ideals of self-restraint and love. At first, this dispute between human nature and human belief seems beyond negotiation. How can exhortations to selflessness be reconciled with the genetic code? (One answer to this question is to construe all religion as hypocrisy in the way that Nietzsche did—as the manipulative ideology of a master class whose purposes it serves.) But if one concedes some ingenuousness to the religious impulse, the question remains: How can a creature revealed by science as *naturally* rapacious be drawn to generosity and love?

A tentative answer, according to Wright's summary of contemporary thinking in the field now known as evolutionary psychology, is that the pleasures of sex (detached from love) or of conquest, or of placated greed, are fleeting and ultimately insufficient to happiness. And since the desire for happiness is a universal craving, religion may express not a futile "defiance of human nature," but the evolution of the species toward satisfactions more enduring than those furnished by the old instincts. "Love, after all, makes us want to further the happiness of others; it makes us give up a little so that others (the loved ones) may have a lot." And if the growth of harmony and the decline of conflict are survival requirements for complex human societies (as they surely must be in the nuclear age), then altruism may turn out to be not just a religious ideal but an evolutionary advantage.

In all these [religious] assaults on the senses there is a great wisdom—not only about the addictiveness of pleasures but about their ephemerality. The essence of addiction, after all, is that pleasure tends to dissipate and leave the mind agitated, hungry for more.[18]

The appetites once known as sin, in other words, can never be satisfied, while the impulse known as love has the astonishing capacity to satisfy itself.

Such propositions are contemporary variants on a moral idea that has been part of Western thought from Judaism through Christianity and into the Enlightenment. They are inevitably speculative and controversial when offered in the guise of science, but they amount to a modern restatement of what the Puritan minister expressed when he wrote three hundred fifty years ago that "Satan . . . may transform himself into an Angel of Light . . . but Satan cannot pacifie the conscience, much less purifie it, himself being an uncleane spirit." Many astute witnesses to the rise of evolutionary psychology (formerly known as sociobiology) suspect its premises and judgments, finding in them echoes not only of ancient religious ideas, but of the eugenicists' more recent claim to have found the biological key to human nature. Indeed the very concept of human nature itself is a specious one to many postmodern intellectuals, who prefer to discount the idea of human nature as "merely the indeterminate material that the social factor molds and transforms."[19]

But the developments in science that Wright reports are, perhaps, reason to believe that one's alarm at the impoverishment of the language of evil may not be merely theological nostalgia. There is reason to hope for a cooperative intellectual venture between religion and science that may lead to a revival of serious moral thinking, in which the category of evil might once again have meaning. And there is certainly no cause to be embarrassed if, like Dr. Selzer, we take recourse to a language that posits Satan as a detectable presence in the world. We want Satan back not just because, as the Romantics knew so well, he exerts an irresistible fascination upon us ("What man," Melville asked, ". . . does not feel livelier and more generous emotions toward the great god of Sin—Satan—than toward yonder haberdasher, who only is a sinner in the small and entirely honorable way of trade?"), but because if there is "no devil," as John Wesley is said to have remarked two centuries ago, then there is "no God." We want Satan back because God depends on him. This is because the essence of religious faith is the idea of transcendence, a concept that contains within itself the idea of its opposite—as in its two Latin elements (*trans-*, beyond or over, and *scandere*, to climb or to scale): limitation, boundedness, the thing to be transcended. As an American evangelical put it a few decades after Wesley, "in all . . . instances of God's permitting sin, he had a view to the manifestation of himself."[20]

[3]

Americans have always wanted Satan back, and, as Melville dramatized in *Moby-Dick*, they raise a hue and cry when he gets away. "It has been one of the great American superstitions," wrote Walter Lippmann at the outset of World War I, "that there is a war between good and bad men"; and when the moral clarities of this perpetual war become blurred, we lose our bearings. Sometimes this war is openly declared— as it was in 1861, or during what I have called the age of blame, or during the seventeenth-century witch-hunts, when, according to the historian John Demos, "to discover the Devil—in a sense both literal and metaphoric—[involved] the naming, the locating, the making tangible, of what had hitherto seemed obscure."[21] At other times, the "war between good and bad" remains a covert war, as it is today, when it is no longer reputable publicly to demonize outsiders or minorities, even as resentment against them patently grows.

This need for the nameable enemy is what Augustine rejected as the Manichean heresy. He understood that among the worst works of the devil is his ability to convince human beings that they have found in him the source of all evil, and that this discovery exonerates themselves. Augustine denounced this objectification of evil as heresy, but the fact is that it is built into the very structure of Christianity itself, whose gospel of love and forgiveness is never fully detached from the excoriating story about an evil people—the Jews—who betrayed and sent Christ to his death. The religion upon which our culture is based is therefore indelibly a religion of love *and* hatred—a duality from which neither Augustine nor any subsequent Christian theologian has been able to free it. Writing in 1964 in a play about a group of men waiting to be interrogated by the Gestapo, each hoping that it will not be he who is detained, Arthur Miller put it this way: "Jew is only the name we give to that stranger, that agony we cannot feel, that death we look at like a cold abstraction. Each man has his Jew; it is the other. And the Jews have their Jews."[22]

This potentiality to seek life through the dehumanization of others lurks within all persons and all cultures—a fact that the great American writers, working within the Augustinian tradition, have tried to resist by exposing it. For Jonathan Edwards, hell is "a world of hatred, where there is no love." For Hawthorne, the unpardonable sinner is the man who is willing to break "the magnetic chain of humanity" by invading the sanctuary of another heart in pursuit of some knowledge, or reward, or power. For Melville, he is a "Cain afloat," convinced that "there was nothing to be believed, nothing to be loved, and nothing worth living for; but everything to be hated, in the wide world." Yet

> there seemed even more woe than wickedness about the man; and his wickedness seemed to spring from his woe; and for all his hideousness, there was that in his eye at times, that was ineffably pitiable and touching; and though there were moments when I almost hated [him], yet I have pitied no man as I have pitied him.[23]

Perhaps the most intricate and refined psychological portrait of evil in our literature was composed in 1881 by Henry James in his great novel *The Portrait of a Lady*. The man's name is Gilbert Osmond, a man of wile and sophistication who ensnares a young woman who sees in him a chance to live more fully than she had imagined possible in her provincial youth. She expects to achieve freedom through Osmond; but he is a prison. Full of resentment at the chances he has been denied, he is sensible that the world is a place of randomly distributed opportunities, but he feels them as fleeting, and is continually on the lookout for the competitors who hunt them alongside him. He apprehends no aesthetic or moral correlation between his own constructed character and some authoritative standard that might exist beyond it. "Under all his culture, his cleverness, his amenity, under his good nature, his facility, his knowledge of life, his egotism lay hidden like a serpent in a bank of flowers."[24]

Osmond's is a consciousness that wakes to self-awareness in the modern world of opportunities, and sets to calculating which ones will help to empower him over other people. A great collector, he "has a genius for upholstery." Chances lost are festering defeats. A miser of time, he sees the world as a storeroom of persons and objects that are available to him as furnishings. When he wakes to the new day, he rolls up his sleeves, and sets to work to hoard the chances that fall within his reach, relishing the knowledge that every augmentation of his own store means that someone else has suffered a loss. "I don't pretend to know what people are meant for," says his mistress, expressing the sensibility she shares with him, "I only know what I can do with them."[25]

What this monster does is to turn other persons into negotiable currency. He has no conscience, scruple, doubt; he has reversed the process by which the fear of external authority is internalized; and, having turned it outward again, he achieves a sinister kind of moral freedom: the only fear he knows is fear of others. Ultimately, the most striking qualities of this frightful modern man are his emptiness and loneliness. "For all his capacity to manipulate and to wound," he is, as the critic R. W. B. Lewis has written, "an essential nothingness." He feels exposed. His instinct is to shutter his windows and pull his collar up about his ears. He lives in a perpetual tantrum, and is an incubator of rage—a man whose closest approach to joy comes in the form of relief when he deflects some blow aimed against him. He is the embodiment of the principle articulated by Kierkegaard, that "the specific character of despair is precisely this: it is unaware of being despair."[26]

Ever since Augustine proposed it, this idea of evil as "an essential nothingness" has been immensely difficult to comprehend, and the events of our own century have only made it more so. How, we ask, can the concept of evil as what one scholar of Augustine's thought calls "a pocket of nothingness in a good world"[27] possibly be adequate to the immeasurable evil of our own time? This question is pressed upon us by every contemplation of how modern rationality and technology have magnified the scale upon which evil is perpetrated in the world.

It is raised, for instance, in Primo Levi's harrowing book about the death camps, *The Drowned and the Saved* (1986), in which he gives an account of a "Kapo" squad in Auschwitz (a group of prisoners selected by the SS to do the work of removing dental gold from the dead and preparing the bodies for the ovens). Amid the tangle of corpses, they come upon a young girl of sixteen who has somehow survived the gassing. She has, by chance, been "sequestered [in] a pocket of air that remained breathable." Faced with this individual life, the cleanup crew does not know what to do. They know that the girl must die because "she has seen." But they cannot bring themselves to kill her. A doctor is summoned, and, perhaps out of some not quite extinct instinct to help a sinking patient, he revives her with an injection. When an SS officer is called, he confirms that she must be killed. But he too cannot bring himself to "kill her with his own hands. [So] he calls one of his underlings to eliminate her with a blow to the nape of the neck."[28]

"Occurrences like this," Levi writes, "astonish because they conflict with the image we have of man in harmony with himself . . . [but] they should not astonish because that is not how man is. Compassion and brutality can coexist in the same individual and in the same moment, despite all logic . . . Not even [the SS officer] was a monolith." The implication here, which is profoundly consistent with the Augustinian conception of evil as privation, is that sin is finally best understood as a failure of knowledge—a lack, an obtuseness, a poverty of imagination. If a man surrenders to his designated function, his victims will be no clearer to him than microbes smeared on a slide as seen with the unaided eye. He will not see beyond the blur into the lives consumed—each singular, each a world unto itself. But if he stands face to face with his victim, he is required to exercise his will in order to evade the beseeching eyes. Somewhere in his soul he has to suppress the knowledge that each kill-able body belongs to a suffering consciousness. It was with incalculable cynicism—but also with great shrewdness about the mentality of modern killers and witnesses—that Stalin made his infamous remark that the death of one man is a tragedy, while the death of a million is a statistic.

In the face of these modern horrors, the idea that evil "radically and fundamentally consists," as Edwards put it, "in what is negative, or privative"—or, as Emerson rephrased it, that "evil is merely privative, not absolute: it is like cold, which is the privation of heat"[29]—may seem pathetically inadequate, even offensive. But to take this idea seriously is to recognize the continuity between our daily disregard for the thoughts and feelings of other persons and the most heinous of crimes:

> Man is tempted to deny the limited character of his knowledge, and the finiteness of his perspectives. He pretends to have achieved a degree of knowledge which is beyond the limit of finite life. This is the "ideological taint" in which all human knowledge is involved and which is always something more than mere human ignorance. It is always partly an effort to hide that ignorance by pretension.[30]

Abstracted from their context, these words (from Niebuhr) could be a description of the dynamics of a bad marriage as well as of the ideology that led to the death camps.

The idea of sin as ignorance is, in other words, an idea—as my thoughtful interlocutor put it to me when I had just begun thinking about this subject—by which it may be possible to "connect Auschwitz with the father who rapes his child." But since, in its essence, this idea of evil as absence requires faith in some knowable presence in the world—a presence that has been variously called God, Reason, Imagination—it is extremely difficult to possess it in an age that has lost faith in all essences. Not long ago, I heard a moral philosopher give an example of this difficulty, when he remarked that the old idea of adultery as sin is surely defunct. He could conceive, he said, of many situations where an adulterous act might be morally irreproachable. But may it not still be a sin to commit adultery, he asked, if one's partner in marriage *feels* the act as a betrayal, as violence against the soul? And does not this shift from a world of prescriptive authority to a world where every self must measure for itself the moral meaning of acts leave us all in a state of unprecedented anxiety? To find one's way through this darkened world requires great exertion of the moral imagination—and the old sources of guidance seem scarcer and more reticent every day. What Judaism codified in the law, and Christianity called love, and the Enlightenment renamed "the categorical imperative" or, simply, the "imagination," is very difficult to maintain when the idea of transcendence has faded away.

Under these trying circumstances, when one must hold oneself to account without benefit of authority for not thinking enough, feeling enough, loving enough, there are signs that the always lurking opposite idea of evil—the conception of evil as some alien invader—is returning in American life. This idea has always been locked in competition with its Augustinian opposite—a dispute expressed in the distinction between Emerson's concept of evil ("sin, seen from the thought, is . . . shade, absence of light, no essence") and Thoreau's ("all sensuality is one, though it takes many forms . . . when the reptile is attacked at one mouth of his burrow, he shows himself at another"). This latter idea is coming back in many forms: in the revival of Satanism as an explanation for cases of child abuse, in the return of open anti-Semitism as a feature of public discourse, and even in the atmosphere of our campuses, where each aggrieved group tends to define itself in terms of the injuries it has suffered at the hands of another. It is back in the form of what has been called the "modern vision of the Dark Woman," the predatory female who has made such a spectacular return in films from *Fatal Attraction* (1987) to *The Last Seduction* (1994),[31] and it is back in numberless horror stories in which evil explodes upon the victims from without. "Anxious to believe in something," as Ann Douglas has put it, "if only in its fear of the epistemological drift to the dead end, the postsecular culture reinvents superstition; it reifies terror."[32]

Evil has returned, in other words, as the blamable other—who can always be counted on to spare us the exigencies of examining ourselves. This form of "evil as the threatening other," as Garry Wills has written, "has taken many forms" in American life. "In our early history, it was that Whore of the Devil, the Church of Rome. More recently, it has been Communism."[33] Now that this last devil (which Ronald Reagan confidently named the "evil empire") has disintegrated—the question is: What will come next in the satanic succession?

This question is particularly urgent for a nation that too often has been driven, as the Canadian novelist Robertson Davies puts it, by "the happy extrovert characteristic of seeing all evil as exterior to itself, and resistance to that evil as a primary national duty."[34] For the party of secular irony, this vision of America as a fortress of virtue has been destroyed, while for the party of nostalgia there is no longer any obvious external enemy upon whom to vent the old righteous anger. Yet even as I write these concluding sentences, the horror in Oklahoma City (whose perpetrators President Clinton properly characterized as "evil") has revealed a subculture within the United States that finds in our own federal government a demonic substitute for the lost foreign enemy.

The subject of this book has been this incessant dialectic in American life between the dispossession of Satan under the pressure of modernity and the hunger to get him back. My driving motive in writing it has been the conviction that if evil, with all the insidious complexity which Augustine attributed to it, escapes the reach of our imagination, it will have established dominion over us all. If the privative conception of evil continues to be lost between liberal irony on the one hand, and fundamentalist demonizing on the other, we shall have no way of confronting the most challenging experiences of our private and public lives. And so, in expounding this theme, I have felt compelled to insist that Satan, always receding and always sought after, has had two very different meanings in our history. Sometimes he has been used for the purpose of construing the other as a monster, and sometimes (as in the lives and writings of figures like Edwards, Emerson, Dewey, Niebuhr, and King) he has been a symbol of our own deficient love, our potential for envy and rancor toward creation. Since the experience of evil will not go away, one or the other of these ways of coping with it sooner or later always comes back.

The former way—evil as the other—is, at least at first, psychically rewarding. The latter way—evil as privation—is much more difficult to grasp. But it offers something that the devil himself could never have intended: the miraculous paradox of demanding the best of ourselves.

Notes

1. In a *New York Times* Op-Ed piece of May 30, 1993 ("Serbian Barbarism—and Ours"), Peter Schneider aptly summed up the American response to the cruel war in Bosnia as "outrage limited to a low sigh before the TV screen."

2. Alexis de Tocqueville, *Democracy in America*, trans. Phillips Bradley (1840; New York: Vintage Books, 1954), 2 vols., I, 27.

3. Henry Murray, "The Personality and Career of Satan," in Edwin S. Shneidman, ed., *Endeavors in Psychology: Selections from the Personology of Henry A. Murray* (New York: Harper & Row, 1981), p. 532.

4. Charles Maier, review of Alan Bullock, *Hitler and Stalin: Parallel Lives, The New Republic*, June 15, 1992, p. 42.

5. John Kekes, *Facing Evil* (Princeton: Princeton University Press, 1990), p. 3.

6. Lionel Tiger, *The Manufacture of Evil: Ethics, Evolution, and the Industrial System* (New York: Marion Boyars, 1991), pp. 5, 4.

7. Henry David Thoreau, *The Maine Woods* (1864), in *A Week on the Concord and Merrimack Rivers; Walden; or, Life in the Woods; The Maine Woods; Cape Cod* (New York: The Library of America, 1985), p. 603.

8. Isser Harrel, *The House on Garibaldi Street* (New York: Viking, 1975), pp. 62–63.

9. Ian McEwan, *Black Dogs* (New York: Doubleday, 1992), p. xxi.

10. Tiger, *The Manufacture of Evil*, pp. 3–4.

11. George Orwell, "Politics and the English Language," in *A Collection of Essays* (New York: Doubleday Anchor, 1954), pp. 165–66; Henry James, Sr., *The Nature of Evil* (New York, 1855), p. 13.

12. See Jeffrey Burton Russell, *Lucifer: The Devil in the Middle Ages* (Ithaca: Cornell University Press, 1984), p. 72; Emerson, *Nature* (1836), in Stephen E. Whicher, *Selections from Ralph Waldo Emerson* (Boston: Houghton Mifflin, 1957), p. 33.

13. Updike, *The Witches of Eastwick* (New York: Ballantine Books, 1985), p. 99.

14. Helen Vendler, review of Melanie Thernstrom, *The Dead Girl, The New York Review of Books*, March 28, 1991, p. 51.

15. Frank Kermode, *The Sense of an Ending* (New York: Oxford University Press, 1967), p. 3.
16. *The Confessions of St. Augustine*, trans. Edward P. Pusey (New York: Collier Books, 1961), p. 34.
17. Quoted in Owen Chadwick, *The Secularization of the European Mind in the Nineteenth Century* (Cambridge: Cambridge University Press, 1975), p. 262.
18. *The New York Times*, July 24, 1993, p. 7.
19. Herman Melville, *Moby-Dick* (1851) (New York: Viking-Penguin, 1992), p. 475.
20. Elaine Scarry, *The Body in Pain: The Making and Unmaking of the World* (New York: Oxford University Press, 1985), pp. 40, 20.
21. Paul Ricoeur, *The Symbolism of Evil*, trans. Emerson Buchanan (Boston: Beacon Press, 1967), pp. 35, 32.
22. Keith Thomas, *Religion and the Decline of Magic* (New York: Charles Scribner's Sons, 1971), p. 91.
23. Georg Lukács, *The Theory of the Novel* (1920), trans. Anna Bostock (Cambridge, Mass.: MIT Press, 1971), p. 29.
24. See Lawrence Wright, *Remembering Satan* (New York: Knopf, 1994), about a rural sheriff's deputy who confessed to participating in a satanic cult that practiced brutal child abuse as part of its ritual worship. In a two-part essay in *The New York Review of Books* ("The Revenge of the Repressed" [November 17 and December 1, 1994]), Frederick Crews attributes belief in such cults (even on the part of putative participants) to a fanciful paranoia that can be triggered in "a community steeped in Biblical literalism on the one hand and *Geraldo* on the other."
25. Benedict Anderson, *Imagined Communities: Reflections on the Origin and Spread of Nationalism* (New York: Verso, 1983), p. 39.
26. Some recent examples are Robert L. Duncan, *The Serpent's Mark* (New York: St. Martin's, 1989), David L. Lindsey, *Mercy* (New York: Bantam Books, 1990), and James Patterson, *Along Came the Spider* (New York: Warner Books, 1992). A nonfictional crime narrative whose author reveals his growing conviction of his subject's guilt is Joe McGinniss, *Fatal Vision* (New York: New American Library, 1983), about Dr. Jeffrey MacDonald, the U.S. Marine officer convicted of murdering his wife and children. McGinniss himself became the subject of a controversial *New Yorker* essay by Janet Malcolm (March 13 and 20, 1989), in which she questions the ethics of publishing a damning account of a man after the author has gained his confidence by professing faith in his innocence.
27. Duncan, *The Serpent's Mark*; Peter Straub, *Koko* (New York: New American Library, 1988); Thomas Harris, *Red Dragon* (New York: Bantam Books, 1982), p. 195.
28. William James, *Pragmatism* (1907; New York: Meridian Books, 1955), p. 32; Lionel Trilling, Introduction to *The Selected Letters of John Keats* (New York: Farrar, Straus and Young, 1951), p. 30.
29. Thomas Harris, *The Silence of the Lambs* (New York: St. Martin's, 1988), p. 21.

I. THE OLD ENEMY COMES
TO THE NEW WORLD

1. Jonathan Edwards, *A Treatise Concerning the Religious Affections* (1746; New Haven: Yale University Press, 1959), p. 87; Baudelaire, quoted in Jeffrey Burton Russell, *Mephistopheles: The Devil in the Modern World* (Ithaca: Cornell University Press, 1986), p. 206; Richard Greenham, quoted in Keith Thomas, *Religion and the Decline of Magic*, p. 476.

2. Quoted in Russell, *Lucifer: The Devil in the Middle Ages*, p. 250; Melville, *Redburn* (1846; Evanston: Northwestern University Press and the Newberry Library, 1967), p. 276.

3. Genesis 3:1–5; Isaiah 14:12; Luke 6:15; 2 Corinthians 6:15; Ephesians 2:2. The devil speaks to Christ in Matthew 4:1–11 and Luke 4:1–13.

4. Chronicles 21:1; Murray, "The Personality and Career of Satan," in Shneidman, ed., *Endeavors in Psychology*, p. 522.

5. Revelation 12:9.

6. Russell, *Satan: The Early Christian Tradition* (Ithaca: Cornell University Press, 1981), p. 45.

7. Revelation 1:18. The classic study of dark romanticism is Mario Praz, *The Romantic Agony* (1930), which includes a chapter entitled "The Metamorphoses of Satan."

8. Ephesians 4:8–9; Hebrews 13:20; 1 Peter 3:17–22, 4:6; and see Russell, *Lucifer*, p. 108.

9. Athanasius, quoted in Russell, *Satan*, pp. 170, 174.

10. Tertullian, quoted in Russell, *Satan*, p. 96 n 50.

11. Russell, *Satan*, p. 191.

12. Hugh Honour, *The New Golden Land: European Images of America from the Discoveries to the Present Time* (New York: Pantheon, 1975), p. 8.

13. Quoted in Honour, *The New Golden Land*, p. 16.

14. Kirkpatrick Sale, *The Conquest of Paradise: Christopher Columbus and the Columbian Legacy* (New York: Knopf, 1990), p. 82.

15. See Sale, *Conquest of Paradise*, p. 147. An exception was the mammoth, which Jefferson, on the evidence of fossil bones, Indian legends, and the pre-Darwinian premise that "the œconomy . . . [has never] permitted any one race of her animals to become extinct," assumed still to exist. See his *Notes on the State of Virginia* (1787), in Jefferson, *Writings*, ed. Merrill E. Peterson (New York: Library of America, 1984), p. 176.

16. Schlesinger, *The Disuniting of America: Reflections on a Multicultural Society* (New York: Norton, 1992), p. 48. For the revision of Columbus, compare Samuel Eliot Morison's hagiographic *Admiral of the Ocean Sea* (1942) with Sale's *Conquest of Paradise*. This change is the scholarly equivalent of what happened in Hollywood between, say, *Destry Rides Again* (1939) and *Dances with Wolves* (1990)—a period in which the cowboy, once a gallant pioneer carrying civilization westward against the resistance of savages, became a repulsive Yahoo defacing the land and brutalizing gentle Indians.

17. See, for example, Francis Jennings, *The Invasion of America: Indians, Colonialism, and the Cant of Conquest* (Chapel Hill: University of North Carolina Press, 1975), a book of unremitting indignation, based on the premise that "the American land was more like a widow than a virgin," and that "Europeans did not find a wilderness here; rather, however involuntarily, they made one" (p. 30).

18. David Ramsay, *The History of the American Revolution* (1789; London, 1793), 2 vols., I, 14. Benjamin Colman, quoted in Edward K. Trefz, "Satan as the Prince of Evil: The Preaching of New England Puritans," *Boston Public Library Quarterly*, 7, no. 1 (1955), 17–18.

19. Thomas Tillam, "Upon the first sight of New England, June 29, 1638," in Harrison T. Meserole, ed., *Seventeenth-Century American Poetry* (New York: Norton, 1968), pp. 397–98.

20. Thomas Hooker, *The Unbeleever's Preparing for Christ* (London, 1638), p. 178.

21. William Perkins, *Works*, 3 vols. (London, 1608–9), I, 755.

22. For elaboration of this argument, see Andrew Delbanco, *The Puritan Ordeal* (Cambridge, Mass.: Harvard University Press, 1989).

23. Philip Stubbes, *The Anatomie of Abuses* (London, 1584), p. 90.

24. Thomas Hooker, *The Saint's Dignity and Duty* (London, 1651), p. 187.

25. Anne Bradstreet, "Verses upon the burning of our house, July 10th, 1666," in J. H. Ellis, ed., *The Works of Anne Bradstreet* (Boston, 1867), p. 41.

26. Thomas Cooper, *Certain Sermons* (1580), quoted in Keith Thomas, *Religion and the Decline of Magic*, p. 79; Thomas Gataker, *On the Nature and Use of Lots* (London, 1619), pp. 2, 17.

27. Gataker, *On the Nature and Use of Lots*, p. 23.

28. M. Halsey Thomas, ed., *The Diary of Samuel Sewall, 1674–1729* (New York: Farrar, Straus and Giroux, 1973), 2 vols., I, 28; II, 731 (entries for November 27, 1676, and October 25, 1713).

29. John Cotton, *A Briefe Exposition upon the Book of Ecclesiastes* (London, 1657), p. 108.

30. John Winthrop, *Journal, 1630–1649*, ed. J. K. Hosmer (New York: Charles Scribner's Sons, 1908), 2 vols., I, 210.

31. John Winthrop, *A Model of Christian Charity* (1630), in Alan Heimert and Andrew Delbanco, eds., *The Puritans in America: A Narrative Anthology* (Cambridge, Mass.: Harvard University Press, 1985), p. 86.

32. Winthrop, *A Model*, in Heimert and Delbanco, *Puritans in America*, p. 86.

33. Roland Bainton, *The Reformation of the Sixteenth Century* (Boston: Beacon Press, 1952), p. 29.

34. John Cotton, *A Treatise of the Covenant of Grace*, p. 204.

35. John Preston, *The New Covenant* (London, 1629), pp. 315–16.

36. Hebrews 8:10–12.

37. John Cotton, *A Practical Commentary upon the First Epistle Generall of John* (London, 1656), p. 40.

38. Thomas Hooker, *The Application of Redemption* (London, 1656), p. 240; *The Soules Humiliation* (London, 1637), p. 150.

39. Quoted in Richard Beale Davis, *Intellectual Life in the Colonial South, 1585–1763* (Knoxville: University of Tennessee Press, 1978), 3 vols., I, 634. See also Davis, "The Devil in Virginia in the Seventeenth Century," *Virginia Magazine of History and Biography*, vol. 65, no. 2 (1957), 131–49.

40. William Hubbard, quoted in John Canup, *Out of the Wilderness: The Emergence of an American Identity in Colonial New England* (Middletown: Wesleyan University Press, 1990), p. 74.

41. Samuel Sewall, quoted in Canup, *Out of the Wilderness*, p. 76.

42. Winthrop Jordan, *White over Black: American Attitudes Toward the Negro, 1550–1812* (Baltimore: Penguin Books, 1969), p. 24.

43. William Byrd, quoted in David Bertelson, *The Lazy South* (New York: Oxford University Press, 1967), p. 68.

44. See Bernard Bailyn, *The Peopling of British North America: An Introduction* (New York: Knopf, 1986), p. 4.

45. Winthrop, *A Model of Christian Charity*, in Heimert and Delbanco, eds., *The Puritans in America*, p. 85.

46. Cotton Mather, *Magnalia Christi Americana* (1702; Hartford, 1853), 2 vols., I, 80.

47. For an account of Puritan entrepreneurial activity, see J. Frederick Martin, *Profits in the Wilderness: Entrepreneurship and the Founding of New England Towns in the Seventeenth Century* (Chapel Hill: University of North Carolina Press, 1991).

48. Richard Sibbes, *Two Sermons upon the First Words of Christ's Last Sermon* (London, 1636), p. 21.

49. Mark 7:18–22.

50. Thomas Hooker, *The Soules Preparation for Salvation* (London, 1628), p. 42.

51. Reinhold Niebuhr, *The Nature and Destiny of Man* (New York: Charles Scribner's Sons, 1941), 2 vols., I, 180.

52. Neil Forsyth, *The Old Enemy: Satan and the Combat Myth* (Princeton: Princeton University Press, 1987), p. 10.

53. Rollo May, quoted in Connie Zweig and Jeremiah Abrams, eds., *Meeting the Shadow: The Hidden Power of the Dark Side of Human Nature* (Los Angeles: Jeremy P. Tarcher, 1991), p. 181.

54. John Murray, *The Origin of Evil* (Newburyport, Mass., 1785), p. 27.

55. Emerson, "Circles" (1840), in Whicher, ed., *Selections from Ralph Waldo Emerson*, p. 176.

56. Russell, *Mephistopheles*, pp. 86–87.

57. Ricoeur, *Symbolism of Evil*, p. 45.

58. Quoted in Roland Frye, *God, Man, and Satan: Patterns of Christian Thought and Life in Paradise Lost, Pilgrim's Progress, and the Great Theologians* (Princeton: Princeton University Press, 1960), p. 22.

59. Augustine, *Confessions*, p. 75.

60. Augustine, *Confessions*, p. 38.

61. Augustine, *Confessions*, pp. 34–35.

62. Jung, in Zweig and Abrams, *Meeting the Shadow*, p. 171.

63. Updike, *Witches of Eastwick*, p. 301.
64. Willard, *A Compleat Body of Divinity* (Boston, 1726), p. 177.
65. Hooker, *The Soules Humiliation*, pp. 36–37.
66. Willard, *Compleat Body of Divinity*, p. 180.
67. Willard, *Compleat Body of Divinity*, pp. 181–82.
68. John Cotton, *The Powring Out of the Seven Vials* (London, 1645), pp. 34–35.
69. Willard, *Compleat Body of Divinity*, p. 180.
70. Samuel Eliot Morison, *Harvard College in the Seventeenth Century* (Cambridge, Mass.: Harvard University Press, 1936), 2 vols., I, 119–20.
71. Mather, *Magnalia Christi Americana*, II, 460; Willard, *Compleat Body of Divinity*, p. 156. And see David D. Hall, *Worlds of Wonder, Days of Judgment: Popular Religious Belief in Early New England* (New York: Knopf, 1989), pp. 23, 38, 162.
72. Willard, *Compleat Body of Divinity*, p. 180.
73. Willard, *Compleat Body of Divinity*, p. 181; Thomas Shepard, *The Sum of Christian Religion* (1648), in *The Works of Thomas Shepard*, ed. John Albro (Boston, 1853), 3 vols., I, 342.
74. Thomas Hooker, *The Soules Exaltation* (London, 1638), p. 215; Milton, *Paradise Lost*, Bk. I, l. 254; Bk. II, ll. 406, 409.
75. Cotton, *Practical Commentary on John*, p. 364.
76. Willard, *Compleat Body of Divinity*, p. 183.

2. THE DEVIL IN THE AGE
OF REASON

1. According to the Oxford English Dictionary, the older, technical sense of the word "fantasy"—"mental apprehension of an object of perception"—began to be differentiated by the fifteenth century from a new meaning—"delusive imagination." The first use of the related word "hallucination" is listed by the OED as occurring in 1652.
2. Cotton Mather, *Memorable Providences, Relating to Witchcraft and Possessions* (1689), in George Lincoln Burr, ed., *Narratives of the Witchcraft Cases* (New York: Charles Scribner's Sons, 1914), pp. 101–2.
3. David Levin, *What Happened in Salem?* (New York: Harcourt, Brace and World, 1960), p. xiv.
4. See Carol F. Karlsen, *The Devil in the Shape of a Woman: Witchcraft in Colonial New England* (New York: Norton, 1987); and Paul Boyer and Stephen Nissenbaum, *Salem Possessed: The Social Origins of Witchcraft* (Cambridge, Mass.: Harvard University Press, 1974).
5. Winthrop, *Journal*, I, 267–68.
6. Herbert Leventhal, *In the Shadow of the Enlightenment: Occultism and Renaissance Science in Eighteenth-Century America* (New York: New York University Press, 1976), p. 82.
7. Perry Miller, *The New England Mind: From Colony to Province* (Cambridge, Mass.: Harvard University Press, 1953), p. 191.

8. Increase Mather, *Cases of Conscience Concerning Witchcrafts* (1692), in Levin, *What Happened in Salem?*, p. 118.
9. Sewall, *Diary*, I, 367.
10. Cotton Mather, *Wonders of the Invisible World* (1692), in Heimert and Delbanco, eds., *The Puritans in America*, p. 340.
11. Robert Calef, *More Wonders of the Invisible World* (1700), in Burr, ed., *Narratives of the Witchcraft Cases*, pp. 325–26; Increase Mather, quoted in Karlsen, *The Devil in the Shape of a Woman*, p. 41.
12. Thomas Brattle, *Full and Candid Account of the Delusion Called Witchcraft*, in *Collections of the Massachusetts Historical Society*, 1st series, 5 (1878), 62.
13. Brattle, *Full and Candid Account*, 63.
14. Herschel Baker, *The Image of Man* (New York: Harper Torchbooks, 1961), p. 60; and see Aristotle, *De Anima*, III, 3.
15. Thomas Hobbes, *Leviathan* (1651; Baltimore: Penguin Books, 1968), p. 88.
16. Hobbes, *Leviathan*, p. 86.
17. Hobbes, *Leviathan*, p. 88.
18. John Locke, *An Essay Concerning Human Understanding* (1690; London: J. M. Dent, 1965), 2 vols., I, 316.
19. Terry Castle, "Phantasmagoria: Spectral Technology and the Metaphorics of Modern Reverie," *Critical Inquiry*, Autumn 1988, 52.
20. *De Anima*, III, 3.
21. *De Anima*, III, 3.
22. Quoted in Ronald Knox, *Enthusiasm* (Oxford: Oxford University Press, 1950), p. 153.
23. *A Full and True Relation of Count Martini* (Philadelphia, 1765), pp. 2, 4.
24. Hezekiah Goodwin, *A Vision* (Burlington, Vt., 1795).
25. *Essex Gazette* (August 6–13, 1771), quoted in Jonathan Dorson, *Jonathan Draws the Long Bow* (Cambridge, Mass.: Harvard University Press, 1946), p. 48.
26. Jane Cish, *The Vision and Wonderful Experience of Jane Cish* (Philadelphia, 1797), p. 10.
27. Cish, *Vision*, p. 6.
28. Increase Mather, *Remarkable Providences* (1684; London: Reeves and Turner, 1890), p. 119.
29. See Ronald A. Bosco, "Early American Gallows Literature: An Annotated Checklist," *Resources for American Literary Study*, 8, no. 1 (Spring 1978), 81–107.
30. Alexander Anderson, *Inaugural Dissertation on Chronic Mania* (New York, 1796), pp. 10, 14.
31. Anderson, *Dissertation*, pp. 15–16.
32. Anderson, *Dissertation*, pp. 13, 15–16.
33. Anderson, *Dissertation*, p. 7.
34. John Cotton, *The Way of Life* (London, 1641), p. 251.
35. Edward Cutbush, *An Inaugural Dissertation on Insanity* (New York, 1794), p. 15.
36. Anderson, *Dissertation*, p. 20; Benjamin Rush, *Medical Inquiries and Observa-*

tions upon the Diseases of the Mind (Philadelphia: Kimber and Richardson, 1812), pp. 43, 104.

37. Michel Foucault, *Madness and Civilization: A History of Insanity in the Age of Reason*, trans. Richard Howard (New York: Vintage Books, 1973), p. 58.
38. Leventhal, *In the Shadow of the Enlightenment*, p. 79.
39. Leventhal, *In the Shadow of the Enlightenment*, p. 85.
40. Jon Butler, *Awash in a Sea of Faith: Christianizing the American People* (Cambridge, Mass.: Harvard University Press, 1990), p. 85.
41. *A New and True Relation, of a Little Girl in Simsbury . . . Bewitch'd, in March 1763* (Boston, 1766), n.p.
42. Philip Vickers Fithian, *Journal and Letters, 1767–1774*, ed. John Rogers Williams (Princeton: Princeton Historical Association, 1900), pp. 214–15; Keith Thomas, *Religion and the Decline of Magic*, p. 77. A little later in his journal, Fithian (the man who had left the room) confesses that although he had made his "impious" friend "think otherwise," he, too, doubted the devil's existence, despite the fact "that it was universally allowed by writers of the greatest reputation for Learning and Religion . . ."
43. Thomas Hooker, *The Soules Exaltation*, p. 83; Leventhal, *In the Shadow of the Enlightenment*, pp. 35, 41.
44. *Virginia Gazette* (September 16, 1775), p. 3.
45. Niebuhr, *The Nature and Destiny of Man*, I, 181.
46. John Lewis in Robert Ross, *A Plain Address to the Quakers, Moravians, Separatists, Separate-Baptists, Rogerenes, and Other Enthusiasts* (New Haven, 1762), p. 3.
47. Lewis, in Ross, *Plain Address*, pp. 7, 47.
48. Thomas Hooker, *The Survey of the Summe of Church Discipline* (London, 1648), Part 2, p. 78.
49. Foucault, quoted in Steven Marcus, *Representations: Essays on Literature and Society* (New York: Columbia University Press, 1990), p. 155; Alcott, *Diary* (December 1838), in George Hochfield, ed., *Selected Writings of the American Transcendentalists* (New York: New American Library, 1966), p. 103.
50. Lewis, in Ross, *Plain Address*, p. 7.
51. James Davenport, *Confession and Retractions* (1744), in Alan Heimert and Perry Miller, eds., *The Great Awakening: Documents Illustrating the Crisis and Its Consequences* (New York: Bobbs-Merrill, 1967), p. 260.
52. H. Richard Niebuhr, *The Kingdom of God in America* (New York: Harper Torchbooks, 1959), pp. 110–11.
53. *Boston Weekly News-Letter*, July 1, 1742, in Richard Bushman, ed., *The Great Awakening: Documents on the Revival of Religion, 1740–1745* (New York: Atheneum, 1970), p. 47; Davenport, in Heimert and Miller, *The Great Awakening*, p. 202; Charles Chauncy, *The New Creature* (Boston, 1741), p. 18.
54. Edwards, *A Careful and Strict Enquiry into the modern prevailing notions of that Freedom of the Will which is supposed to be essential to Moral Agency, Virtue and Vice, Reward and Punishment, Praise and Blame* (1754; New Haven: Yale University Press, 1957), pp. 357–58.

55. Franklin, *A Dissertation on Liberty and Necessity, Pleasure and Pain* (1725), in Chester E. Jorgenson and Frank Luther Mott, eds., *Benjamin Franklin: Representative Selections* (New York: Hill and Wang, 1962), pp. 117–18.
56. William Godwin, *Enquiry Concerning Political Justice* (1793; Oxford: Oxford University Press, 1971), p. 36.
57. Edwards, *Freedom of the Will*, p. 164.
58. Noah Worcester, *Some Difficulties Proposed for Solution* (Boston, 1793), p. 39; Edwards, *Freedom of the Will*, pp. 326–27.
59. Patricia J. Tracy, *Jonathan Edwards, Pastor: Religion and Society in Eighteenth-Century Northampton* (New York: Hill and Wang, 1980), p. 106.
60. Esther Rogers, in John Rogers, *Death the Wages of Sin* (1701), p. 130. (I owe this reference to Laura Henigman.)
61. Noah Worcester, *Some Difficulties*, p. 34; E. L. Doctorow, *The Waterworks* (New York: Random House, 1994), p. 236.
62. Samuel Whitman, *A Dissertation on the Origin of Evil* (Northampton, 1797), p. 9.
63. Whitman, *A Dissertation*, pp. 5–6.
64. William James, *Pragmatism*, pp. 97–98.
65. Fyodor Dostoevsky, *The Brothers Karamazov*, trans. Constance Garnett (New York: Random House, 1912), p. 290.
66. Edwards, *Treatise on the Religious Affections*, p. 274.
67. Kant, *On the Failure of All Attempted Philosophical Theodicies* (1791), trans. Michel Despland, in *Kant on History and Religion* (Montreal: McGill-Queen's University Press, 1973), p. 290.
68. Kant, *Failure of All Philosophical Theodicies*, p. 290.
69. Kant, *Failure of All Philosophical Theodicies*, p. 293.

3. THE BIRTH OF THE SELF

1. Bernard Bailyn, *The Ideological Origins of the American Revolution* (Cambridge, Mass.: Harvard University Press, 1967), p. 147; Lydia Dittler Schulman, *Paradise Lost and the Rise of the American Republic* (Boston: Northeastern University Press, 1992), p. 160.
2. Schulman, *Paradise Lost*, pp. 162–63.
3. Philip Freneau, "On the Fall of General Earl Cornwallis" (1781), in Harry Hayden Clark, ed., *Poems of Freneau* (New York: Harcourt, Brace, 1929), p. 63.
4. Dwight, "The Triumph of Infidelity," (1788), in V. L. Parrington, ed., *The Connecticut Wits* (New York: Crowell, 1969), p. 262; Royall Tyler, "The Origin of Evil" (1793), in Marius B. Peladeau, ed., *The Verse of Royall Tyler* (Charlottesville: University Press of Virginia, 1968), pp. 13–15.
5. Dorson, *Jonathan Draws the Long Bow*, p. 49; George B. Cheever, *Deacon Giles's Distillery* (1835; New York, 1859), p. 9.
6. Robert Bailey, *The Life and Adventures of Robert Bailey, from his infancy up to

December, 1821, interspersed with anecdotes, and religious and moral admonitions (Richmond, 1822), pp. 12–13.

7. David Young, *The Wonderful History of the Morristown Ghost* (Newark, 1826), p. 12; Harry Levin, *The Power of Blackness* (New York: Vintage Books, 1958), p. 11; Dorson, *Jonathan Draws the Long Bow*, p. 51; "Miss Emily and Miss Olive and the Legend of the Devil's Hoof Prints of Bath," *North Carolina Folklore Journal*, 36, no. 2 (1989), 121–27.

8. Lewis O. Saum, *The Popular Mood of Pre-Civil War America* (Westport, Conn.: Greenwood Press, 1980), p. 35.

9. Edward Taylor, "Meditation" (1690), in *The Poems of Edward Taylor*, ed. Donald E. Stanford (New Haven: Yale University Press, 1960), p. 63.

10. Schulman, *Paradise Lost*, p. 13 and passim.

11. Whittier, *The Supernaturalism of New England* (London, 1847), p. 42.

12. Evan S. Connell, *Son of the Morning Star: Custer and the Little Big Horn* (New York: HarperCollins, 1985), p. 124.

13. William Ramsay, *Spiritualism: A Satanic Delusion and a Sign of the Times* (Boston, 1864), pp. 11–12.

14. Lawrence Fuchs, *The American Kaleidoscope: Race, Ethnicity and the Civic Culture* (Middletown: Wesleyan University Press, 1990), p. 38.

15. See Alice Kessler-Harris, *Out to Work: A History of Wage-Earning Women in the United States* (New York: Oxford University Press, 1982), pp. 20–72.

16. See Avery Craven, *The Coming of the Civil War* (Chicago: University of Chicago Press, 1957), pp. 125–29.

17. *Southern Literary Messenger*, March 1861, p. 344.

18. Craven, *Coming of the Civil War*, p. 295.

19. Emerson, "Self-Reliance" (1840), in Whicher, ed., *Selections from Emerson*, p. 150.

20. Quoted in Joan Hedrick, *Harriet Beecher Stowe: A Life* (New York: Oxford University Press, 1994), p. 72.

21. Joseph G. Baldwin, *The Flush Times of Alabama and Mississippi* (New York, 1853), pp. xx, xix.

22. Edward K. Spann, *The New Metropolis: New York City, 1840–1857* (New York: Columbia University Press, 1981), p. 73.

23. Emerson, "Experience" (1844), in Whicher, ed., *Selections from Emerson*, p. 265.

24. Melville, *Redburn*, p. 261.

25. Melville, *Redburn*, p. 261.

26. Hawthorne, *The Scarlet Letter* (1850; Boston: Little, Brown, 1960), pp. 61, 128; Alcott, *A Modern Mephistopheles* (1877; New York: Bantam Books, 1987), p. 4.

27. Emerson, *Representative Men* (1850; Boston: Houghton Mifflin, 1903), p. 22.

28. Caroline Kirkland, *A New Home: Who'll Follow?* (1839; New Haven: College and University Press, 1965), p. 58.

29. Joel Porte, ed., *Emerson in His Journals* (Cambridge, Mass.: Harvard University Press, 1982), p. 161 (April 22, 1837).

30. Emerson, "Historic Notes on Life and Letters in New England" (1880), in

The American Transcendentalists, ed. Perry Miller (New York: Doubleday Anchor, 1957), p. 18.

31. Porte, ed., *Emerson in His Journals*, p. 390 (June 1848).

32. Brownson, quoted in Nelson Aldrich, *Old Money* (New York: Vintage Books, 1989), p. 38.

33. Aldrich, *Old Money*, p. 57.

34. Charles Taylor, *Multiculturalism and "The Politics of Recognition"* (Princeton: Princeton University Press, 1992), p. 29.

35. Tocqueville, *Democracy in America*, II, 147.

36. Fuller, *Summer on the Lakes in 1843* (1844), in Bell Gale Chevigny, ed., *The Woman and the Myth: Margaret Fuller's Life and Writings* (New York: The Feminist Press, 1976), p. 317.

37. Henry Adams, *History of the United States During the Administrations of Adams and Jefferson* (New York, 1898), 9 vols., I, 175; Kirkland, *A New Home*, p. 80; Adams, *History*, I, 160.

38. See Stuart Bruchey, "Law and Economic Change in the Early American Republic," in *American Industrialization, Economic Expansion, and the Law*, ed. Joseph R. Frese, S.J., and Jacob Judd (New York: Sleepy Hollow Press, 1981), esp. pp. 103–7.

39. Kirkland, *A New Home*, p. 63.

40. Thoreau, *Walden: or, Life in the Woods* (1854), in *Walden and Other Writings*, ed. Brooks Atkinson (New York: Modern Library, 1950), pp. 27–28.

41. Lincoln, "Address to the Wisconsin Agricultural Society" (1859), in *The Portable Abraham Lincoln*, ed. Andrew Delbanco (New York: Viking-Penguin, 1992), p. 158.

42. Emerson, "The Divinity School Address" (1838), in Whicher, ed., *Selections from Emerson*, p. 111.

43. Tocqueville, *Democracy in America*, I, 381; Augustus Foster, quoted in Adams, *History*, I, 186; and see David Hackett Fischer, *The Revolution of American Conservatism* (New York: Harper Torchbooks, 1968).

44. Lionel Trilling, *The Liberal Imagination* (New York: Viking, 1950), p. ix.

45. Hawthorne, *The House of the Seven Gables* (1852; New York: Washington Square Press, 1966), p. 39.

46. George Templeton Strong, quoted in Daniel Aaron, *The Unwritten War* (New York: Oxford University Press, 1973), p. 23.

47. William Smith, quoted in Gordon Wood, *The Radicalism of the American Revolution* (New York: Knopf, 1992), p. 66.

48. Johnson, quoted in John C. Miller, *The Wolf by the Ears: Thomas Jefferson and Slavery* (New York: New American Library, 1980), p. 8.

49. J. Hector St. John de Crevecoeur, *Letters from an American Farmer* (1782; New York: E. P. Dutton, 1957), pp. 166–67.

50. John Marshall, *Cherokee Nation* v. *State of Georgia* (1831), in Wilcomb E. Washburne, ed., *The Indian and the White Man* (New York: Doubleday Anchor, 1964), pp. 121, 118; John Ehle, *Trail of Tears: The Rise and Fall of the Cherokee Nation* (New York: Doubleday Anchor, 1988), p. 275.

51. Jefferson, *Notes on the State of Virginia*, in Jefferson, *Writings*, p. 289.
52. Lincoln, letter to Albert G. Hodges (1864), and letter to Joshua F. Speed (1855), in *The Portable Abraham Lincoln*, pp. 304, 85.
53. George Fitzhugh, *Cannibals All: or, Slaves Without Masters* (1857; Cambridge, Mass.: Harvard University Press, 1960), pp. 24–25.
54. Bernard Bailyn et al., *The Great Republic: A History of the American People* (Lexington: D. C. Heath, 1992), 2 vols., I, 398.
55. George Fredrickson, *The Black Image in the White Mind* (New York: Harper Torchbooks, 1972), pp. 57, 75; Henry Gansevoort, quoted in Stanton Garner, *The Civil War World of Herman Melville* (Lawrence: University Press of Kansas, 1993), p. 23.
56. Robert Bailey, *Life and Adventures*, pp. 37–38.
57. Herman Melville, *The Confidence-Man: His Masquerade* (1857; Evanston: Northwestern University Press and the Newberry Library, 1984), p. 190.
58. Lincoln, "Speech at New Haven, Connecticut" (1860), in *Speeches and Writings*, ed. Don E. Fehrenbacher (New York: The Library of America, 1989), 2 vols., II, 144.
59. Quoted in Aldrich, *Old Money*, p. 42.
60. Kenneth Lynn, Introduction to Harriet Beecher Stowe, *Uncle Tom's Cabin* (1852; Cambridge, Mass.: Harvard University Press, 1962), p. vii.
61. George Fredrickson, ed., *William Lloyd Garrison: Great Lives Observed* (Englewood Cliffs, N.J.: Prentice-Hall, 1968), p. 143; Marshall Berman, *All That Is Solid Melts into Air: The Experience of Modernity* (New York: Penguin, 1988), p. 67.
62. Fredrickson, ed., *Garrison*, p. 141.
63. Emerson, "The Transcendentalist" (1841), in Whicher, ed., *Selections from Emerson*, pp. 193–94.
64. Lincoln, Second Inaugural Address (1865), in Delbanco, ed., *The Portable Lincoln*, p. 321; David Reynolds, *Beneath the American Renaissance: The Subversive Imagination in the Age of Emerson and Melville* (Cambridge, Mass.: Harvard University Press, 1989), p. 64.
65. Butler, *Awash in a Sea of Faith*, p. 270.
66. Saum, *Popular Mood*, pp. 59–63.
67. Whittier, *Supernaturalism of New England*, p. 3.
68. Timothy J. Gilfoyle, *City of Eros: New York City, Prostitution, and the Commercialization of Sex* (New York: Norton, 1992), p. 129.
69. Mark Holloway, *Heavens on Earth: Utopian Communities in America, 1680–1880* (New York: Dover Books, 1966), p. 104.

4. THE LOSS OF PROVIDENCE

1. Niebuhr, *Nature and Destiny of Man*, I, 182.
2. Thoreau, *Walden*, p. 17.
3. Porte, ed., *Emerson in His Journals*, p. 197 (Sept. 16, 1838); Emerson, "The American Scholar" (1837), in Whicher, ed., *Selections from Emerson*, p. 64.

4. Hegel, *Phenomenology of Spirit* (1807), quoted in Charles Taylor, *Multiculturalism*, p. 50.

5. Hawthorne, quoted in Garner, *The Civil War World of Herman Melville*, pp. 88–89; Emerson, quoted in Aaron, *Unwritten War*, p. 35.

6. *Southern Literary Messenger*, November 1860, quoted in Aaron, *Unwritten War*, p. 19.

7. Lincoln, "Fragment on Slavery" (c. 1854), in Delbanco, ed., *The Portable Lincoln*, p. 41.

8. Brown, Letter of November 8, 1859, in *Old South Leaflets*, no. 85, p. 20 (my italics).

9. Longfellow, quoted in Garner, *The Civil War World of Melville*, p. 44; Melville, "The Portent," in *Battle-Pieces and Aspects of the War* (1866; New York: Thomas Yoseloff, 1963), p. 35; Oliver Wendell Holmes, *Writings* (Boston, 1894–95), 14 vols., VIII, 87–88.

10. Thoreau, "A Plea for Captain John Brown" (November 30, 1859), in *Walden and Other Writings*, p. 704.

11. George Templeton Strong and Oliver Wendell Holmes, quoted in Aaron, *Unwritten War*, pp. 23, 28.

12. Henry Howard Brownell, quoted in Garner, *The Civil War World of Melville*, p. 74; Whitman, *Specimen Days* (1882), in Whitman, *Poetry and Prose* (New York: The Library of America, 1982), p. 706; Hawthorne, quoted in Garner, p. 88.

13. Bell Irvin Wiley, *The Life of Billy Yank: The Common Soldier of the Union* (Baton Rouge: Louisiana State University Press, 1978), p. 21; Edward Everett and Lowell, quoted in Aaron, *Unwritten War*, pp. 343, 344.

14. Quoted in Craven, *Coming of the Civil War*, p. 439.

15. Lincoln, "Speech to the 140th Indiana Regiment" (1865), in Delbanco, ed., *The Portable Lincoln*, p. 323.

16. Emerson, "Divinity School Address" (1838), in Whicher, ed., *Selections from Emerson*, pp. 106, 107.

17. Lincoln, "Speech on the Kansas-Nebraska Act" (1854); "Handbill Replying to Charges of Infidelity" (1846); "Letter to Edward Everett" (November 20, 1863), in Delbanco, ed., *The Portable Lincoln*, pp. 75, 27–28, 296; Stephens, quoted in Edmund Wilson, *Patriotic Gore: Studies in the Literature of the American Civil War* (New York: Oxford University Press, 1962), p. 97.

18. Herndon and Keckley, quoted in Philip B. Kunhardt, Jr., et al., *Lincoln: An Illustrated Biography* (New York: Knopf, 1992), pp. 85, 363; Melville, *Moby-Dick*, pp. 178, 174; J. S. Potter to Francis W. Pickens, March 30, 1861, quoted in Steven A. Channing, *Crisis of Fear: Secession in South Carolina* (New York: Norton, 1970), p. 274; Lincoln, "Speech at Independence Hall, Philadelphia" (1861), in Lincoln, *Speeches and Writings*, II, 213.

19. Joseph P. Thompson, *Abraham Lincoln: His Life and Its Lessons. A Sermon Preached April 30, 1865*, in Frank Freidel, ed., *Union Pamphlets of the Civil War* (Cambridge, Mass.: Harvard University Press, 1967), 2 vols., II, 1160, 1162.

20. Lincoln, "Eulogy on Henry Clay" (1852), in *Speeches and Writings*, I, 261.

21. Strong, quoted in Aaron, *Unwritten War*, p. 345.
22. Melville, "Apathy and Enthusiasm," in *Battle-Pieces*, p. 41.
23. Thomas Wentworth Higginson, *Army Life in a Black Regiment* (1869; Boston: Beacon Press, 1962), p. 255.
24. McFeely, *Grant: A Biography* (New York: Norton, 1981), p. 78; Anne C. Rose, *Victorian America and the Civil War* (Cambridge: Cambridge University Press, 1992), p. 62.
25. *Selected Letters of William Dean Howells* (Boston: Twayne, 1979), p. 77.
26. Mary Chesnut, quoted in Rose, *Victorian America*, p. 61; Mary Todd Lincoln, quoted in Kunhardt, *Lincoln*, p. 240.
27. Melville, "The House-top," in *Battle-Pieces*, pp. 89–90.
28. James M. McPherson, ed., *The Negro's Civil War* (New York: Vintage Books, 1965), p. 22.
29. Allan Nevins, ed., *The Civil War Diary of George Templeton Strong* (New York: Macmillan, 1962), p. 337.
30. Whitman, *Specimen Days*, in *Poetry and Prose*, p. 707.
31. Charles Royster, *The Destructive War: William Tecumseh Sherman, Stonewall Jackson, and the Americans* (New York: Knopf, 1991), p. 256.
32. Hofstadter, *The American Political Tradition* (New York: Knopf, 1948), p. 135; Diana Trilling, *Claremont Essays* (London: Secker and Warburg, 1965), p. 182; and see Robert Wiebe, *The Search for Order: 1877–1920* (New York: Hill and Wang, 1967), p. 7, who speaks of the nation gripped by "a haunting sense of the war's failure."
33. McFeely, *Grant*, p. 64.
34. McFeely, *Grant*, p. 67.
35. Wilson, *Patriotic Gore*, p. 140.
36. Henry James, *Hawthorne* (1879; New York: St. Martin's, 1967), p. 135.
37. T. Jackson Lears, *No Place of Grace: Antimodernism and the Transformation of American Culture, 1880–1920* (New York: Pantheon, 1981), p. 10.
38. Alan Trachtenberg, *The Incorporation of America: Culture and Society in the Gilded Age* (New York: Hill and Wang, 1982), pp. 99, 129.
39. Veblen, "The Theory of Business Enterprise" (1904), in Max Lerner, ed., *The Portable Veblen* (New York: Viking, 1948), p. 338.
40. Lerner, ed., *The Portable Veblen*, p. 342.
41. Quoted in Tom Lutz, *American Nervousness, 1903: An Anecdotal History* (Ithaca: Cornell University Press, 1991), p. 79.
42. Adams, "A Letter to American Teachers of History" (1910), in *The Degradation of the Democratic Dogma* (1919; New York: Capricorn, 1958), p. 138.
43. David Montgomery, *The Fall of the House of Labor* (New York: Cambridge University Press, 1989), pp. 17, 21.
44. John W. DeForest, *Miss Ravenel's Conversion from Secession to Loyalty* (1867; New York: Rinehart, 1955), p. 279.
45. Emerson, "Nature" (1836), in Whicher, ed., *Selections from Emerson*, pp. 39, 48.

46. Mason Lock Weems, *The Life of George Washington* (1800; Cambridge, Mass.: Harvard University Press, 1962), p. 14.

47. John J. McDermott, *Streams of Experience: Reflections on the History and Philosophy of American Culture* (Amherst: University of Massachusetts Press, 1986), p. 81; Emerson, Sermon 59 (1829), in *The Complete Sermons of Ralph Waldo Emerson*, ed. Teresa Toulouse and Andrew Delbanco (Columbia: University of Missouri Press, 1990), 4 vols., II, 102; *Commercial Advertiser*, August 2, 1832, quoted in Charles Rosenberg, *The Cholera Years* (Chicago: University of Chicago Press, 1987), p. 43.

48. Bell Irvin Wiley, *Johnny Reb: The Common Soldier of the Confederacy* (Baton Rouge: Louisiana State University Press, 1978), p. 40.

49. Lewis O. Saum, *The Popular Mood of America, 1860–1890* (Lincoln: University of Nebraska Press, 1990), pp. 21, 29. (My italics)

50. Bernard Bailyn, *Education in the Forming of American Society* (Chapel Hill: University of North Carolina Press, 1960), p. 14.

51. Quoted in Walter Benn Michaels, *The Gold Standard and the Logic of Naturalism: American Literature at the Turn of the Century* (Berkeley: University of California Press, 1987), p. 219.

52. Weber, *The Protestant Ethic and the Spirit of Capitalism* (1905), trans. Talcott Parsons (New York: Charles Scribner's Sons, 1958), p. 182; Twain, letter to Howells (January 22, 1898), in *Selected Mark Twain–Howells Letters*, ed. Frederick Anderson et al. (Cambridge, Mass.: Harvard University Press, 1967), p. 317.

53. Robert Jay Lifton, *Death in Life: Survivors of Hiroshima* (New York: Vintage Books, 1969), p. 55.

54. John V. Canfield, ed., *Purpose in Nature* (Englewood Cliffs, N.J.: Prentice-Hall, 1966), p. 3.

55. Edward Arlington Robinson, *Credo* (c. 1890).

56. Written, respectively, by Stephen Crane, Robert Herrick, Ellen Glasgow, and Willa Cather.

57. Adams, *The Education of Henry Adams* (1907; Boston: Houghton Mifflin, 1973), p. 460.

58. Kenneth M. Stampp, *America in 1857: A Nation on the Brink* (New York: Oxford University Press, 1990), p. 18.

59. Quoted in Stampp, *The Imperiled Union: Essays on the Background of the Civil War* (New York: Oxford University Press, 1980), p. 221.

60. Marcus, *Representations*, p. 6.

61. Adams, *Degradation of the Democratic Dogma*, p. 127.

62. Joanne J. Meyerowitz, *Women Adrift: Independent Wage Earners in Chicago, 1880–1930* (Chicago: University of Chicago Press, 1988), pp. 106, 105.

63. William James, *Pragmatism*, p. 79.

64. Porte, ed., *Emerson in His Journals* (entry for June 21, 1838), p. 190; Chauncey Wright, quoted in David E. Shi, *Facing Facts: Realism in American Thought and Culture* (New York: Oxford University Press, 1995), p. 67; Emerson, "Self-Reliance," in Whicher, ed., *Selections*, p. 156.

65. Zygmunt Bauman, review of Barbara Goodwin, *Justice by Lottery*, *Times Literary Supplement*, March 12, 1993, p. 23.
66. Lloyd, quoted in Daniel Aaron, *Men of Good Hope* (New York: Oxford University Press, 1951), p. 143.
67. Howells, *A Hazard of New Fortunes* (1890; New York: New American Library, 1965), pp. 159–60.
68. John Bigelow, "What Is Gambling?" (1895), quoted in Michaels, *The Gold Standard*, p. 225.
69. Bigelow, quoted in Michaels, *The Gold Standard*, p. 223.
70. Greeley, quoted in Spann, *The New Metropolis*, p. 78.
71. Keith Thomas, *Religion and the Decline of Magic*, p. 111.
72. Thomas Carver, "The Economic Basis of the Problem of Evil," *Harvard Theological Review*, 1 (1908), 105.
73. Susan Blow, quoted in Lears, *No Place of Grace*, p. 157.
74. Thomas Pynchon, *V* (New York: Bantam Books, 1964), p. 66.

5. THE AGE OF BLAME

1. Genesis 3:9–13.
2. Nietzsche, quoted in Karl Löwith, *From Hegel to Nietzsche: The Revolution in Nineteenth Century Thought*, trans. David E. Green (New York: Doubleday Anchor, 1967), p. 365.
3. Freud, *Civilization and Its Discontents*, trans. James Strachey (New York: Norton, 1961), pp. 75, 72.
4. Emerson, "Nature" (1836), in Whicher, ed., *Selections from Emerson*, p. 33.
5. Stephen Crane, *The Red Badge of Courage* (1895), in Stephen Crane, *Prose and Poetry* (New York: The Library of America, 1984), p. 126.
6. Walter Benjamin, "Unpacking My Library," in *Illuminations*, trans. Harry Zohn (New York: Schocken, 1969), p. 60; Simon Schama, *Dead Certainties: "Unwarranted Speculations"* (New York: Knopf, 1991), p. 33; Crane, quoted in R. W. Stallman, *Stephen Crane: A Biography* (New York: George Braziller, 1968), p. 73.
7. Edith Wharton, *The House of Mirth* (1905; New York: New American Library, 1964), p. 334.
8. David Charles Sloane, *The Last Great Necessity: Cemeteries in American History* (Baltimore: Johns Hopkins University Press, 1991), p. 145.
9. James Hart, *The Popular Book: A History of America's Literary Taste* (Berkeley: University of California Press, n.d.), pp. 120, 121.
10. Joseph Story, quoted in Garry Wills, *Lincoln at Gettysburg: The Words That Remade America* (New York: Simon & Schuster, 1992), p. 74.
11. Alexander Borthwick, quoted in Saum, *Popular Mood of America, 1860–1890*, pp. 125–26.
12. Phelps, quoted in Sloane, *Last Great Necessity*, p. 146.
13. Saum, *Popular Mood of America, 1860–1890*, p. 126.
14. Wirt Sikes, quoted in Peter G. Beidler, *Ghosts, Demons, and Henry James: The*

Turn of the Screw at the Turn of the Century (Columbia: University of Missouri Press, 1989), p. 20.

15. Royce, "The World and the Individual" (1899), in John K. Roth, ed., *The Philosophy of Josiah Royce* (New York: Crowell, 1971), p. 240; James, *The Varieties of Religious Experience* (1902; New York: Collier, 1961), pp. 354, 120.

16. Wills, *Lincoln at Gettysburg*, p. 76.

17. Paul McArthur, *Modern Spiritualism* (Progressive Spiritualist Association of Missouri, 1908), p. 9.

18. McArthur, *Modern Spiritualism*, pp. 41, 45, 11; Wills, *Lincoln at Gettysburg*, p. 72.

19. W. M. Lockwood, *The Molecular Hypothesis of Nature; the relation of its Principles to continued existence and to the philosophy of Spiritualism* (Chicago, 1895), p. 5.

20. Quoted in Russell M. and Clare R. Goldfarb, *Spiritualism and 19th-Century Letters* (Cranbury, N.J.: Associated University Press, 1978), p. 129. The amazingly strong appeal of spiritualism is suggested by George Templeton Strong's remark that "hundreds of thousands of people in this country," including "ex-judges of the Supreme Court, senators, clergymen, professors of physical sciences . . . believe themselves able to communicate daily with the ghosts of their grandfathers." (Quoted in R. Laurence Moore, "Spiritualism and Science: Reflections on the First Decade of the Spirit Rappings," *American Quarterly*, 24 [1972], 475.) Something similar was happening in England, where a collection called *Real Ghost Stories* was published in a print run of 100,000 that "went off like snow in a fresh"; and the Society for Psychical Research (which invited William James to become its president in 1894) included among its members "prime ministers, bishops, titled persons, scientists of various persuasions, and . . . such literary men as Tennyson and Ruskin." (Beidler, *Ghosts, Demons*, p. 25.)

21. Newton Crosland, *Apparitions* (1873), quoted in Beidler, *Ghosts, Demons*, p. 32; Lutz, *American Nervousness*, p. 185.

22. *New York Daily Tribune*, January 25, 1881.

23. *New York Daily Tribune*, March 6, 1881.

24. James, *Varieties of Religious Experience*, p. 124.

25. Cyrus Bartol, *Radical Problems* (1872), quoted in David Robinson, *The Unitarians and Universalists* (Westport, Conn.: Greenwood Press, 1985), p. 111.

26. James, *Varieties of Religious Experience*, p. 124.

27. Ignatius Donnelly, *Caesar's Column: A Story of the Twentieth Century* (1889; Cambridge, Mass.: Harvard University Press, 1960), p. 71.

28. Otto Rank, quoted in Ernest Becker, *The Denial of Death* (New York: The Free Press, 1973), p. 99; A. Mitchell Palmer, "The Case Against the Reds" (1920), in Loren Baritz, ed., *The Culture of the Twenties* (New York: Bobbs-Merrill, 1970), p. 78; Lewis P. Simpson, *The Brazen Face of History* (Baton Rouge: Louisiana State University Press, 1980), p. 110; Kenneth Burke, *The Philosophy of Literary Form* (Berkeley: University of California Press, 1973), p. 39.

29. Dixon, *The Clansman* (New York: Doubleday, Page, 1905), p. 214; Dixon, *The Leopard's Spots* (1902), quoted in Fredrickson, *The Black Image in the White Mind*, p. 280; Du Bois, *Dusk of Dawn: An Essay Toward an Autobiography of a Race Concept* (1940; New York: Schocken, 1968), p. 67.

30. Josiah Strong (1885), and Thomas E. Watson (1912), quoted in Richard Hofstadter, *The Age of Reform* (New York: Vintage Books, 1955), pp. 82–83.

31. William Byrd, *Diary* (May 22, 1712), in *The Great American Gentleman*, ed. Louis B. Wright and Marion Tinling (New York: Capricorn, 1963), p. 229; Poe, *The Narrative of Arthur Gordon Pym* (1838), in W. H. Auden, ed., *Edgar Allan Poe: Selected Prose, Poetry, and Eureka* (New York: Rinehart, 1950), p. 309; Melville, *Typee* (1846; Evanston: Northwestern University Press and the Newberry Library, 1968), p. 205.

32. See Thomas Jefferson, *Notes on the State of Virginia*, in *Writings*, pp. 266–70. At one moment, Jefferson speculates that blacks are "in reason much inferior" to whites, but a few sentences later he cautions that "I advance it as a suspicion only, that the blacks . . . are inferior to the whites in the endowments both of body and mind," and insists that "the opinion, that they are inferior in the faculties of reason and imagination, must be hazarded with great diffidence."

33. Nebraska senator William Allen (in the 1890s), quoted in Stuart Creighton Miller, *"Benevolent Assimilation": The American Conquest of the Philippines, 1899–1903* (New Haven: Yale University Press, 1982), p. 15.

34. Montgomery, *Fall of the House of Labor*, pp. 81, 24.

35. Woodberry (1903), quoted in W. B. Carnochan, *The Battleground of the Curriculum* (Stanford: Stanford University Press, 1993), p. 83; Taft and Kipling, quoted in Thomas F. Gossett, *Race: The History of an Idea in America* (Dallas: Southern Methodist University Press, 1975), p. 332; Harry H. Powers, "The Ethics of Expansion" (1900), in Milton Plesur, ed., *Creating an American Empire, 1865–1914* (New York: Pitman, 1971), p. 129.

   In response to these sorts of claims, and to the actions they were meant to justify, Mark Twain rewrote in 1901 "The Battle Hymn of the Republic":

> Mine eyes have seen the orgy of the launching of the Sword;
> He is searching out the hoardings where the stranger's wealth is stored;
> He hath loosed his fateful lightnings, and with woe and death has scored;
> His lust is marching on.

36. Melville, quoted in Garner, *The Civil War World of Melville*, p. 54.

37. Thomas Bailey Aldrich, "Unguarded Gates" (1895).

38. Melville, *White-Jacket* (1850; Evanston: Northwestern University Press and the Newberry Library, 1970), p. 151.

39. Democratic Party Platform, quoted in Fuchs, *The American Kaleidoscope*, p. 112; James, *The American Scene* (1907; Bloomington: Indiana University Press, 1968), p. 131; Roosevelt, quoted in Alex Zwerdling, "Anglo-Saxon Panic: The

Turn-of-the-Century Response to 'Alien' Immigrants," *Ideas* (Bulletin of the National Humanities Center), 1, no. 2 (1993), 38.

40. Charles Loring Brace, *The Dangerous Classes of New York* (New York, 1880), pp. 25–26.
41. Christopher Benfey, *The Double Life of Stephen Crane* (New York: Knopf, 1992), p. 171.
42. *The Literary Digest* (1919), quoted in John Higham, *Strangers in the Land: Patterns of American Nativism, 1860–1925* (New York: Atheneum, 1974), p. 229.
43. Paul M. Winter (1928), quoted in David Brion Davis, ed., *The Fear of Conspiracy: Images of Un-American Subversion from the Revolution to the Present* (Ithaca: Cornell University Press, 1971), p. 245.
44. Ann Fabian, "Making a Commodity of Truth: Speculation on the Career of Bernarr Macfadden," *American Literary History*, 5, no. 1 (1993), 51–76.
45. Bailyn et al., *The Great Republic*, p. 233.
46. Quoted in Gossett, *Race*, p. 372.
47. It was in the 1880s and 1890s that football became a "central feature of college social life." Elliott J. Gorn and Warren Goldstein, *A Brief History of American Sports* (New York: Hill and Wang, 1993), p. 131.
48. Quoted in Stallman, *Stephen Crane*, p. 238.
49. Gossett, *Race*, p. 364.
50. Charles H. Reeve, *The Prison Question* (Chicago: Knight and Leonard, 1890), p. 152.
51. Eugene S. Talbot, *Degeneracy: Its Causes, Signs and Results* (London, 1898), pp. 13–14.
52. Havelock Ellis, quoted in Talbot, *Degeneracy*, p. 17.
53. Carl N. Degler, *In Search of Human Nature: The Decline and Revival of Darwinism in American Social Thought* (New York: Oxford University Press, 1991), pp. 37, 41, 45.
54. Holmes, quoted in Degler, *In Search of Human Nature*, p. 47.
55. For the place of eugenicist ideas in Nazism, see Degler, *In Search of Human Nature*, esp. pp. 202–5, and Stefan Kühl, *The Nazi Connection: Eugenics, American Racism, and German National Socialism* (New York: Oxford University Press, 1994), which details the intellectual indebtedness of Nazi ideologues to the American eugenicist movement.
56. Degler, *In Search of Human Nature*, p. 22.
57. Joseph LeConte, quoted in Degler, *In Search of Human Nature*, p. 24.
58. Amos Warner, quoted in Degler, *In Search of Human Nature*, p. 24.
59. On Augustine's view of the transmission of sin, see Elaine Pagels, *Adam, Eve, and the Serpent* (New York: Vintage Books, 1988), p. 109; Jefferson, *Writings*, pp. 290–91; Thomas Hooker, *The Soules Preparation for Christ* (London, 1632), p. 54.
60. Carroll Smith-Rosenberg, *Disorderly Conduct: Visions of Gender in Victorian America* (New York: Oxford University Press, 1986), p. 91.
61. Randolph Bourne, "Trans-National America" (1916), in David A. Hollinger and Charles Capper, eds., *The American Intellectual Tradition* (New York: Ox-

ford University Press, 1993), 2 vols., II, 179; Dewey, *Democracy and Education* (1916; New York: The Free Press, 1966), p. 86; Emerson, "Circles" (1840), in Whicher, ed., *Selections from Emerson*, p. 171.

62. Wiebe, *Search for Order*, p. 4; John F. Kasson, *Rudeness and Civility: Manners in Nineteenth-Century Urban America* (New York: Hill and Wang, 1990), p. 121; Emile Durkheim, quoted in Kai Erikson, *Wayward Puritans: A Study in the Sociology of Deviance* (New York: John Wiley, 1966), p. 4.

63. Quoted in Stallman, *Stephen Crane*, p. 219. (My italics)

64. W.T. Hornaday, *Awake! America: Object Lessons and Warnings* (1918), in Davis, ed., *The Fear of Conspiracy*, p. 216; Arthur Schlesinger, Jr., quoted in Stephen J. Whitfield, *The Culture of the Cold War* (Baltimore: Johns Hopkins University Press, 1991), p. 43.

65. Gilman, "Education for Motherhood," in *The Forerunner*, 4 (October 1913), 262 (I owe this reference to Maria Russo); Sheila M. Rothman, *Woman's Proper Place: A History of Changing Ideals and Practices, 1870 to the Present* (New York: Basic Books, 1978), p. 28.

66. Degler, *In Search of Human Nature*, p. 28.

67. Adams, *The Education*, p. 384; see Rothman (on the birth-control pioneer Margaret Sanger), *Woman's Proper Sphere*, p. 195, and Elaine Tyler May, *Great Expectations: Marriage and Divorce in Post-Victorian America* (Chicago: University of Chicago Press, 1980), p. 102; Scott Fitzgerald, *The Beautiful and Damned* (1922; New York: Charles Scribner's Sons, 1950), p. 150.

68. George Stade, "Dracula's Women and Why Men Love to Hate Them," in Gerald I. Fogel et al., eds., *The Psychology of Men: New Psychoanalytic Perspectives* (New York: Basic Books, 1986), p. 42.

69. M. O. Terry, "On the Cure of Insanity by the Operative Procedure," *Medical Times*, November 1900, 324.

70. Ernest A. Hooton, *Crime and the Man* (Cambridge, Mass.: Harvard University Press, 1939), pp. 252, 269, 273, 271.

71. J. Fred Larsen, quoted in Timothy Spears, "All Things to All Men: The Commercial Traveler and the Rise of Modern Salesmanship," *American Quarterly*, December 1993, 547, 554.

72. Doris Kearns Goodwin, *No Ordinary Time: Franklin and Eleanor Roosevelt, the Home Front in World War II* (New York: Simon & Schuster, 1994), p. 172.

73. *Meet the Press*, October 23, 1994.

74. Melville, *Moby-Dick*, p. 200.

75. Melville, *Moby-Dick*, p. 200.

76. Bilbo, *Take Your Choice: Separation or Mongrelization* (Poplarville, Miss.: Dream House Publishing Co., 1947), p. 8.

77. *Father Coughlin's Radio Sermons* (Baltimore: Knox and O'Leary, 1931), pp. 200–1.

78. Melville, *Moby-Dick*, pp. 176, 177.

79. Richard Hofstadter, *The Paranoid Style in American Politics* (New York: Knopf, 1966), p. 36.

80. Quoted in Claudia Koonz's review of Ralf Georg Reuth, *Goebbels*, *The New York Times Book Review*, January 16, 1995, p. 14.

6. THE CULTURE OF IRONY

1. Quoted in Lawrence M. Friedman, *Crime and Punishment in American History* (New York: Basic Books, 1993), p. 339.
2. Paul Fussell, *The Great War and Modern Memory* (New York: Oxford University Press, 1975), p. 79.
3. Darrow, "Address to the Prisoners in Cook County Jail," in Richard J. Jensen, ed., *Clarence Darrow: The Creation of an American Myth* (New York: Greenwood Press, 1992), p. 271; Mencken, *The Philosophy of Friedrich Nietzsche* (1913; Port Washington, N.Y.: Kennikat Press, 1967), p. 3.
4. Nietzsche, *The Genealogy of Morals*, trans. Francis Golffing (New York: Doubleday Anchor, 1956), pp. 277–78.
5. Fitzgerald, *The Beautiful and Damned*, p. 3; Hemingway, *The Green Hills of Africa* (1935; New York: Charles Scribner's Sons, 1963), p. 21. The view of the Puritans as "oligarchs" emerged in the 1920s in the work of Brooks Adams (*The Emancipation of Massachusetts* [1919]) and V. L. Parrington (*Main Currents of American Thought: The Colonial Mind* [1927]), and by the time of Thomas Jefferson Wertenbaker, *The Puritan Oligarchy* (1947), it had become a kind of orthodoxy of its own.
6. Ann Douglas, *Terrible Honesty: Mongrel Manhattan in the 1920s* (New York: Farrar, Straus, and Giroux, 1995), p. 54; Lippmann, *A Preface to Morals* (New York: Macmillan, 1929), p. 4.
7. Clifton Fadiman, review of Lionel Trilling, *The Liberal Imagination*, *The New Yorker*, April 22, 1950, p. 118.
8. F. Scott Fitzgerald, letter to Marya Mannes, in Baritz, ed., *Culture of the Twenties*, p. 308.
9. George Steiner, *In Bluebeard's Castle: Some Notes Toward the Re-definition of Culture* (London: Faber and Faber, 1971), p. 48.
10. Douglas, *Terrible Honesty*, p. 57; Tillich, quoted in Roland Frye, *God, Man, and Satan*, p. 23.
11. Ernst Cassirer, *An Essay on Man* (New Haven: Yale University Press, 1944), p. 228; *The Myth of the State* (New Haven: Yale University Press, 1946), pp. 296, 298.
12. Cassirer, *Essay on Man*, pp. 5, 14.
13. Lewis Mumford, "The Corruption of Liberalism," *The New Republic*, April 29, 1940, pp. 569–70. (I owe this reference to Daniel Terris.) As late as the summer of 1944, when the daily press began to pick up accounts of mass extermination in the concentration camps in German-occupied Poland, the news remained subsidiary to the battlefield bulletins. In the case of *The New York Times*, the gas chambers never made the front page. See Deborah Lipstadt, *Beyond Belief: The American Press and the Coming of the Holocaust, 1933–1945* (New York: The Free Press, 1986), p. 235.

14. Frances Perkins, *The Roosevelt I Knew* (New York: Viking, 1946), pp. 147–48. (I owe this reference to Ann Douglas.)
15. David S. Wyman, *The Abandonment of the Jews: America and the Holocaust, 1941–1945* (New York: Pantheon, 1984), p. 311; David Eisenhower, *Eisenhower at War: 1943–1945* (New York: Random House, 1986), pp. 762–63. Shortly after visiting the camp, Eisenhower wrote to his wife, Mamie, that he had gone for the purpose of gathering "*first hand* evidence," so that "if ever, in the future, there develops a tendency to charge these allegations merely to propaganda," he would be able to testify to the truth. (Quoted in Lipstadt, *Beyond Belief*, pp. 254–55.)
16. Niebuhr, *Nature and Destiny of Man*, I, 35.
17. Niebuhr, *The Children of Light and the Children of Darkness* (New York: Charles Scribner's Sons, 1944), p. 9; Melville, *Moby-Dick*, p. 230.
18. Quoted in Marshall Berman, *All That Is Solid Melts into Air*, p. 67. I have drawn here on Berman's discussion, esp. pp. 60–71.
19. Trilling, *The Middle of the Journey* (New York: Viking, 1947), pp. 138, 75.
20. Miller, *All My Sons*, in Henry Hewes, ed., *Famous American Plays of the 1940s* (New York: Dell, 1967), p. 236.
21. Trilling, *Middle of the Journey*, p. 145.
22. Trilling, *The Liberal Imagination*, pp. x–xi.
23. Joseph R. McCarthy, *America's Retreat from Victory: The Story of George Catlett Marshall* (New York: Devin-Adair, 1951), pp. 167, 166, 163.
24. McCarthy, *America's Retreat*, pp. 69, 67, 168, 171.
25. Alsop, quoted in Victor S. Navasky, *Naming Names* (New York: Viking, 1980), p. 29.
26. Spillane, quoted in Whitfield, *Culture of the Cold War*, p. 35.
27. Saul Bellow, *Herzog* (1964; New York: Fawcett Crest, 1965), pp. 289–94.
28. See Leslie T. Hatamiya, *Righting a Wrong: Japanese Americans and the Passage of the Civil Liberties Act of 1968* (Stanford: Stanford University Press, 1993).
29. Oppenheimer, quoted in Dietrich Schroeer, *Physics and Its Fifth Dimension: Society* (Reading, Mass.: Addison-Wesley, 1972), p. 220. (I owe this reference to John Kasson.)
30. Auchincloss, quoted in Carol Gelderman, *Louis Auchincloss: A Writer's Life* (New York: Crown, 1993), p. 99.
31. Carson, *Silent Spring* (Boston: Houghton Mifflin, 1962), p. 6; Donald Fleming, "Roots of the New Conservation Movement," in *Perspectives in American History*, 6 (1972), 34.
32. Marcuse, *Eros and Civilization* (1955; New York: Vintage Books), p. 184.
33. Hofstadter, *American Political Tradition*, p. v.
34. King, "Letter from Birmingham Jail," in Capper and Hollinger, eds., *American Intellectual Tradition*, II, 238.
35. Kierkegaard, *The Concept of Irony*, trans. Howard V. Hong and Edna H. Hong (1841; Princeton: Princeton University Press, 1992), pp. 248, 253.
36. Emerson, "Self-Reliance" (1840), in Whicher, ed., *Selections from Emerson*, p.

150; Walker Percy, *The Last Gentleman* (1966; New York: Ballantine Books, 1989), p. 280.

37. Irving Howe, *Decline of the New* (New York: Harcourt, Brace, 1970), p. 253.

38. Trilling, *Beyond Culture* (New York: Viking, 1965), p. 26.

39. Fitzgerald, letter to Marya Mannes, in Baritz, ed., *Culture of the Twenties*, p. 308.

40. Susan Sontag, *Against Interpretation* (1966; New York: Dell, 1981), pp. 279–80.

41. Mailer, "The White Negro," in *Advertisements for Myself* (1959; New York: New American Library, 1960), pp. 304, 305.

42. Sontag, *Against Interpretation*, pp. 279, 280, 150.

43. Capote, *In Cold Blood* (1965; New York: New American Library, n.d.), pp. 286, 56, 189.

44. Capote, *In Cold Blood*, p. 29.

45. Emerson, "Nature," in Whicher, ed., *Selections from Emerson*, p. 44; Melville, *White-Jacket*, p. 186.

46. Howe, *Decline of the New*, p. 253.

47. Hayden White, *Metahistory: The Historical Imagination in Nineteenth-Century Europe* (Baltimore: Johns Hopkins University Press, 1973), p. 233.

48. Alasdair MacIntyre, *After Virtue* (Notre Dame: Notre Dame University Press, 1984), p. 19; Walker Percy, *Lancelot* (New York: Ballantine Books, 1979), p. 45.

49. Walker Percy, *The Last Gentleman*, p. 303.

50. Jürgen Habermas, *Legitimation Crisis*, trans. Thomas McCarthy (Boston: Beacon Press, 1975), p. 4.

51. Whitman, *Democratic Vistas* (1870), in *Poetry and Prose*, p. 937; White, *Metahistory*, p. 232.

52. Abner Kneeland, *Review of the Trial, Conviction and Final Imprisonment in the Common Jail of the County of Suffolk of Abner Kneeland for the Alleged Crime of Blasphemy* (Boston, 1838), pp. 13–14. (I owe this reference to John Matteson.)

53. Doctorow, interview in press release announcing *The Waterworks*, 1994.

54. Dulles, "Address at the General Conference of the Methodist Church, Boston, May 4, 1948," in *The Spiritual Legacy of John Foster Dulles*, ed. Henry P. Van Dusen (Philadelphia: Westminster Press, 1960), pp. 152–53.

55. Ricoeur, *Symbolism of Evil*, p. 43.

56. Mary Ellmann, *Thinking about Women* (New York: Harcourt Brace Jovanovich, 1968), p. 30.

57. Melville, *Pierre, or the Ambiguities* (1852; Evanston: Northwestern University Press and the Newberry Library, 1971), p. 285.

58. David A. Hollinger, "How Wide the Circle of the 'We'? American Intellectuals and the Problem of the Ethnos Since World War II," *American Historical Review*, 98, no. 2 (1993), 326.

59. Richard Rorty, *Contingency, Irony, and Solidarity* (Cambridge: Cambridge University Press, 1989), p. 75.

60. Fredric Jameson, *The Prison-House of Language* (Princeton: Princeton University Press, 1972), p. 138.

61. Hardwick, "The Menendez Show," *The New York Review of Books*, February 17, 1994, p. 14; *The New York Times*, January 19, 1994, p. B7.
62. Charles Baxter, "Dysfunctional Narratives, or 'Mistakes Were Made,' " *Ploughshares*, 20, nos. 2 & 3 (1994), p. 68; Alice Miller, *Banished Knowledge* (New York: Doubleday Anchor, 1991), p. 4. For a more extended version of Miller's argument about Hitler's childhood, see her *For Your Own Good* (1983).

  Another recent instance of a legal action centering on the idea of the coerced will is the case of Leonard Tose, former owner of the Philadelphia Eagles football team. Tose took legal action against the Taj Mahal Casino in Atlantic City, which had sued him for the recovery of gambling debts. Tose, who had lost hundreds of thousands of dollars, countersued the casino for permitting him to gamble while he was under the influence of alcohol. (*New Jersey Law Journal*, April 18, 1994.)
63. Niebuhr, *Nature and Destiny of Man*, I, 257.
64. Telford Taylor, *The Anatomy of the Nuremberg Trials* (New York: Knopf, 1992), pp. 51, 167.
65. Michael Wood, *America in the Movies* (1975; New York: Columbia University Press, 1989), p. 145.
66. Wood, *America in the Movies*, p. 145, 27.

7. PROSPECTS

1. Increase Mather, *A Discourse Concerning Comets* (Boston, 1683), sig. A3.
2. Mather, *Discourse Concerning Comets*, sig. A3.
3. Simpson, *Brazen Face of History*, p. xii.
4. Poe, *Eureka* (1848), in Auden, ed., *Selected Prose, Poetry, and Eureka*, p. 512.
5. Mailer, "The White Negro," in *Advertisements for Myself*, p. 303.
6. Rorty, *Contingency, Irony, and Solidarity*, pp. 5–6, 22.
7. Trilling, *Beyond Culture*, p. 8.
8. *Encyclopaedia Britannica*, 15th edition.
9. Poe, "Sonnet—to Science" (1829), in Auden, ed., *Selected Prose, Poetry, and Eureka*, p. 458.
10. Garry Wills, *Under God: Religion and American Politics* (New York: Touchstone, 1990), p. 29.
11. See Stephen L. Carter's astute *The Culture of Disbelief* (New York: Basic Books, 1993).
12. Niebuhr, "The Truth in Myths" (1937), in Capper and Hollinger, eds., *American Intellectual Tradition*, II, 204; Jean-François Lyotard, *The Postmodern Condition: A Report on Knowledge* (Minneapolis: University of Minnesota Press, 1984), pp. 41, xxiv; Antonio Gramsci, *Selections from the Prison Notebooks*, ed. Quintin Hoare and Geoffrey Nowell Smith (New York: International Publishers, 1971), p. 324.
13. Sontag, *Illness as Metaphor* (New York: Farrar, Straus and Giroux, 1978), p. 3.
14. Quoted in Rorty, *Contingency, Irony, and Solidarity*, p. 46.
15. Whittier, *Supernaturalism of New England*, pp. 42–43; Sontag, *Illness as Metaphor*, p. 85.

16. Richard Selzer, "The Art of Surgery," *Harper's*, October 1975, pp. 30, 34.
17. Robert Wright, *The Moral Animal: Evolutionary Psychology and Everyday Life* (New York: Pantheon, 1994), p. 368.
18. Wright, *The Moral Animal*, pp. 341, 369.
19. John Cotton, *Practical Commentary on John*, p. 364; Emile Durkheim, quoted in Wright, *The Moral Animal*, p. 5.
20. Melville, *Pierre*, pp. 177–78; Joseph Bellamy, "God's Wisdom in the Permission of Sin," in Bellamy, *Works* (Boston, 1853), 2 vols., II, 22.
21. Lippmann, *A Preface to Politics* (1914; Ann Arbor: University of Michigan Press, 1962), p. 7; John Demos, *Entertaining Satan: Witchcraft and the Culture of Early New England* (New York: Oxford University Press, 1982), pp. 129–30.
22. Arthur Miller, *Incident at Vichy* (1964), in Harold Clurman, ed., *The Portable Arthur Miller* (New York: Viking, 1971), p. 339.
23. Edwards, *Charity and its Fruits* (Boston, 1852), p. 359; Hawthorne, "Ethan Brand" (1850), in James McIntosh, ed., *Nathaniel Hawthorne's Tales* (New York: Norton, 1987), p. 241; Melville, *Redburn*, pp. 104–5. Earlier in the story, Hawthorne defines the unpardonable sin as "the sin of an intellect that triumphed over the sense of brotherhood with man and reverence for God, and sacrificed everything for its own mighty claims" (p. 235).
24. James, *The Portrait of a Lady* (1881; New York: New American Library, 1963), p. 396.
25. James, *The Portrait of a Lady*, pp. 356, 222.
26. R. W. B. Lewis, *The Jameses: A Family Narrative* (New York: Farrar, Straus and Giroux, 1991), p. 332; Kierkegaard, quoted by Walker Percy as the epigraph to *The Moviegoer* (1960).
27. G. R. Evans, *Augustine on Evil* (Cambridge: Cambridge University Press, 1982), p. 35.
28. Primo Levi, *The Drowned and the Saved*, trans. Raymond Rosenthal (New York: Vintage Books, 1988), pp. 55–57.
29. Edwards, *Treatise on the Religious Affections*, p. 118; Emerson, "The Divinity School Address" (1838), in Whicher, ed., *Selections*, p. 103.
30. Niebuhr, *Nature and Destiny of Man*, I, 182.
31. Emerson, "Experience" (1845), in Whicher, ed., *Selections*, p. 270; Thoreau, *Walden*, p. 198; Susan Faludi, *Backlash: The Undeclared War Against American Women* (New York: Crown, 1991), pp. 112–39. See especially Faludi's illuminating discussion (pp. 117–23) of how the idea for *Fatal Attraction* began as a story about a man struggling with his responsibility for the effects of his casual affair upon a victimized woman, and became the story of a lunatic woman who is "a raging beast underneath."
32. Ann Douglas, "The Dream of the Wise Child," in *Prospects: The Annual of American Cultural Studies*, 9 (1984), 309.
33. Garry Wills, *Under God*, p. 72.
34. Robertson Davies, in the *Times Literary Supplement*, September 30–October 6, 1988, p. 1070.

Acknowledgments

This book was begun at the National Humanities Center, during a precious semester of reading and reflection that enabled me to get the topic into focus. I am grateful as well to the John Simon Guggenheim Foundation and the American Council of Learned Societies for supporting my work with grants that made it possible for me to complete it. I have been ably assisted by several research assistants at Columbia University, especially Linda Ainsworth, who checked references and made the index, and Michael Elliott, who got used to receiving late-night or early-morning phone calls when I needed to find a book or confirm a fact, and who always came through. Angela Darling was a great help in preparing the manuscript for copy-editing. Several audiences gave me valuable responses, especially at the Massachusetts Institute of Technology, where Alvin Kibel and Harriet Ritvo made remarks that they are unlikely to remember but that proved fruitful for me in the ensuing months. Michael Stoller, whose grasp of the history of Christian doctrine is remarkable, was kind enough to read the pages on Augustine and the early church. And although this is the first book of mine over which my teacher Alan Heimert has not exerted a direct influence, I have been continually conscious of his lessons on how to read and think about culture and religion in American history.

I am indebted to my agent, Virginia Barber, who went beyond the call of duty and read the book in several versions, offering astute suggestions and moral support along the way; and to Elisabeth Sifton, who signed it up when it was nothing more than a half-articulated idea in my mind, waited for it patiently, and then greeted it with the highest compliment any author can wish for—strenuous and precise criticism. Elisabeth is a

263

living refutation of the notion that great editors are a phenomenon of the past.

Among family and friends, my brothers Nicholas and Thomas read the manuscript with care, as did my father and my good friend Eric Himmel, who also helped me with the maddening work of tracking down the illustrations. My children, Benjamin and Yvonne, have had their patience tested over the last few years, when Dad sometimes emerged from his study as a pretty good imitation of the devil. I thank them, with love, for putting up with me. Finally, I have dedicated this book to my wife, Dawn, because it is her presence in my life that more than anything else enables me to experience the world as a place of beauty and grace.

Index

abolitionism, 100, 116, 117; *see also* Civil War, slavery
Adams, Brooks, 257n5
Adams, Henry, 141, 146, 148, 178
Adams, John, 93, 132
Alcoholics Anonymous, 221
Alcott, Bronson, 78
Alcott, Louisa May: *A Modern Mephistopheles*, 101
Aldrich, Thomas Bailey, 178–79
Alger, Horatio, 148
Allen, William, 254n33
Allen, Woody, 148
Alsop, Joseph, 197
Altman, Robert: *M*A*S*H**, 209
Anderson, Alexander, 243n30, 243n31, 243n32, 243n33, 243n36
Anderson, Benedict, 238n25
Anderson, Sherwood, 176
anti-Catholic exposés, 119
Aquinas, St. Thomas, 201
Arendt, Hannah, 7–8
Aristotle, 67
Athanasius, 27
Auchincloss, Louis, 199
Augustine, St., 12, 48, 70, 87, 88, 134, 135, 174, 183, 193, 208, 229, 230, 231, 233, 234; *see also* evil, sin
Awful Disclosures of . . . the Hotel Dieu Nunnery at Montreal, 119

Bad Seed, The, 195
Bailey, Robert, 245n6
Bailyn, Bernard, 241n44, 248n54, 251n50

Bainton, Roland, 37
Baker, Herschel, 243n14
Baldwin, Joseph G., 246n21
Banks, Russell: *The Sweet Hereafter*, 19
Barnum Museum, 112
Bartol, Cyrus, 253n25
Baudelaire, Charles, 23, 239n1
Bauman, Zygmunt, 252n65
Baxter, Charles, 215
Beecher, Henry Ward, 143
Bellamy, Joseph, 261n20
Bellow, Saul, 194; *Herzog*, 197–99
Benedict, Ruth, 187
Benjamin, Walter, 158
Berger, Thomas: *Meeting Evil*, 18
Berlin, Isaiah, 224
Berman, Marshall, 248n61, 258n18
Bierce, Ambrose, 179
Bigelow, John, 252n68, 252n69
Big Sleep, The, 216
Bilbo, Theodore, 182
Blow, Susan, 252n73
Boas, Franz, 182
Bobbitt, Lorena, 215
Borthwick, Alexander, 252n11
Bourne, Randolph, 175
Boyer, Paul, 242n4
Brace, Charles Loring, 255n40
Bradstreet, Anne, 240n25
Brattle, Thomas, 243n12
Brooks, Preston, 148
Brown, John, 129, 131; and Harper's Ferry, 128–29, 130
Brownell, Henry Howard, 249n12
Brownson, Orestes, 103

Bruchey, Stuart, 247n38
Buber, Martin, 201
Buchanan, James, 148
Bullock, Alan, 237n4
Burke, Kenneth, 253n28
Butler, Jon, 244n40, 248n65
Byrd, William, 254n31
Byron, Lord, 25

Calef, Robert, 63
Calvin, John, 48, 193
Cape Fear, 195
capitalism: nineteenth-century dissat-
    isfaction with, 120–21; and sin, 125
Capote, Truman, 208; *In Cold Blood*,
    139, 205
Carnegie, Andrew, 142
Carson, Rachel, 201; *Silent Spring*, 200
Carter, Stephen L., 260n11
Cartier, Jacques, 29
Carver, Thomas, 252n72
Casablanca, 217
Cassirer, Ernst: *The Philosophy of Sym-
    bolic Forms*, 189–90
Castle, Terry, 243n19
Cather, Willa: *Obscure Destinies*, 147
Chadwick, Owen, 238n17
chance, 35, 107; post-Civil War belief
    in, 143–46, 148–53
Chauncy, Charles, 244n53
Cheever, George B., 245n5
Cherokee removal, 109–10
Chestnut, Mary, 250n26
Chopin, Kate: *The Awakening*, 141
Cish, Jane, 69–70
Civil War, 107, 110, 119, 120, 126–33,
    136–38, 140, 146, 147, 148, 152,
    159, 160, 193, 208, 222; as Holy
    War, 130, 131; legacies of, 142–47;
    156–57, 164; *see also* abolitionism,
    slavery
class, and conceptions of sin, 40–41
Clay, Henry, 133–34
Clement of Alexandria, 48
clergy, as necessary interpreters of
    scripture, 78–79
Clinton, Bill, 6, 234
Cold War, 193, 197; language of, 13,
    202
Coleridge, Samuel Taylor, 97

Colman, Benjamin, 240n18
Columbus, Christopher, 29, 30–31
Communism, 196; as evil, 197, 234
confidence man as manifestation of
    Satan, 100
Connell, Evan S., 246n12
Conrad, Joseph, 193
consciousness, rationalist view of, 67
Cooper, Thomas, 240n26
Cotton, John, 240n29
Coughlin, Charles, 182–83
Crane, Stephen, 177; "The Open
    Boat," 147; *The Red Badge of Cour-
    age*, 156
Craven, Avery, 246n16, 246n18,
    249n14
Crevecoeur, J. Hector St. John de,
    247n49
Crews, Frederick, 238n24
Cromwell, Oliver, 135
Crosland, Newton, 253n21
Custer, George Armstrong, 97
Cutbush, Edward, 243n35

da Gama, Vasco, 29
Dances with Wolves, 239n16
Dante, 43
Darrow, Clarence, 186
Darwin, Charles, 147, 174
Darwinism, 149; influences on foreign
    policy, 167; *see also* evolution
Davenport, James, 79–80
Davies, Robertson, 234
Davis, Jefferson, as Satan, 130–31,
    134, 145; *see also* Civil War
Davis, Richard Beale, 241n39
Deacon Giles's Distillery, 94
De Antonio, Emile: *Point of Order*,
    204
death, modern views of, 158–60,
    172; Victorian fear of, 157–58,
    167–68
DeForest, John W., 250n44
Degler, Carl N., 255n53, 255n54,
    255n56, 256n66
demagoguery, 181–83, 197, 203
democracy, as religion, 132, 151
Demos, John, 229
Descartes, Réné: *Discourse on Method*,
    64

Destry Rides Again, 239n16
devil, 4, 5, 10, 32; as fallen angel, 26;
as fraud, 95; as mythic figure, 82,
95; as prankster, 69; as source of all
evil, 229; Christian, as historical and
linguistic amalgamation, 24–26; decline into invisibility, 23; dissociation from self, 58; exorcisms of, 14;
New England conceptions of, 43,
52, 54, 62; representations of, 26,
27, 28, 52, 70, 92; Southern concep-
tions of, 42–43; *see also* evil, Satan,
sin
Devil Among the Taylors, The, 93
Devil in Love, The, 93
Devil's Comical Almanac, The, 93
Devil Turned Doctor, The, 93
Dewey, John, 175–76, 234
diabolism, 28, 43, 46; *see also*
Manicheans
Dickens, Charles, 102, 117
disease, moral explanations of, 14,
15–16; *see also* Sontag, Susan
Dixon, Senator, 134
Dixon, Thomas: *The Clansman*, 164
Doctorow, E. L., 85, 210
Donahue, Phil, 216
Donne, John, 31
Donnelly, Ignatius, 253n27
Dorson, Jonathan, 243n25
Dostoevsky, Fyodor, 118, 193
Douglas, Ann, 187, 188, 234
Douglas, William O., 185
Doyle, Arthur Conan, 161
Dreiser, Theodore: *Sister Carrie*, 149,
158; *see also* naturalists
Du Bois, W.E.B., 165, 182
Dulles, John Foster, 210
Dunbar, Paul Laurence: *The Sport of
the Gods*, 146
Duncan, Robert L., 238n26, 238n27
Dunster, Henry, 53
Durkheim, Emile, 256n62, 261n19
Dwight, Timothy: "The Triumph of
Infidelity," 93

Eddy, Mary Baker, 47
Eden, Garden of, *see* Garden of Eden
Edison, Thomas Alva, 142
Edwards, Jonathan, 80–83, 86, 87–88,

93, 193, 216, 230, 232, 234; *see also*
Great Awakening
Ehle, John, 247n50
Eichmann, Adolf, 7, 8
Eisenhower, Dwight D., 192, 258n15;
see also World War II
Eliot, Charles W., 173
Ellis, Bret Easton, 206
Ellis, Havelock, 255n52
Ellison, Ralph: *Invisible Man*, 200
Ellmann, Mary, 211, 212
Emancipation Proclamation, 136; *see
also* Civil War, slavery
Emerson, Ralph Waldo, 11, 47, 100,
101, 102–3, 106, 117, 118, 126,
129–30, 132, 143, 144, 149, 156,
157, 175, 187, 202, 203, 205, 232,
233, 234; "The American Scholar,"
248n3; "Circles," 241n55; "The Divinity School Address," 247n42;
"Experience," 261n31; "Historic
Notes on Life and Letters in New
England," 246n30; *Journals*, 103;
Nature, 237n12, 250n45; "Self-
Reliance," 246n19; "The Transcendentalist," 248n63
epistemology, and problem of evil,
8
eugenics, 172–75, 185, 228; and Nazi
ideologies, 255n55; liberal support
for, 173; *see also* fascism
Eusebius, 47
Evans, G. R., 261n27
evil: and effects of technology, 3; and
contemporary fiction, 18–19; and
cultural identity, 6; and historical
events, 5–6; and illness, 15–16;
and irony, 185–91; and liberalism,
196; and post-modernism, 8; and
social mobility, 41, 43–44; and un-
Americanism, 165–72; as bad luck,
153; as departure from norm, 176–
77; as deviance, 179; as disease,
175; as epistemological problem, 8;
as estrangement from God, 70, 87;
as madness, 71–76; as pride, 57, 72;
as privation, 46–51, 131, 175, 231–
32; as synonym for physical illness,
76; as superstition, 69; denial of,
195; estrangement from, 6, 9–10;

evil (*cont.*)
   images of, 6, 7, 24; lack of language for, 224; language of, 10–11, 13, 17, 19; manifested in fascism, 191–92; manifested in racism, 168–72; manifested in slavery, 109–15, 116, 125–35; Marxist conceptions of, 9, 192–93; media accounts of, 3, 7, 19; modern characteristics of, 193–99; moral, 12, 14; mythological vs. historical modes, 46; names for, 4, 9; natural, 12, 13, 14; need for, 227; nostalgia for, 68–69, 76; objectification of, 229, 233–34; personifications of, 10–11, 24; physiological views of, 71–73; psychological portrait of, 230–31; psychoanalytical conceptions of, 9; Puritan conceptions of, 4, 50; responsibility for, 4, 6, 82, 86, 215; scientific theories of, 172–75; visibility of in contemporary society, 3; *see also* devil, Satan, sin
evolution, 174, 210; and theories of social progress, 173; *see also* Darwinism
evolutionary psychology, 226–27

Fabian, Ann, 255n44
Fadiman, Clifton, 188
Faludi, Susan, 261n31
fascism, 185, 189, 190–91, 196, 199–200; *see also* eugenics
Fatal Attraction, 233, 261n31
Female Convents, 118
feminism, 211
Fischer, David Hackett, 247n43
Fithian, Philip Vickers, 244n42
Fitzgerald, F. Scott, 188, 203
Fitzhugh, George, 248n53
Fleming, Donald, 258n31
Forsyth, Neil, 241n52
Foucault, Michel, 244n37
Fox, George, 67–68
Franco, Generalissimo Francisco, 196
Frank, Waldo, 190
Franklin, Benjamin, 216; *Autobiography*, 76, 81–82, 216
Fredrickson, George, 248n55

Freeman, Mary Wilkins, 179
Free Soilers, 128; *see also* Civil War, Kansas–Nebraska Act
Freneau, Philip, 245n3
Freud, Sigmund, 67, 156, 187, 201
Frick, Henry Clay, 158
Friedan, Betty, 200
Frye, Roland, 241n58
Fuchs, Lawrence, 246n14, 254n39
Fugitive Slave Law, 100, 126–27; *see also* Civil War
Fuller, Margaret, 103–4
Fulton, Robert, 152
Fussell, Paul, 257n2

gambling, popularity of, 96, 145
Gansevoort, Henry, 248n55
Garbo, Greta, 204
Garden of Eden, 4, 14, 24, 38, 155; Gnostic interpretations of, 25
Gataker, Thomas, 240n26, 240n27
ghosts, 67–69, 210; stories, modern popularity of, 161; *see also* spiritualism
Gilfoyle, Timothy J., 248n68
Gilman, Charlotte Perkins, 177
Gingrich, Newt, 181
Glasgow, Ellen: *Barren Ground*, 147
Godwin, William, 82–83
Goebbels, Joseph, 5, 183
Goethe, Johann Wolfgang von, 193; *Faust*, 117, 194
Goodwin, Doris Kearns, 256n72
Goodwin, Hezekiah, 243n24
grace, Enlightenment views of, 75, 80; Puritan belief in, 32, 38
Gramsci, Antonio, 260n12
Grant, Ulysses S., 139–40, 145; *Memoirs*, 140; *see also* Civil War
Great Awakening, 79–81; *see also* Edwards, Jonathan
Great Depression, 152–53
Greeley, Horace, 152
Greenham, Richard, 239n1
Griffith, D. W.: *The Birth of a Nation*, 164–65

Habermas, Jurgen, 208
Hall, David D., 242n71
hallucinations, 67

Hardwick, Elizabeth, 214
Hardy, Thomas, 149
Harrel, Isser, 237n8
Harrington, Michael, 200, 201
Harris, Joel Chandler, 114
Harris, Thomas: *The Silence of the Lambs*, 19
Hart, James, 252n9
Harvey, William, 165
Hatamiya, Leslie T., 258n28
Hawthorne, Nathaniel, 101, 107–8, 119, 126, 130, 230; "Ethan Brand," 261n23; *The House of Seven Gables*, 247n45; *The Marble Faun*, 156; "The Minister's Black Veil," 116; *The Scarlet Letter*, 40, 116; "Wakefield," 110
Hay, John, 134
health: and gender, 178; regimens for women, 178; spiritual and physical, 169
Hearst, Randolph, 142
Hedrick, Joan, 246n20
Hegel, Georg Wilhelm Friedrich, 47, 126
hell, Christ's descent into, 25–26; conceptions of, 25, 54; *see also* devil, evil, Satan, sin
Heller, Joseph: *Catch-22*, 201
Hellman, Lillian: *The Little Foxes*, 194
Hemingway, Ernest, 187, 188, 203
Herblock, 199
Herndon, Billy, 133
Herrick, Robert: *Waste*, 147
Hersey, John, 201; *Hiroshima*, 200
Higginson, Thomas Wentworth, 250n23
High Noon, 197
Hitchcock, Alfred: *Shadow of a Doubt*, 194
Hitler, Adolf, 4, 5, 183, 210, 215, 260n62
Hobbes, Thomas: *Leviathan*, 65, 67, 71
Hofstadter, Richard, 138, 182, 201
Hollinger, David, 213
Holloway, Mark, 248n69
Holmes, Oliver Wendell, 130, 173
Holocaust, 6, 199
Honour, Hugh, 239n12, 239n13

Hooker, Thomas, 240n20, 240n24
Hooten, Ernest A., 256n70
Hoover, J. Edgar, 196
horror, images of, 3, 6, 19
horror fiction, popularity of, 17–18
Howe, Irving, 202–3
Howe, Julia Ward, 130
Howells, William Dean, 136, 146, 162, 176; *Between the Dark and the Daylight*, 161; *A Hazard of New Fortunes*, 150; *Questionable Shapes*, 161
Hubbard, William, 241n40

identity, cultural, effects of evil on, 6
imagination, rationalist view of, 65, 66
immigration, 98, 166, 169, 171, 173
individualism, 103, 107, 212; *see also* self
industrialization, 98
Irenaeus, 26
irony, 187–92, 202, 205, 208–14, 216, 220, 223, 234

Jackson, Andrew, 103, 105, 110, 118
Jackson, Robert, 216
James, Henry, 140, 168; *The American Scene*, 254n39; *Hawthorne*, 250n36; *The Portrait of a Lady*, 141, 230–31; *The Turn of the Screw*, 161
James, Henry Sr., 11
James, William, 18, 67, 87, 159–60, 161, 162, 253n20
Jameson, Fredric, 214
Japanese Internment Camps, 199
Jefferson, Thomas, 30, 92, 104, 106–7, 110, 132, 175
Jennings, Francis, 240n17
Jewett, Sarah Orne: *The Country of the Pointed Firs*, 141
Johnson, Lyndon B., 223
Johnson, Samuel, 68, 108, 119
Jordan, Winthrop, 241n42
Jung, Carl, 51

Kafka, Franz, 118; *Trial*, 216
Kansas–Nebraska Act, 127–28, 132; *see also* Civil War
Kant, Immanuel, 88, 159, 193
Karlsen, Carol F., 242n4
Kasson, John F., 256n62

Keckley, Elizabeth, 133
Kekes, John, 237n5
Kennedy, John F., 169
Kermode, Frank, 11–12
Kessler-Harris, Alice, 246n15
Khrushchev, Nikita, 197
Kierkegaard, Soren, 191, 202, 231, 261n26
King, Martin Luther Jr., 234; *Letter from Birmingham Jail*, 201
Kipling, Rudyard, 167
Kirkland, Caroline, 246n28, 247n37
Kiss of Death, 194–95
Klement, Ricardo, *see* Eichmann, Adolf
Kneeland, Abner, 209
Knox, Ronald, 243n22
Krafft-Ebing, Richard von: *Psychopathia Sexualis*, 179
Kubrick, Stanley: *Dr. Strangelove*, 201
Kühl, Stefan, 255n55
Ku Klux Klan, 169, 182

Lactantius, 26
LaLanne, Jack, 169
Lamarck, Jean-Baptiste, evolutionary theories of, 173
language, 145, 221; and evil, 3, 4–5, 9, 11, 13–14, 17, 19; of Providence, 148
Larsen, J. Fred, 256n71
Laski, Harold, 173
Last Seduction, The, 233
Lears, T. Jackson, 250n37
le Carré, John, 197
LeConte, Joseph, 255n57
Lee, Robert E., 129, 140
Leventhal, Herbert, 242n6
Levi, Primo: *The Drowned and the Saved*, 231–32
Levin, David, 242n3
Levin, Harry, 246n8
Lewis, John, 77–78
Lewis, R.W.B., 231
Lewis, Sinclair, 190
L'Heureux, John: *The Shrine at Altamira*, 18
Lifton, Robert Jay, 146
Lincoln, Abraham, 105, 110, 115–16, 118, 127–28, 131–39, 148, 151,
160, 197, 208; as Augustinian, 135; compared to Captain Ahab, 133; compared to Christ, 133; conception of evil, 131–35
Lincoln, Mary Todd, 139, 160
Lindsey, David L., 238n26
Lippmann, Walter, 187–88, 207, 213, 229
Lipstadt, Deborah, 257n13
Lloyd, Henry Demarest, 150
Locke, John, 66, 67, 71
Lockwood, W. M., 253n19
Long, Huey, 182
Longfellow, Henry Wadsworth, 129, 187
Lowell, James Russell, 131
Lukacs, Georg, 238n23
Luther, Martin, 37
Lynn, Kenneth, 248n60
Lyotard, Jean-François: *The Postmodern Condition*, 223

McArthur, Paul, 253n17, 253n18
McCarthy, Joseph, 182, 196, 197, 204
McCarthyism, 199
McDermott, John J., 251n47
McEwan, Ian, 9; *Black Dogs*, 18–19
Macfadden, Bernarr, 169–70
McFeely, William, 135
McGinniss, Joe, 205
McInerney, Jay, 206
MacIntyre, Alasdair, 259n48
Magellan, Ferdinand, 29
Maier, Charles, 237n4
Mailer, Norman, 197, 203–4; *The Executioner's Song*, 139; "The White Negro," 259n41
Malamud, Bernard, 194
Malcolm, Janet, 238n26
Manicheans, 48, 50, 131, 229
Manifest Destiny, 118, 168
Marcus, Steven, 244n49, 251n60
Marcuse, Herbert: *Eros and Civilization*, 201
Marlowe, Christopher, 23
Marshall, George C., 196
Marshall, John, 109, 110, 118
Martin, J. Frederick, 241n47
Martyr, Justin, 26

Marxism, and evil, 9, 192–93, 196
Massachusetts Bay Colony, 32, 37, 43, 61; *see also* Puritans
Mather, Cotton, 28, 62, 63, 64
Mather, Increase, 63, 70; *Cases of Conscience*, 61
May, Elaine Tylor, 256n67
May, Rollo, 241n53
Mazzini, Giuseppe, 133
Mead, Margaret, 187
media, accounts of evil, 3
medicine, and treatment of evil, 71–73
Melville, Herman, 23–24, 129, 136, 193–94, 205, 212, 222, 228, 230; "Apathy and Enthusiasm," 250n22; "Bartleby, the Scrivener," 119; *Billy Budd*, 169; *The Confidence-Man*, 248n57; "The Housetop," 250n27; *Moby-Dick*, 13, 99, 101, 126, 133, 181, 183, 229; *Pierre, or the Ambiguities*, 259n57; *Redburn*, 117, 239n2; *Typee*, 254n31; *White-Jacket*, 254n38
Mencken, H. L., 186
Menendez brothers, 214–15
Mephistopheles, 5, 10, 23; *see also* devil, Satan
Mesmer, Anton, 160
mesmerism, 160; *see also* spiritualism
Metcalfe, Deborah, 70–71
Meyerowitz, Joanne J., 251n62
Miller, Alice, 260n62
Miller, Arthur, 229; *All My Sons*, 195; *The Crucible*, 197
Miller, Perry, 242n7
Milton, John, 43, 69; descriptions of Satan, 4, 52; *Paradise Lost*, 14, 26, 44, 53, 54, 93, 130, 134, 155
mind, 79; conceived of as machine, 64–66, 70
minimalism, 206
Missouri Compromise, 128; *see also* Civil War
monism, 46, 47; *see also* Augustine, St.
Montgomery, David, 250n43, 254n34
Morgan, J. P., 158
Morison, Samuel Eliot, 239n16
Mumford, Lewis, 190
Murray, Henry, 4, 237n3, 239n4

Native Americans, as personifications of evil, 29, 42, 52–53
natural selection, 174
naturalists, 150
Nazism, 7, 8, 9, 10, 192, 199–200, 208, 231; *see also* fascism
Newman, Barnett, 206
New World: as playground of devil, 42; importance of, to changing conception of Satan, 29
Nicolay, John, 134
Niebuhr, Reinhold, 76, 85, 189, 190, 192–93, 195, 200, 201, 215, 216, 223, 232, 234
Nietzsche, Friedrich, 156, 186, 187, 188, 227
Night of the Hunter, The, 195
Nissenbaum, Stephen, 242n4
Nixon, Richard M., 215
Norris, Frank, 149; *see also* naturalists

Oppenheimer, J. Robert, 199
Origen, 26
original sin, 4, 81, 82, 93, 174, 191, 227; *see also* evil, Garden of Eden, sin
Orwell, George, 11, 237n11
Owen, Robert, 120

Pagels, Elaine, 255n59
Paine, Thomas: *Common Sense*, 92
Palmer, A. Mitchell, 253n28
Parrington, V. L., 257n5
Parry, Oliver Hazard, 202
Patterson, James, 238n26
Paul, St., 39, 50, 117, 134
Peale Museum, 96
Percy, Walker, 202, 208; *Lancelot*, 206–7; *The Last Gentleman*, 207, 213; *The Moviegoer*, 261n26
Perkins, Frances, 190–91
Perkins, William, 240n21
Phelps, Elizabeth Stuart: *The Gates Ajar*, 158, 159
Phillips, Jayne Anne: *Shelter*, 19
phrenology, 172
Pickens, Francis W., 249n18
Poe, Edgar Allan, 221; *The Devil in the Belfry*, 100–1; *Eureka*, 260n4; *The Narrative of Arthur Gordon Pym*,

Poe, Edgar Allan (*cont.*)
    254n31; "Sonnet—to Science,"
    260n9
Pope, Alexander, 68
populism, 165
Potter, J. S., 249n18
Powers, Harry H., 254n35
Praz, Mario, 239n7
Preston, John, 240n35
pride, as source of evil, 26–27
Providence: language of, 148; erosion
    of belief in, 144–48
psychoanalysis, and evil, 9
psychology, accounts of evil, 4
Puritans, 32–40, 91; as modified dual-
    ists, 51; respect for St. Augustine,
    48; conception of evil, 50;
    conception of Satan, 41, 45, 52, 53,
    64; conception of sin, 37, 41, 43;
    viewed from twentieth century,
    187, 257n5
Pynchon, Thomas, 197

racism, 165–72, 180; scientific bases
    for, 171
Raleigh, Sir Walter, 30
Ramsay, David, 31
Rank, Otto, 253n28
Reagan, Ronald, 119, 234
Reeve, Charles H., 255n50
Reinhardt, Ad, 206
religious revivalism, 119; and Civil
    War, 138
responsibility: Enlightenment views
    of, 84–85; for evil, 4, 7, 82, 212–17
Reynolds, David, 248n64
Rice, Anne, 179
Ricoeur, Paul, 47, 211
Robinson, Edwin Arlington, 147
Rogers, Esther, 245n60
Rogers, John, 245n60
Roosevelt, Franklin D., 180, 190, 191,
    192
Roosevelt, Theodore, 168, 169, 177
Rorty, Richard, 221–22; *Contingency,
    Irony, and Solidarity*, 213–14
Rose, Anne C., 250n24
Ross, Edward, 168
Ross, Robert, 244n46, 244n47
Roth, Philip: *Portnoy's Complaint*, 156

Rothman, Sheila M., 256n65
Royce, Josiah, 159
Royster, Charles, 138
Rush, Benjamin, 73
Russell, Jeffrey Burton: *Lucifer: The
    Devil in the Middle Ages*, 239n2;
    *Mephistopheles: The Devil in the Mod-
    ern World*, 239n1, 241n56; *Satan:
    The Early Christian Tradition*, 27,
    239n6, 239n9, 239n10, 239n11

Sagan, Françoise, 211
Sale, Kirkpatrick, 239n14, 239n15,
    239n16
Salem witch trials, 35, 58–64
Satan, 4, 9, 18, 24, 81, 224, 229, 234–
    35; as antithesis of Christ, 27; as
    confidence man, 100; as museum
    exhibit, 96; Augustinian views on,
    48–49; images of, 27–28; and pa-
    gan tradition, 26; dissociation from
    self, 64; Enlightenment views of,
    57, 69, 70, 74–75, 78; nineteenth-
    century views of, 92–93, 95, 96, 97,
    102, 114–15, 126; pride of, 26–27,
    43, 54, 57, 72; psychological ac-
    counts of, 4; Puritan conceptions of,
    32, 40, 41, 43–45, 51, 53–55, 60,
    62, 64; represented in Hebrew
    scripture, 25; reemergence of, 16–
    17; ubiquity of, 23; *see also* devil,
    evil, sin
Saum, Lewis O., 246n8, 248n66,
    251n49, 252n11, 252n13
Sayers, Dorothy, 191
Scarry, Elaine, 238n20
Schama, Simon, 252n6
Schlesinger, Arthur M. Jr., 30
Schneider, Peter, 237n1
Schulman, Lydia Dittler, 245n1
Schweitzer, Albert, 200
science: as replacement for God, 75;
    excluding idea of God, 148
Scott, Dred, 128; *see also* Civil War
secularism, 11
secular liberalism, 223
segregation, 199; as sin, 201; legality
    of, 170
self: as source of evil, 8, 58, 64; En-
    lightenment views of, 83; fragmen-

tation of, 13; nineteenth-century
views of, 97–107; responsibility for,
82–85, 214
Selzer, Richard, 225–26, 227
Sewall, Samuel, 35, 62
sexuality, and sin, 16, 27, 227–28,
233–34; *see also* evil, original sin,
sin
Shakespeare, William, 23; *King John*,
160; *King Lear*, 146
Shepard, Thomas, 242n73
Shirer, William L., 190
Sibbes, Richard, 241n48
Sikes, Wirt, 252–253n14
Simpson, Lewis P., 253n18
sin, 4, 9, 16, 229; as error, 76; as hereditary, 175; as ignorance, 232; as
limitation, 175; as pathology, 187;
Augustinian conceptions of, 48–49;
in Garden of Eden, 155–56; loss of
concept of, 189; manifested in segregation, 201; New England conceptions of, 41, 43–44, 55;
Southern conceptions of, 41–43; *see
also* devil, evil, Satan
Six Months in a Convent, 118
slavery, 6, 98–100, 108–15, 118, 125,
126–134, 193; Jefferson's views on,
110; Southern arguments for, 111–
12; *see also* Civil War
slaves, as personifications of devil, 42
Sloane, David Charles, 252n8
Smith, John, 30
Smith-Rosenberg, Carroll, 175
Sontag, Susan, 203, 204; *Illness as Met-
aphor*, 223–24, 225
Spanish-American War, 177
Spillane, Mickey, 197
Spinoza, 47
spiritualism, 160–64, 253n20
Stade, George, 256n68
Stalin, Joseph, 4, 196, 197, 210, 232
Stampp, Kenneth M., 251n58
Steinbeck, John, 149–50
Steiner, George, 257n9
Stephens, Alexander, 132
sterilization, 173, 185; *see also* eugenics
Stevens, Army Secretary, 204
Stoker, Bram, 179
Story, Joseph, 252n10

Stowe, Harriet Beecher: *Uncle Tom's
Cabin*, 127
Straub, Peter, 238n27
Strong, George Templeton, 134,
253n20
Strong, Josiah, 254n30
Stubbes, Philip, 240n23
Sumner, Charles, 148
Supreme Court, 170, 173, 185, 199
Swaggart, Jimmy, 223
Symington, Stuart, 204

Taft, William Howard, 167
Talbot, Eugene S., 255n51
Tanny, Vic, 169
Taylor, Charles, 247n34
Taylor, Edward, 246n9
Taylor, Telford, 215–16
Tennyson, Alfred Lord, 161
Terry, M. O., 256n69
Tertullian, 27
Thomas, Keith, 75
Thompson, Jim, 139
Thompson, Joseph, 249n19
Thoreau, Henry David, 7–8, 105,
119, 129, 138, 143, 233; *The Maine
Woods*, 237n7; *Walden*, 100, 125
Tiger, Lionel, 6, 11
Tillam, Thomas, 240n19
Tillich, Paul, 189
Tituba, 59; *see also* Salem witch trials
Tocqueville, Alexis de, 4, 103, 107–8
totalitarianism, 189; struggle against,
197
Trachtenberg, Alan, 250n38
Tracy, Patricia, 84
Trefz, Edward K., 240n18
Trilling, Diana, 250n32
Trilling, Lionel, 18, 107, 195–96, 201,
202, 203, 222; *The Middle of the Jour-
ney*, 195
Twain, Mark, 146, 254n35; *The Adven-
tures of Huckleberry Finn*, 43, 100,
114; "The United States of
Lyncherdom," 165
Tyler, Royall, 245n4; "The Origin of
Evil," 94

Updike, John: *The Witches of Eastwick*,
11, 51

Veblen, Thorstein, 141
Vendler, Helen, 237n14
Very, Jones, 78
Vespucci, Amerigo, 29
Vietnam, 6, 202
Village of the Damned, 195
virtue, physical strength as, 170
Voltaire, 68; *Candide*, 86
voyeurism, as leading theme in post-Civil War fiction, 140

Warner, Amos, 255n58
Washington, George, 144
Watson, Thomas, 254n30
Webb, Beatrice and Sidney, 173
Weber, Max, 146; *The Protestant Ethic and the Spirit of Capitalism*, 40
Webster, Daniel, 100
Weems, Mason Lock, 251n46
Weimar Republic, 208
Welch, Joseph, 204
Wertenbaker, Thomas Jefferson, 257n5
Wesley, John, 228–29
Wharton, Edith, 176; *Ethan Frome*, 150; *The House of Mirth*, 158; *Men and Ghosts*, 161
White, Hayden, 209
Whitman, Samuel, 86
Whitman, Walt, 130, 137, 208, 210
Whittier, John Greenleaf, 97, 119, 187, 224

Wiebe, Robert, 250n32, 256n62
Wiley, Bell Irvin, 249n13, 251n48
Willard, Samuel: *A Compleat Body of Divinity*, 53
Wills, Garry, 223, 234
Wilson, Edmund, 143
Winfrey, Oprah, 216
Winter, Paul M., 255n43
Winthrop, John, 37
witchcraft, 42, 73–75, 96; tradition in New England, 59, 60, 61, 63–64; *see also* Salem witch trials
Wood, Elizabeth, 71
Wood, Gordon, 247n47
Wood, Michael, 216–17
Woodberry, George Edward: "Race Power," 167
Worcester, Noah, 245n58
World War I, 177, 185–86, 229
World War II, 53, 146, 193, 202
Wright, Chauncey, 149
Wright, Lawrence, 238n24
Wright, Richard: *Native Son*, 194
Wright, Robert: *The Moral Animal*, 226–27, 228
Wyler, William: *Detective Story*, 194
Wyman, David S.: *The Abandonment of the Jews*, 192

Young, David, 246n7